True to Our Vision

Home-O-Nize

HON INDUSTRIES

HNI Corporation

True to Our Vision

Home-O-Nize

HON INDUSTRIES

HNI Corporation

Jeffrey L. Rodengen & Richard F. Hubbard

Edited by Melody Maysonet & Heather Deeley
Design and layout by Dennis Shockley

Dedicated to Jake Burstein,

Remember your Torah as well as the lines from My Cousin Vinny
on this very special day. You're no longer a "yout."

—Jeffrey L. Rodengen

Write Stuff Enterprises, Inc.
1001 South Andrews Avenue
Second Floor
Fort Lauderdale, FL 33316
1-800-900-Book (1-800-900-2665)
(954) 462-6657
www.writestuffbooks.com

Also by Jeffrey L. Rodengen

The Legend of Chris-Craft

*IRON FIST:
The Lives of Carl Kiekhaefer*

*Evinrude-Johnson
and The Legend of OMC*

*Serving the Silent Service:
The Legend of Electric Boat*

The Legend of Dr Pepper/Seven-Up

The Legend of Honeywell

The Legend of Briggs & Stratton

The Legend of Ingersoll-Rand

*The Legend of Stanley:
150 Years of The Stanley Works*

The MicroAge Way

The Legend of Halliburton

The Legend of York International

The Legend of Nucor Corporation

*The Legend of Goodyear:
The First 100 Years*

The Legend of AMP

The Legend of Cessna

The Legend of VF Corporation

The Spirit of AMD

The Legend of Rowan

*New Horizons:
The Story of Ashland Inc.*

The History of American Standard

The Legend of Mercury Marine

The Legend of Federal-Mogul

*Against the Odds:
Inter-Tel—The First 30 Years*

The Legend of Pfizer

*State of the Heart:
The Practical Guide to Your Heart
and Heart Surgery*
with Larry W. Stephenson, M.D.

*The Legend of
Worthington Industries*

The Legend of IBP, Inc.

*The Legend of
Trinity Industries, Inc.*

*The Legend of
Cornelius Vanderbilt Whitney*

The Legend of Amdahl

The Legend of Litton Industries

The Legend of Gulfstream

*The Legend of Bertram
with David A. Patten*

*The Legend of
Ritchie Bros. Auctioneers*

*The Legend of ALLTEL
with David A. Patten*

*The Yes, you can of
Invacare Corporation
with Anthony L. Wall*

*The Ship in the Balloon:
The Story of Boston Scientific
and the Development of
Less-Invasive Medicine*

The Legend of Day & Zimmermann

The Legend of Noble Drilling

*Fifty Years of Innovation:
Kulicke & Soffa*

*Biomet—From Warsaw
to the World
with Richard F. Hubbard*

NRA: An American Legend

*The Heritage and Values
of RPM, Inc.*

*The Marmon Group:
The First Fifty Years*

The Legend of Grainger

*The Legend of
The Titan Corporation
with Richard F. Hubbard*

*The Legend of Discount Tire Co.
with Richard F. Hubbard*

*The Legend of Polaris
with Richard F. Hubbard*

*The Legend of La-Z-Boy
with Richard F. Hubbard*

*The Legend of McCarthy
with Richard F. Hubbard*

*InterVoice:
Twenty Years of Innovation
with Richard F. Hubbard*

*Jefferson-Pilot Financial:
A Century of Excellence
with Richard F. Hubbard*

*The Legend of HCA
with Richard F. Hubbard*

*The Legend of Werner Enterprises
with Richard F. Hubbard*

*The History of J. F. Shea Co.
with Richard F. Hubbard*

Publisher's Cataloging-in-Publication

Rodengen, Jeffrey.
    True to Our Vision/[Jeffrey L. Rodengen,
Richard F. Hubbard]. —1st ed.
    p. cm.
    Includes bibliographical references and index.
    LCCN 2003108360
    ISBN 1-932022-03-1

    1. HON Industries—History. 2. Office furniture industry—United States—History.
3. Conglomerate corporations—United States—History. I. Hubbard, Richard F. II. Title

    HD9803.U64H6673 2004   388.7'6841'00973
                                  QBI04-200128

Library of Congress
Catalog Card Number 2003108360

ISBN 1-932022-03-1

Completely produced in the
United States of America
10 9 8 7 6 5 4 3 2 1

Table of Contents

Introduction

MANY COMPANIES TODAY STRIVE TO create a company culture not so much to guide their actions, but merely as a means to market the company to others. Not HNI Corporation. HNI was founded on a set of values that has shaped its culture for 60 years.

The company that evolved into HNI Corporation began with an idea. Not a product idea. Not a factory in search of something to manufacture. An idea about how a company should treat the people who work for it. Those who work for the company are not merely *employed* by the company; they are *members* and *owners* of the company.

Throughout its history, HNI Corporation has followed a consistent course, guided by the high value that its founders placed on treating every person with fairness and respect. Out of that value grew a company that has shared its profits with members and has paid dividends every quarter since 1955 to its owners, including its member-owners.

The company's personal commitment to its members has paid another sort of dividend over the years. Members are committed to HNI's success. Never satisfied with the status quo, its members constantly work to find a better way. Time and again throughout its history, HNI has faced challenges, and in each instance its members have helped meet those challenges head-on to ensure the enduring success of the company.

Over 60 years, the members of HNI have held true to these founding ideals and have acted accordingly. Today, the company that began with little more than an unshakeable commitment to the people who made it work is sharing the rewards of its success with all of its stakeholders—members, customers, suppliers, the public, and shareholders.

HNI begins its seventh decade as an industry leader in its core business—office furniture and hearth products. It enjoys the admiration of business authorities, who hold it up as an example of how a company should be run. Hardly complacent, HNI is making strategic moves to ensure its bright future.

This is the legacy of HNI Corporation, true to a 60-year-old vision.

Acknowledgments

MANY DEDICATED PEOPLE ASSISTED IN the research, preparation, and publication of *True to Our Vision.*

The principal research and assembly of the narrative time line was accomplished by research assistant Fred Anderson. Senior editors Melody Maysonet and Heather Deeley oversaw the text and photos from beginning to end, and art director Dennis Shockley's graphic design brought the story to vivid life.

Several key people associated with HNI lent their invaluable efforts to the book's completion, sharing their experience, providing valuable oversight for accuracy, and helping guide the book's development from outline to final form: Chairman and CEO Jack Michaels; Vice President, Member and Community Relations Jeff Fick; and Susan Cradick, secretary and treasurer, HNI's Charitable Foundation, who served as our tireless and efficient liaison. HNI also acknowledges Patricia Corriell's assistance in grammatical editing and Peggy VanZandt for member photography.

Many other HNI Corporation executives, employees, retirees, family members, and friends greatly enriched the book by discussing their experiences. The authors extend particular gratitude to these men and women for their candid recollections and guidance: Stan Askren, Pete Atherton, Roger Behrens, Lee Benjamin, Dave Burdakin, Robert Carl, Mike DeRosier, Brad Determan, Jerry Dittmer, Melinda Ellsworth, Malcolm C. Fields, David Gardner, Thomas E. Hammer, Jim Hanson, Tony Hayden, Robert Hayes, Tom Head, Phillip E. Hecht, Stanley M. Howe, James Johnson, Jeffrey L. Jollay, Eric Jungbluth, Jim Kane, James Knutson, Jim Littich, Kevin Mathis, Lyle McCullough, Don Mead, Ken Meyerholz, Thomas Miller, Jean Reynolds, Josh Slowik, Richard Stanley, Tim Summers, Jerry Vande Kieft, and Julie Zielinski.

Special thanks are extended to the dedicated staff and associates at Write Stuff Enterprises, Inc.: Jon VanZile, former executive editor; Torey Marcus, executive editor; Peter Donald and Debra Kronowitz, senior editors; Bonnie Freeman and Kevin Allen, copy editors; Sandy Cruz, senior art director; Rachelle Donley, art director; Mary Aaron, transcriptionist; Barbara Koch, indexer; Bruce Borich, production manager; Marianne Roberts, vice president of administration; Sherry Hasso, bookkeeper; Julie Castro, executive assistant to Jeffrey L. Rodengen; and Lars Jessen, director of worldwide marketing.

Typical of a Home-O-Nize installation is this unit consisting of two 18″ and two 12″ sections—five feet of counter working space. Can be installed as easily as a stove or a refrigerator —*packaged merchandise in fact.*

The Lyric

Home-O-Nize, the predecessor to HON INDUSTRIES, intended to manufacture and sell a unique line of kitchen cabinets, but a shortage of steel after World War II kept the company from moving beyond the prototype designs.

CHAPTER ONE

The Idea That Became a Company

1943–1947

[To form] a company where employees . . . would be treated with dignity and fairness, not exploited in the interest of profits.

—HON INDUSTRIES founders
C. Maxwell Stanley and Clement T. Hanson,
early mission statement

THE COMPANY THAT eventually became HON INDUSTRIES began with an idea—not a product idea, not a factory in search of something to manufacture—but an idea about how a company should treat its employees. The people who worked at the company would not be considered mere employees but would be members who shared in the company's success.

The idea originated with C. Maxwell Stanley and Clement T. Hanson, who had been friends for many years. The two met while they were students at the University of Iowa in the 1920s. Stanley, an engineering student, and Hanson, who was enrolled in the university's College of Commerce, dated the Holthues sisters, whom they eventually married.

After college, the friends went their separate ways for a time. Stanley worked for a Chicago engineering firm for a year, returned to the University of Iowa to earn a master's degree in hydraulic engineering, and served as a consulting engineer in Chicago and Dubuque, Iowa. Meanwhile, Hanson became a reporter for the *Des Moines Register,* later moving to the Quad Cities where he had a ten-year career with a Davenport advertising agency.

By 1943, Max Stanley, 39, and his wife Elizabeth lived in Muscatine, Iowa, where he had become the senior partner of Stanley Engineering Company, a consulting firm that helped build air bases and other military installations during the early years of World War II. A pillar of the Wesley United Methodist Church of Muscatine, Stanley taught Sunday school for several years and was instrumental in starting the church-sponsored Boy Scout Troop 127. (Oddly enough, one of his Sunday school students and a member of his troop, Stanley M. Howe, would be instrumental in HON INDUSTRIES' future). Clem Hanson, 42, and his wife Sylvia lived some 30 miles away in Moline, Illinois, where he was in charge of sales at the Tri-City Blue Print Company.[1]

A Sunday Conversation

As they had done many times before, the two families gathered at the Hanson home for dinner one Sunday afternoon in June 1943. After dinner, the wives retreated to the kitchen, and the husbands pulled lawn chairs together so they could exchange ideas. Around them in the yard swirled the Stanley children—David, 15, Richard, 11, and Jane, 7—and the Hanson boys—James, 10, and Thomas, 5. "The mental image I have," Richard "Dick" Stanley recalled, "is of my dad and Clem sitting in these lawn

The Home-O-Nize logo was designed by founders Clem Hanson and Wood Miller in 1944.

chairs, the kind that have the canvas seat that stretches from a wooden frame, and we kids were playing around, throwing balls back and forth."[2]

Conversation between the longtime friends turned logically to the war and other current events. There was certainly much to talk about in the spring and early summer of 1943. In the North Africa campaign, Allied forces had recently captured 275,000 German and Italian soldiers. After three weeks of fighting in the Aleutians, U.S. troops had liberated Attu. Thanks to British intelligence and code work, not one North Atlantic convoy had been attacked during June although German U-boats had been observed off the Azores. Two small Italian islands off Malta had surrendered to the Allies. In the Pacific, U.S. forces under Admiral "Bull" Halsey resumed moving up the Solomon Islands. On the home front, more than 500,000 coal miners went on strike for about a week when wage negotiations broke down.[3]

Talk of the war and labor unrest turned to speculation about conditions after the war ended, specifically what would happen to the job market as millions of soldiers and sailors returned home

and the U.S. economy moved away from wartime production. "Clem and I were worried, as many people then were, that employment would be a major problem when, at war's end, the country converted to a peacetime economy," Max Stanley wrote years later in *The HON Story.*[4]

Their concerns were not in vain. Industries and families adjusted as soldiers returned. Unemployment led to labor unrest and even violence. Workers went on strike and labor organizations competed for control of industries and workers. Tensions would not calm until the mid-1950s. "We both believed that there was a need in our country for more enlightened approaches to employer-employee relations," Stanley wrote. "We joined others in criticizing many industries for an all-too-prevalent 'public-be-damned' attitude toward consumers of their products. We had often expressed the egotistical belief that we could do better."[5]

Above: The yard of the Hanson home on 30th Street in Moline, Illinois, where Max Stanley and Clem Hanson pulled up lawn chairs to discuss their idea for a company.

Right: Max Stanley, cofounder of Home-O-Nize, the company that would later become HON INDUSTRIES. *(Photo courtesy of Fabian Bachrach)*

Thus the stage was set for the brothers-in-law to take the step from conversation to action. Stanley recalled saying, "Clem, what do you think about starting a manufacturing enterprise of some kind when peace comes?" Hanson thought it was a good idea. They agreed that such a venture could address several of the issues that had been frequent topics of their conversations in recent years. Theirs would be "a company that handled relations between employer and employee well," one where "employees, as fellow human beings, would be treated with dignity and fairness, not exploited in the interest of profits." Further, a manufacturing company would provide jobs for returning veterans and help offset the predicted widespread unemployment as the U.S. economy readjusted to peacetime.

The challenge of creating and operating a company excited them. The brothers-in-law spent the remainder of that afternoon's conversation taking a kind of inventory of the assets they would bring to their dream company.

"To me, it's fascinating that the impetus to start a company was first the belief that there were better ways to run a company than was common at the time," Dick Stanley recalled. "There was a lot of labor strife, a lot of difficulties taking place in the late- and postwar period that they felt could be eliminated. They believed that the stakeholders in a company—the owners, managers, customers, suppliers, and employees—all have a common interest in having a successful, profitable company. And if one can manage well, one can align those interests in a way that produces far better results than if a lot of energy is spent struggling amongst the various stakeholders on how the pie is divided rather than on how we work together to increase the overall success of the enterprise."[6]

Assembling the Pieces

The two men knew they had many of the right ingredients for starting a manufacturing company. Max Stanley wrote that "at age 39, I had developed strong confidence in my talents, not only in engineering, but also in organization and management." Hanson laid claim to expertise in marketing, sales, and advertising.

Still, the brothers-in-law thought they needed to add another dimension to the leadership of their

Clem Hanson, left, and Wood Miller, who with Max Stanley cofounded Home-O-Nize.

enterprise: experience in developing product ideas and converting those ideas into a workable design. To acquire that talent, Hanson suggested they ask H. Wood Miller, a friend and colleague from Hanson's days at the Davenport advertising agency, to join them. A graduate of the Art Institute of Chicago, Miller, 42, owned his own industrial design firm in Davenport. His previous experience as a consulting designer for an appliance manufacturer provided him with a vast array of ideas for kitchen cabinets and appliances.

Miller agreed to join the venture, and the trio set out to invent their company—to name and incorporate it, to select and develop the product to produce and market that product, and, in what turned out to be a challenge for a number of years, finance the entire venture. These beginning steps occupied the three men for the remainder of 1943, 1944, and well into 1945.[7] Securing financing and acquiring production facilities and material would take even longer. "A significant amount of family resources went into the company," said Hanson's son James. "It made a difference in the way we lived for a while. My mother made all our shirts, for example. We didn't buy shirts for a long time."[8]

First, the founders came up with a general idea of the kinds of products the new company would manufacture. From their earliest conversations, the partners focused on home-related products. The war would end, they reasoned, and GIs would return home eager to resume their lives. They would get married and start families. All those young families would need homes, and those homes would need furnishings. That's where the new company would find its niche, the partners planned.

Miller focused on product development and soon created the concept for what Max Stanley described as "some exciting kitchen cabinet concepts. He proposed electrically operated upper cabinets that could be raised or lowered for the home-maker's convenience."[9] Dick Stanley recalled seeing prototypes of the "very modernistic" cabinet designs his father and his father's partners were developing: "Tops of the lower cabinets could be pulled out so you could sit down and be chopping vegetables or whatever you wanted to do," the younger Stanley recalled. Available in a variety of widths and configurations, the fully assembled modular units could be installed easily and could be removed when the owners moved to a new home.[10]

The new company's name was inspired by Clem Hanson's marketing-oriented creative thinking. After some initial attempts containing the word "home," the partners settled on "Home-O-Nize." The name

contained the destination of the company's intended products, and its last syllable rhymed with words they could use to create advertising slogans such as "Economize with Home-O-Nize," "Modernize with Home-O-Nize," and "Harmonize with Home-O-Nize," Hanson and Miller devised a company logo using an easily read script font with two stylized musical notes inside the capital O.[11]

While they felt satisfied about the progress they were making into the autumn of 1943, the partners realized their work would be academic without a manufacturing facility. They began looking for expertise in sheet metal fabrication.

Miller had extensive connections among Quad City manufacturers. His friend Dale Hermes of the Herman Nelson Division of the American Air Filter Company, introduced the partners to Albert Uchtorff, president of the Davenport-based Uchtorff Company, which manufactured sheet metal products, including some conventional, square-cornered kitchen cabinets. It was with great anticipation that "in November 1943, the four of us signed a partnership agreement to establish an organization for the design, manufacture and sale of home appliances and other apparatus," Stanley wrote.[12] Unfortunately, the partnership with Uchtorff would cause the founding partners the first of many difficult challenges.

Making It Official

Now that they had apparently secured the means to produce their kitchen goods, the partners decided to formalize their arrangements. Stanley used the services of two Muscatine lawyers, Matthew Westrate and Harvey Allbee, to work on the incorporation. Allbee's son, Harvey Allbee Jr., recalled that his father was paid for his work in Home-O-Nize stock, "plus cash for the income tax portion."[13] On

Below: The promise of a postwar housing boom as returning GIs bought homes gave Home-O-Nize the hope of success.

Below right: Home-O-Nize was incorporated on January 6, 1944, after the state of Iowa granted the company a charter.

Iowa Charter Asked by Home Appliance Concern

Articles of incorporation were filed with the Iowa secretary of State in Des Moines today by the Home-O-Nize company of Davenport. The firm is capitalized at $50,000 and will design and manufacture household appliances, according to a United Press dispatch.

Officers are C. Maxwell Stanley, Muscatine, president; Albert F. Uchtorff, Davenport, vice president; H. Wood Miller, Davenport, vice president, and C. T. Hanson, Moline, secretary-treasurer.

Every home would have a kitchen, Home-O-Nize's founders reasoned, so they planned to sell kitchen cabinets to the new homeowners.

January 6, 1944, The Home-O-Nize Co. became incorporated with headquarters at Wood Miller's office at 315 ½ West Fourth Street in Davenport. The officers were C. Maxwell Stanley, president; Albert F. Uchtorff, vice president; H. Wood Miller, vice president; and Clement T. Hanson, secretary-treasurer. The capital consisted of 500 shares of preferred stock with $100 par value plus 500 shares of common stock without par value. That same day, the four officers pledged to buy ten shares each within three weeks, giving the fledgling company a badly needed $4,000 bank account.[14]

A little more than two months later, on March 15, 1944, the partners approved the bylaws at the first annual meeting of stockholders. The sign on their new office door read, "THE HOME-O-NIZE CO.—MAKERS OF HOME APPLIANCES." They paid $10 per month rent.[15]

The Cabinet Designs

By mid-1944, Miller was devoting a substantial part of his time designing products for the new company under a retainer arrangement. Later in the year, Hanson resigned from Tri-City Blue Print to become the first full-time employee of The Home-

O-Nize Co., working on marketing materials and sales strategies, at a salary of $400 per month.[16]

Miller's first completed design was for a home freezer. Stanley obtained a compressor unit for the prototype, and Uchtorff built the model. The partners took the model to Stanley's garage for testing. "It was a crudely made freezer," Dick Stanley said. "It was a sort of test product. It was a flat-topped freezer rather than a front-door opening one. The lid would lift off the top and the frozen product would set down inside it."[17] But the freezer idea seemed to have waned at that point as the partners' enthusiasm grew for the kitchen cabinets.

Miller continued to work on the design for the cabinets. He and Hanson set up a model shop at the Davenport office, and with some hired assistance from retired sheet metal worker William Booth, they developed a working model and detailed designs that would guide production.[18]

By October 1944, events seemed to be moving ahead so well that Stanley, Miller, and Hanson set an early December date for unveiling their new products to some Midwest distributors of kitchen products. G. W. Timmerman & Company, a Davenport distributor of home appliances (and an enthusiastic supporter of the Home-O-Nize venture), had invited some other Midwest dealers to Davenport in early December to see and test the working models of the cabinets and to listen to Hanson's marketing proposals. The promotional literature Hanson had prepared claimed the units could be "installed as easily as a stove or a refrigerator." The literature described the cabinets as having "attractive curves and round corners [that] add to beauty and style." Moreover, they were easily accessible. "Press the button, and lo, the shelves descend for easy access," the brochure said. "Shelves that were beyond reach are now at eye level. No more risky, tiresome climbing on chairs."[19]

The Face of Adversity

Virtually on the eve of their presentation to dealers, the three founding partners faced a crisis. Uchtorff pulled out of The Home-O-Nize Co. and took the company's manufacturing capability with him. As Stanley described it, "Uchtorff... did not like the highly styled, ingeniously designed kitchen cabinets that we proposed. He was negative toward plans to tap so large a market that The Home-O-Nize Co. would ultimately need a plant of its own. In short, he seemed determined to limit The Home-O-Nize Co.'s production... to levels compatible with the capacity of his own plant."[20]

The new company was stopped dead. Typically sanguine, Stanley later wrote, "We were compelled for the first time, but not for the last, to deal with adversity, rise above disappointment, and move ahead, albeit on an altered course.... In retrospect, I am convinced that the parting of ways with Uchtorff was not only inevitable but beneficial, at least in the long run. His interests and objectives were obviously different from those of the three founders."[21]

Home-O-Nize's kitchen cabinets featured easy-rolling ball bearings that permitted drawers to slide in and out smoothly. The illustrations at left show several easy-to-access ways the cabinets could store pots, pans, dishes, and other commonly used kitchen aids.

Max Stanley was ever adaptable to changing circumstances, a characteristic his biographer later described as "his most serviceable trait. Change challenged him, not to take a defensive stance, but to take hold of an opportunity to turn new conditions into favorable ones. . . . His own willingness to change was, in many ways, one of his most valuable strengths."[22]

The three remaining partners commenced with the planned December 9, 1944, presentation to Midwest kitchen cabinet dealers. "Following the luncheon, we unveiled a working model of the Home-O-Nize kitchen cabinet with power-operated upper shelves," Stanley recalled. "Hanson presented data targeting a huge potential market: the more than 18 million families in the United States with annual incomes of over $2,500 in 1944. The uniquely designed Home-O-Nize units were packaged items, not tailor-made or built-in cabinets. They could be stocked, installed and moved just like a range or a refrigerator." Stanley's note in his logbook after the dealers departed said, "Showing of cabinets to distributors. All were enthusiastic: reception exceeded our fondest hopes!"[23]

The First Plant

Based on the reaction to their kitchen cabinet concept, the three partners plunged ahead to arrange financing, locate and equip a manufacturing plant, complete detailed product designs, recruit employees, and develop production and marketing programs. On the heels of Uchtorff's departure, they moved their offices to the second floor of Muscatine's Central State Bank building, where Stanley Engineering was located.[24] Although they no longer had a factory, they confidently projected they would start rolling cabinets off the assembly line during the first quarter of 1947. Unfortunately, they failed to consider one essential element for the success of their new company: they needed sheet steel from which to make the cabinets.[25]

They also needed capital. Although the stock that Stanley, Hanson, and Miller had purchased gave them enough funds to operate to the end of 1944, they knew they would need more working capital to truly get the company off the ground. Stanley put together a proposal with the Central State Bank that would have raised start-up funds through the sale of 1,000 shares of common stock, but, by mid-1945, only one shareholder outside the partnership was found. By early 1946, Stanley had purchased 380 shares, Hanson 60, and Miller 36—nearly all the 500 total shares the bank would permit them to own together. They knew The Home-O-Nize Co. would need a fresh infusion of funds soon.[26]

Meanwhile, the partners were reaching other start-up goals they had set for their little company. The Home-O-Nize trademark was registered in July 1945.[27] By autumn, they had located a suitable manufacturing site, the largely unused U.S. Button Company factory at Third and Oak streets in downtown Muscatine.

In early October, before The Home-O-Nize Co. took possession of that property, Stanley encountered Lyle McCullough at church. McCullough was a returned Army Air Corps veteran. Stanley soon offered him a job, and McCullough became the first full-time employee of The Home-O-Nize Co. outside of the founders. "I made the decision to go with Max because I had a lot of faith in him," McCullough recalled years later.[28]

McCullough first reported for work at the Stanley Engineering office, but it wasn't long until Stanley told him to set up a model shop in one corner of the button plant and "handed me the keys," McCullough recalled. As McCullough turned the key in the lock, he noticed the glass on the door was engraved with "Boepple Button Company." John Frederick Boepple, a German immigrant, started the pearl button industry that once employed thousands in Muscatine. "Of course, being an old button factory," McCullough said, "everything that was horizontal was built up with button dust as high as you could pile it." After cleaning and enclosing an area big enough for the model shop, McCullough installed heat, water, and electricity.[29]

Soon, William Booth, the retired sheet metal worker from Davenport, arrived in his Ford Model A truck with the materials from the model shop in Davenport, where work on the Home-O-Nize prototypes had begun. Working in the makeshift facility inside the old button factory, McCullough and Booth labored to perfect the models of the kitchen cabinets. Booth commuted to Muscatine every day from Davenport in his old truck.

The concept of the cabinets "was far in advance of anything that was available at that time,"

The vacant U.S. Button Company factory on Muscatine's Oak Street became the first location for the factory and office of The Home-O-Nize Co.

McCullough said. "Ten years after we developed them, General Electric came out with the kitchen of the future. They had the same thing, the same concept. It had electric shelves moving down and the door up."[30]

Miller continued to devote part of his time to his consulting business, and Hanson divided his time between the Muscatine company and his own advertising firm, which he had founded in Moline earlier in 1945. Occasionally during the winter of 1945–46, Hanson and Miller drove to the model shop from the Quad Cities to supervise McCullough

and Booth's work.[31] With additional working models to test, product design development progressed to the point where the partners knew what equipment would be needed to produce their revolutionary kitchen cabinets.[32]

Still working at Stanley Engineering, Max Stanley set up a small office on the third floor of the Third and Oak building, where he also worked part-time. "The first president's office had an old oak desk, a wobbly swivel chair and a folding chair for visitors," he wrote. "The most extraordinary feature was the door. An eye-level knothole about three inches in diameter...allowed almost anyone to look through at me."[33]

The button factory occupied three lots with a total floor space of 18,000 square feet. It had enough land around the three buildings to enclose an additional 18,700 square feet. The Home-O-

The Mississippi River Button Industry

IN THE 19TH CENTURY, THE UNITED States imported most of its buttons, many from Germany and Austria where they were made from seashells. Meanwhile along the Mississippi River, people harvested mussels, primarily for freshwater pearls, discarding most of the shells.

That all changed after a German named John Frederick Boepple moved to Muscatine, Iowa, in 1887. Years earlier, a family friend living in the United States had sent him some Mississippi River shells. Boepple, a skilled "turner"—an artisan who used a lathe to cut blanks out of hard materials—found he could cut those shells into buttons.

Arriving in Muscatine, Boepple wanted to start a button-making business, but he had no money, and his broken English kept him from persuading others that he had a good idea. He supported himself doing odd jobs in Columbus Junction, Iowa, and Petersburg, Illinois. As he walked from place to place, he asked farmers to give him small wooden or metal wheels they no longer wanted. With those and other scrounged materials, he fashioned a foot-powered lathe that he used to cut blanks from Mississippi River shells.

The McKinley Tariff of 1890 sent the price of imported seashell mother-of-pearl, from which buttons at the time were made, sky high. Seeing an opportunity, Boepple returned to Muscatine and again approached investors. This time they listened, and on January 26, 1891, Boepple opened the first freshwater pearl button factory in the world.

The business soon outgrew its first head-quarters in the basement of the Davis Cooper Shop, and Boepple moved his equipment to space above Nester's Blacksmith Shop. Seeing the growth, his investors wanted him to automate, but they bought inadequate machines; Boepple, who thought of himself as an Old World craftsman, preferred manual machines. The partners fell out over the issue, and the business failed.

Undaunted, Boepple found other investors and opened a new factory at Third and Oak Streets in Muscatine that employed more than 100. Over time, some of his employees left, taking his "secrets" with them, and started rival button-making companies. By 1897, Muscatine had 53 button factories and hundreds of home operations. It was known as the Pearl Button Capital of the World. Towns as far away as Prairie du Chien, Wisconsin, and Louisiana, Missouri, shipped shells to Muscatine.

Boepple lived to see the button industry he started in a cooper shop basement reach unimagined heights. In 1905 Muscatine alone produced 1.5 billion buttons—almost 40 percent of the world's output. Four years after his death, at the industry's zenith, some 9,500 button factory workers made 6 billion buttons, worth about $12.5 million. Most plants were in Iowa, New York, and New Jersey.[1] HON INDUSTRIES took over several button buildings when the button industry declined due to the advent of plastics.

Nize Co. hired Ed Doonan, then city engineer at Waverly, Iowa, to plan and supervise an expansion and rehabilitation of the plant, beginning in November 1945. Doonan later became plant superintendent. According to the building permit issued for the project, the cost of the addition "of steel and concrete block construction" was set at $13,000.[34] The basement was filled with sand, and a concrete floor was poured. The wooden second floor was removed, except for office space above the corner of Third and Oak streets. Stanley Engineering Company developed detailed plans for the addition that connected the button factory buildings, and construction began in May 1946. The construction crew included McCullough and other returned World War II veterans, among them Harold Barton, Ray Shellabarger, Edmund Metz, and Raymond Wichers, all of whom stayed with the company for long careers. Production equipment, much of it used, was purchased and installed, with full-scale production still expected to begin by January 1947.[35]

In February 1946, with the help of Central State Bank, The Home-O-Nize Co. had managed to obtain a $100,000 loan from a federal agency, the Smaller War Plants Corporation. In September, the company used those funds to buy the former button factory, one of four abandoned mother-of-pearl button factories the company purchased as it expanded over the years.[36]

By late autumn of 1946, construction on the Home-O-Nize plant was nearing completion. Production equipment—shears, punch presses, press brakes, tools, and dies—was arriving at the site and being installed. The gas-fired finishing oven and paint spray equipment, which Doonan told reporters would "assure a baked enamel finish of the highest quality to be found in the home appliance industry," was in place before Thanksgiving.[37]

As work on prototypes of kitchen cabinets continued in the winter of 1945–1946, Clem Hanson (pictured) often visited the model shop in the Oak Street plant. This photo shows kitchen cabinet prototypes immediately to Hanson's right and in the corner of the room.

Machinery Arriving for New Home-O-Nize Firm

Construction work in preparation for the introduction of a new Muscatine product upon the market early next year is preceeding according to schedule at the manufacturing plant being completed by the Home-O-Nize co. at East Third and Oak streets, it is announced by C. M. Stanley, president.

The firm will produce metal kitchen cabinets and is expected to furnish employment to approximately 100 persons when the plant is in full production.

Equipment and machinery ordered last summer is now starting to arrive at the factory and installation is in progress. In the stage of erection at present is the gas fired finishing oven and paint spray equipment which R. G. Doonan, plant manager, reports is the most up to date to be installed anywhere and will assure a baked enamel finish of the highest quality to be found in the home appliance industry upon Home-O-Nize kitchen cabinets.

Arrangements for the distribution of Home-O-Nize metal kitchen cabinets have been made with leading appliance wholesale firms which will absorb the firm's entire production for the first several years of operation. Acceptance of the Home-O-Nize line of cabinets is reported by sales personnel to be extremely satisfactory.

Advertising and promotion plans have crystallized under the direction of C. T. Hanson, vice president, and W. C. Newsom, sales manager.

Home-O-Nize co. officials plan to be ready for production around the first of the year at which time personnel will be added to the force as required until the required complement has been reached.

Present personnel includes, in

C. M. STANLEY

ddition to the construction crew, red Winn, Jr., auditor, Elmer ossman and Arthur Dahl in the anning department, and Lyle Cullough, Ray Zeidler, Bob gren, Ray Shellabarger and old Barton, who are ...rolled a GI training program for men and junior plant executives.

Above and right: Even in its early days, The Home-O-Nize Co. made headlines in the local news. The local press followed closely the progress in establishing the Oak Street plant. These articles appeared in the *Muscatine Journal*.

Four Building Permtis Totaling $15,000 Issued

Four building permits totaling $15,000, including one for a new addition to the Home-O-Nize Co., at $13,000, have been issued by F. E. Tewksbury, acting city engineer.

The Home-O-Nize addition will be of steel and concrete block construction and will be started within about 10 days, Ed Doonan of the company said this morning. The company sometime ago acquired the old U. S. Button Co. building on East Third street at Oak street and the new addition will be adjacent to that building.

The company will manufacture metal kitchen cabinets just as soon as the construction is completed and materials are available, Mr. Doonan said.

Another permit for a new home was issued to Marvin Burke, the structure to be erected on First Avenue between Monroe and Jackson streets at a cost of $1,500.

A permit to repair a concrete block building at the rear of East Third street between Walnut and Cedar streets at a cost of $350 was issued to C. W. Ramseyer and Donald McDaniel was issued a permit to remodel a frame garage on Hershey avenue between Taylor and Clinton streets at a cost of $150.

Speculative Stock

Faced with a pressing need for funds, the stockholders voted to try again to sell stock in their fledgling company. This time it worked. The Iowa Commissioner of Insurance gave them permission to sell 2,500 shares of common stock at $100 each and raised to 1,000 the number of shares the partners could buy. They hired William C. Newsom, a returned veteran with sales experience, to sell the stock. The company was not yet operating, not to mention profitable, so the insurance commissioner insisted each certificate be stamped "speculative stock."

"There were those in Muscatine who thought it would be money down the tube," recalled Dick Stanley. "The new company wasn't anything that everybody thought, at first blush, was ever going to get off the ground."[38]

Still, by January 1947, Newsom had sold enough stock that the first $50,000 in proceeds could be released from escrow. By March 1947, a total of 998 shares at $100 apiece had been sold to the public, and the founding partners had bought another 500 shares—at $50 apiece, since they received no other compensation.[39]

Speculating on why this stock sale succeeded, Max Stanley wrote, "Undoubtedly, it had something to do with the fact that most of our new shareholders were acquainted with me or one of the other founders. In addition, the many Muscatine investors were concerned about local employment, as the community's major employers, the pearl button and the sash and door industries, were on the decline."[40]

McCullough, who was then in his first year of employment with the company, took a leap of faith. "My wife and I had $400 we scraped together, and we bought four of the original shares." Their faith paid off; nearly 60 years later he noted, "Now each of the original four shares is worth 15,552 shares."[41]

While the plant was under construction during 1946, the leaders of the new company were busy building their management team and workforce. Doonan would continue as plant superintendent, and Newsom would become sales manager after the stock sales concluded. Fred S. Winn,

Left: Art Dahl, head of The Home-O-Nize Co.'s planning division, is shown at work in 1947 in what had served as a carding and sorting room for the U.S. Button Company. The assembly line system design is illustrated on the chalkboard.

Below: These new shears were installed in the Oak Street plant in late 1946 or early 1947. Much of the early equipment was purchased used to save money.

Four new spot welding stations at the Oak Street plant stand ready for action.

a Quartermaster Corps captain during the war, was hired as bookkeeper and chief clerk. With an accounting degree from the University of Illinois, Winn eventually became corporate secretary-treasurer. Arthur Dahl, a draftsman at Stanley Engineering, moved to The Home-O-Nize Co. to prepare the plant for production of kitchen cabinets. Later he would head production control and planning and eventually would become senior vice president of HON INDUSTRIES. Louis York left his position at the Herman Nelson Division of the American Air Filter Company to become plant

foreman. Returned veterans Harold Barton, Ray Shellabarger, Robert Nygren, and Raymond Zeidler participated in an on-the-job training program. McCullough, newly appointed as company purchasing agent, ordered parts and supplies to meet Stanley's ambitious production plan, which called for ramping up to a rate of 4,000 kitchen cabinets per month by August 1947.[42]

Anticipation for those new cabinets was growing among distributors who were following the new company's progress. G. W. Timmerman & Company in Davenport placed an order for about 7,500 cabinets. Hanson, in his role as head of marketing and advertising, sent copies of a sales brochure, "Cabinets for modern kitchens," to distributors, many of whom had attended the December 1944 demonstration, and they were excited.[43]

The Bonderite finishing system cleaned and etched the metal's surface and applied a coat of phosphorus in preparation for painting.

Steel Shortage

Unfortunately, the distributors were about to be disappointed. As McCullough later recalled, "When we had the building ready to go, the machinery in place, the Bonderite cleaning-and-painting system set up and ready to manufacture, we didn't have anything to do because we didn't have any steel at that time."[44]

Companies such as Home-O-Nize that did not exist before the war could not find steel to buy. During the war, most available steel had gone toward the war effort, and the postwar economy was frantically working to satisfy pent-up demand among manufacturers of consumer goods. Hanson had tried for months to find a source from which they could buy the needed steel, but domestic steel mills worked on a quota system—for established customers only. Nor was there foreign steel in the North American market at the time.[45]

"I can remember my dad coming back from Granite City, Illinois, where he was trying to requisition some steel from a mill," recalled James Hanson. "The mill finally told him, 'We're awfully sorry, but it's going to be years before we can supply any new account at all. We can't help you.'"[46]

The leaders of The Home-O-Nize Co. faced their worst crisis since Uchtorff pulled out of the partnership and left them without a factory. They examined their few options and quickly concluded that if the company was going to survive, it would have to contract out its manufacturing capacity to other companies. Ads announcing the availability of manufacturing capacity appeared in area newspapers.[47]

Ironically, Wood Miller's friend Dale Hermes, who had introduced the three founders to Uchtorff in 1943, provided the most important solution to this crisis. Hermes managed a new company called Stampings Inc., a Davenport-based bottled gas supplier that had been founded by Stanley and James Leach of Bettendorf.[48] Stampings needed aluminum hoods, bases, and other accessories for its gas bottles. The Home-O-Nize Co. had most of the equipment needed to make the products. Stampings and The Home-O-Nize Co. signed a contract on November 28, 1946, and the new Muscatine company was able to celebrate a happy Thanksgiving.

Stanley's logbook for the date noted, "Closed deal with Stampings Inc. for work for The Home-O-Nize Co. Will aggregate $88,500 in 1947 on estimated schedule. This means production and revenue soon!" The company ended 1946 with its income statement showing $14,501 in red ink.[49]

In Summary

THE COMPANY THAT BECAME HON INDUSTRIES began with a unique idea—not for a particular product, but with a noble ideal about how a company should treat its employees.

The idea originated with C. Maxwell Stanley and Clement T. Hanson, friends for many years since the 1920s. The fast friends even married sisters.

When their two families gathered for dinner at the Hanson home one fateful Sunday afternoon in June 1943, the conversation turned to their dream of founding an employee-friendly company after the conclusion of World War II.

To develop practical product ideas, Hanson suggested the brothers-in-law invite H. Wood Miller, who owned an industrial design firm in Davenport, Iowa, to join them. The trio set out to invent the company and pick a home-related product to manufacture. The Home-O-Nize Co. was incorporated in 1944, as Miller worked on designs for a kitchen cabinet product line.

The three plunged ahead with their concept, but the fledgling company was plagued by war-related steel shortages in 1944–46. To keep The Home-O-Nize Co. alive, what could it manufacture?

Home-O-Nize member Leonard McEvoy assembles a combination file cabinet at the Oak Street plant. By 1950 the company was manufacturing eight models of file or file-and-storage cabinets.

CHAPTER TWO

A Rough Start

1947–1950

Why not use the word "member" to designate everyone in the Home-O-Nize organization—whether in office, in shop, or an officer.

—Clem Hanson, handwritten note, 1947

GOLDEN DAWN

CHRISTMAS OF 1946 MUST HAVE been a happy time for the employees of The Home-O-Nize Co. At last the fledgling company had a manufacturing contract, and production would begin soon. The first products, aluminum hoods for bottled gas canisters used commonly by farm families, were loaded onto a truck and delivered to Stampings Inc. on April 5, 1947. Innovative for their time, the Stampings gas bottle hoods boasted "a one-piece housing—no welds—no seams—no hinges. *Made entirely of aluminum, it will not rust....* Fits all standard regulators and manifold assemblies."[1]

In the deep-draw technology used to manufacture the bottle hoods, the aluminum drawing press would press a flat piece of aluminum into a shape of nearly one foot in depth by 18 inches across. Each hood fit over two bottles of gas and covered up the valving and tubing that would connect into the house.[2]

Putting Scrap to Good Use

The dream that had begun in June 1943 was being realized—in a sense. The Home-O-Nize Co. was making products and employing returned war veterans. The company was not, however, producing the kitchen cabinets the founders had envisioned, and it seemed unlikely that shareholders would get a return on their investment from the

cabinets. The company had just one customer, and that customer did not use Home-O-Nize's manufacturing capacity to its fullest. Some equipment lay idle, including the enamel finishing system of which Ed Doonan had been so proud. Moreover, The Home-O-Nize Co. had very little cash. The company was not yet profitable, and until it secured further financing, this would be a problem.[3]

Within two weeks of making that first shipment in early April, 540 gas bottle hoods crossed the loading dock of the plant at Oak and Third streets each day on their way to Stampings. The client was impressed enough to move its warehouse operation to Muscatine. However, The Home-O-Nize Co.'s output was so good that it exceeded Stampings' needs, and production had to be slowed for a while. As welcome as the Stampings contract was, this incident showed the vulnerability of the company's position: the fortunes of The Home-O-Nize Co. were tied to those of one client.[4]

To solve this dilemma, Home-O-Nize members realized they needed to diversify and exhibited the kind of ingenuity that would benefit the company

---

In the company's early lean days, it made use of scrap metal to help bring in revenue. Clem Hanson conceived the idea of welding together two pieces of drop-off aluminum to create identifying tags for flower enthusiasts' gardens.

repeatedly over the years. The manufacture of gas bottle hoods produced waste aluminum. At first the company sold the odd bits of aluminum as scrap, but at a much lower price per pound than the metal cost originally. The members thought they could do better. Within a few weeks, The Home-O-Nize Co. was manufacturing aluminum beverage coasters and selling them to businesses to be used as gifts. The coasters bore the name of the business to which they were sold and became the first product to bear the Home-O-Nize name. Some of those businesses, in addition to The Home-O-Nize Co. itself, included some familiar names— G. W. Timmerman & Company; Appliance Distributors of Davenport, which had earlier hoped to distribute The Home-O-Nize Co.'s kitchen cabinets; Tri-City Blue Print Company, where Clem Hanson worked; and Swan Engineering & Machinery Company in Bettendorf, which had

Right: The Home-O-Nize Co. manufactured aluminum housings on contract for Stampings Inc. from 1947 to 1959. These hoods were the first products the new company made. The scrap aluminum left after their manufacture was turned into recipe card file boxes, and the boxes eventually led the company into office supplies and furniture.

Below: The Home-O-Nize Co. also made aluminum coasters from scrap and marketed them to businesses for use as gifts and promotional items.

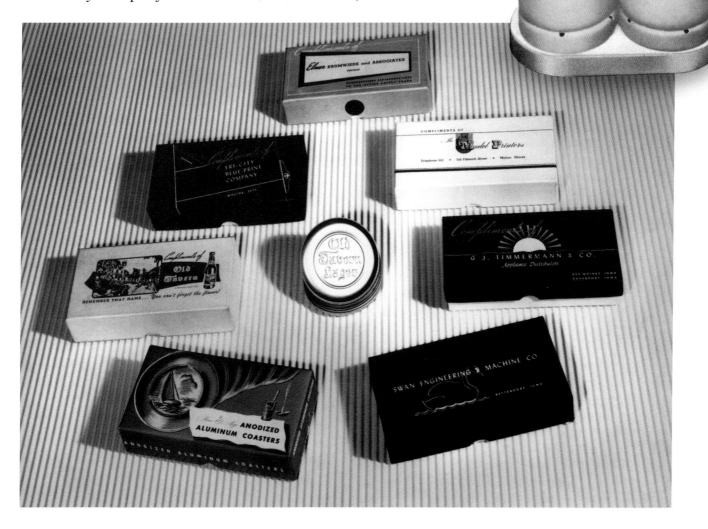

supplied a major portion of the equipment for the company's factory.[5]

The beverage coasters were only the beginning of The Home-O-Nize Co.'s diversification efforts. Other products came from the Stampings project's scrap pile. The process of making the aluminum hoods involved punching slugs from the aluminum. Hanson, a rose fancier, found a way to turn the slugs into durable labels (marketed under the brand Flower Names Limited) that identified flowers in the garden. To make the flower labels, one slug, about 1½ inches by 4 inches with a rounded end, was spot-welded to a 10-inch-long, quarter-inch-wide slug, which could be inserted into the soil beside the flower. Common plant names were silk-screened onto labels, and others were left blank. The product never took off.[6]

Although the coasters and the flower labels brought in some revenue, the third attempt to utilize the drop-off aluminum raised more significant income in 1947—and led the company a step closer to its future in office furniture. The Home-O-Nize Co. began manufacturing 3-by-5-inch aluminum card file boxes. The boxes had "rounded corners," Max Stanley wrote, "piano hinges and baked-on enamel finish." Producing the card files used many

Ray Shellabarger, one of the first employees (foreground) and Harold "Peewee" Whisler assemble flower markers in 1947 at the Oak Street plant.

of the company's expensive machines, including the enamel finishing equipment and the heavy-duty press to deep-draw the boxes and lids.[7]

The aluminum file boxes sold well because steel card files were so scarce. At first, consistent with The Home-O-Nize Co.'s market niche, the card files were marketed primarily as recipe boxes. One version was painted white with a red lid. Because the card files were relatively easy to produce, the company soon had more than enough of them to satisfy demand.

Searching for additional markets for the item, the company sent Hanson and William Newsom to the National Stationers Show in Chicago in September 1947. Elmer Krumweide & Associates of Chicago, a national distributor, took on the product, and sales began to climb. An early sales flyer pointed out, "This file blends nicely with the finest home or office surroundings. Usable for many purposes in both places." Led by the card file sales, The

Home-O-Nize Co.'s own products earned the company about $20,000 that year.[8]

Member Benefits

As the company's income stream began flowing in 1947, Hanson and Stanley produced the first handbook for employees. That document may have been the first formal document to refer to company employees as "members."

"The concept of members was very important to my dad," James Hanson said. "He was one of those people who had a very strong human relations quotient. His thinking was primarily about people rather than machines."[9]

Using that term, Max Stanley said, "projects a greater sense of belonging and participation." The handbook set out policies that embodied the founders' opinions and beliefs on how a company should be run—what they called "basic and fundamental truths." They were:

1. *That the welfare of the members of this organization and of the company itself [are] inter-dependent; neither can prosper unless the other likewise prospers.*
2. *That maximum productivity and its fruits can be attained only by wholesome, open-minded relationships among the entire personnel of the organization.*

Left: Home-O-Nize's recipe boxes were sold with index tabs. Painting them green turned the recipe box for the kitchen into a card file for the office.

Below: In 1947, The Home-O-Nize Co. displayed aluminum coasters and 3-by-5 card files (hanging on wall right side) at the National Stationers Show in Chicago at a booth it shared with two other companies.

3. *That every member is entitled to fair treatment from the company and to an equitable share in the fruits of quality performance and high production.*
4. *That every permanent employee is a full-fledged member of this organization and assumes individual responsibility for the quality and efficiency of his work.*
5. *That the customer who buys is the final judge of our products and neither the member nor the company can long prosper unless the customer is provided with a good product at a fair price. Continued customer satisfaction is a goal that must be maintained in order to achieve any real success.*[10]

After a 90-day probationary period, Home-O-Nize employees became full-fledged members and were eligible for sick leave, vacations, and health insurance. They could also participate in the company's profit sharing, which, the handbook noted, would "become operative immediately upon elimination of the deficit that has accumulated during development of the plant."[11] A retirement fund, incentive bonuses, and other benefits would come later. Wages were established in seven job classifications with five rate levels in each class; they ranged from 70 cents to $1.20 per hour. Beginning in 1947, the company adjusted workers' wages consistent with the federal cost-of-living index, becoming one of the first companies to do so.[12]

With remarkable foresight for the time, The Home-O-Nize Co. gave all permanent members the right to serve on planning committees. Five committees existed from the beginning:

- *General Policy, which made major decisions, including deciding on general shop rules, supervising plant elections, setting up additional committees, and helping formulate the profit-sharing plan*
- *Health and Security, which covered all member welfare matters, including insurance and retirement plans*
- *Safety, which acted to ensure a safe workplace and investigated any accidents*
- *Sports and Recreation, which oversaw many off-duty activities involving members, such as picnics and sports teams*

- *Civic Affairs, which kept track of members' involvement in charities and other community matters, including governmental actions*[13]

Consistent with the values they expressed on that Sunday afternoon in June 1943, Stanley and Hanson established regular employee communication meetings in which company executives talked directly with members about any matter of company interest and then answered members' questions. At first Stanley or another top officer would personally conduct the meetings, which everyone in the plant attended. Later, as the company grew larger and occupied more locations, the pattern continued with local officials in charge at each company site. Dick Stanley, who worked summers at the Oak Street plant during his school years, remembered an informal extension of the practice. "The conveyor belt would stop in the morning, and they'd blow a horn," he recalled. "Everybody would go down to a central location in the factory. The front office folks would come down too, and everyone would stand around chatting a little bit, kind of reviewing what was going on."[14]

Contacts and Contracts

In the search for more contract work to broaden the company's client base, once again a Quad City connection paid off for the young Muscatine

A counter display for The Home-O-Nize Co.'s aluminum card files calls the product an "Easy Way to Save and to Use Your Favorite Recipes." In mid-1948, The Home-O-Nize Co. began making red and white recipe boxes.

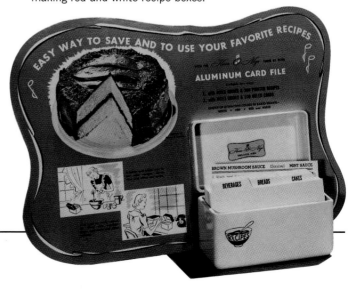

Max Stanley and Clem Hanson persuaded John Deere & Company to give The Home-O-Nize Co. a contract to manufacture pick-up attachments for combines, although the new company didn't yet have a track record.

company. Hanson and Stanley persuaded John Deffenbaugh, the manager of the John Deere Harvester Works in Moline, to contract with The Home-O-Nize Co. to manufacture a belt pick-up attachment for its combines. Demand for farm implements was so brisk that Deere didn't have enough manufacturing capacity to meet it. Deere and The Home-O-Nize Co. signed the contract on August 26, 1947.

The next month, Robert Carl, who later became secretary of HON INDUSTRIES, started his Home-O-Nize/HON INDUSTRIES career as a stock inventory and production control clerk. He remembered the combine pick-up attachment well. "Deere supplied most of the parts, and we assembled them and did some of the sheet metal because we knew how to bend sheet metal," he said.[15] Although The Home-O-Nize Co. performed well and Deere was satisfied with the work, the contract lasted just one year. Deere had purchased a former defense plant in Ankeny, Iowa, and was moving production, including the combine pick-up attachment, to that site.[16]

From Home-O-Nize to Office Supplies

By early 1948, new companies such as Home-O-Nize still could not buy steel in large quantities, so manufacturing the kitchen cabinets remained in limbo. The success of the file card boxes, however, helped lead the board of directors to make an important decision at its meeting of March 30, 1948; the board passed a resolution that "Home-

O-Nize's efforts in sales, advertising, and product development should be directed to the office supply and equipment field." The board at that time was made up of Stanley, Hanson, Wood Miller, plant superintendent Ed Doonan, and a new director who represented local investors, A. J. Whitsitt, manager of Muscatine's Batterson's, a well respected local department store. Production of a 4-by-6-inch deep-drawn aluminum card file began two months later, doubling the company's product line.[17]

A second board decision in 1948 reinforced the new direction Home-O-Nize would take. In August, faced with the lingering reality that the steel shortages would not permit the company to pursue its original production plans, the board "authorized the officers to dispose of materials, tooling, and equipment assembled specifically for the manufacture of kitchen cabinets and, if possible, to sell the design and patent applications." Established manufacturers in home furnishings had been able to obtain steel and, in doing so, had moved ahead in their product development and production. The Home-O-Nize Co. officially acknowledged that it was bowing to reality and revising its original goal.[18]

Capital Quandaries

Those two decisions eventually would lead the company to a bright financial future, but The Home-O-Nize Co. faced deep capital pressures and other serious challenges for the next several years.

The Home-O-Nize Co. reached the end of 1947, its first year of manufacturing, with operating losses of $30,000, despite respectable sales of about $90,000. Meanwhile, stock sales were dismal. Newsom managed to sell only $21,400 worth of stock to outside investors; Clem Hanson, Max Stanley, and Stanley's extended family purchased an additional $20,000 in stock. Stanley tersely wrote, "The aggregate amount was inadequate to cover the combined losses."[19]

As tenuous as the company's future appeared, some accounts accepted Home-O-Nize stock as payment. For example, in payment for a $200 bill, the partners in the Muscatine-based Ioway-Record Printing Company each accepted a share of common stock. Years later, Stanley recalled one of those partners saying his only regret was that The Home-O-Nize Co. had not owed the printer more money.[20]

The second year of manufacturing, 1948, ended with black ink on the company's bottom line. On sales of $419,700, the company realized net profit of $39,900, but stock sales of just $25,600 again did not provide adequate working capital. As in the previous year, the Stanleys and the Hansons purchased the largest portion of the stock. Whitsitt, the newest director, bought $3,000 worth. Other members of the company acquired $2,600 worth of stock, some of it in lieu of full salaries. To ease its financial constraints, the company persuaded its primary bank, the Central State Bank of Muscatine, to factor accounts receivable on its sales of office products.[21]

The Stanley family felt the strains from the company's financial problems. "I can recall the summer of '48," Dick Stanley said. "I wanted to go to the national Boy Scout Jamboree. The deal that I worked out with my folks was, if I could get a summer job and earn so much of the Jamboree cost, then they'd help with so much more. For whatever reason, I wasn't able to line up a summer job, and I didn't go." The younger Stanley also remembered his father talking with his mother about mortgaging the house to raise more capital for The Home-O-Nize Co., "but she drew the line on that point," Dick Stanley said.[22]

Progressive Management

As if the financial difficulties were not traumatic enough, Max Stanley faced a problem in the summer of 1948 that shook him personally and altered the company's management team. The Home-O-Nize Co.'s managers needed to exercise strong

A Birkhofer delivery truck backs up to The Home-O-Nize Co.'s loading dock to pick up a shipment of gas bottle hoods for Stampings. This truck was the model for a toy produced to commemorate HON INDUSTRIES' 50th anniversary.

leadership, especially because the three founders were dividing their attentions between the new company and their own enterprises. Stanley, as CEO, still spent about half his time at Stanley Engineering, Miller gave much attention to his design firm in Davenport, and Hanson was forming the Clement T. Hanson Advertising Agency in Moline.

The management team at The Home-O-Nize Co. in early 1948 consisted of Ed Doonan as plant superintendent, Louie York as foreman, W. C. Newsom as sales manager, Fred Winn as office manager, Lyle McCullough as purchasing agent, John Van Lent as personnel director, and Art Dahl in charge of production planning, control, and engineering.[23]

It was a close-knit group, and all were friends as well as colleagues—which made Stanley's decision in the summer of 1948 to seek Doonan's resignation as plant superintendent and as a board member doubly difficult. In Stanley's estimation, Doonan, after ably leading the planning and construction of the factory, had not adapted to his new role as plant superintendent. "Despite repeated counseling, he was not providing satisfactory leadership," wrote Stanley, who seemed to have agonized over the decision:

I had faced, for the first time but not the last, the difficult decision to terminate a manager who, despite demonstrated loyalty and effort, did not fit.... Over the years, I have observed that failure to deal directly, positively, but kindly with such situations is always a disservice to the organization and to its other members. Moreover, it is usually a disservice to the individual involved. Dealing frankly with such situations often allows that person to redirect his or her career objectives along more satisfactory lines.[24]

In Doonan's case, that meant becoming a county engineer.

Stanley possessed a trait that served him well as he juggled his responsibilities at the top of two companies. "He had an unusual ability to spot the hidden flaw," his son Dick recalled. "That's a skill that few people have: being able to take what

In the Oak Street plant (front to rear), Dale Shellady, Ray Meyer, and Butch Zeidler operate punch presses in 1947.

In 1947, Oak Street plant manager Ed Doonan (in suit) talks with an unidentified press operator in the aluminum drawing press room. Dale Shellady is at far left, and Bob Nygren is at far right.

would appear to be a cursory look at something and realizing there was a major glitch."[25]

Robert Carl experienced this ability early in his career as he struggled with his job as production control clerk, a function that was new to him and at which he admittedly was not very skilled. "I didn't do the timekeeping," Carl said, "but I reviewed the information, and every day we had to calculate a production report. And then we had to calculate the production index. Max Stanley used to check that report daily. He'd just quickly look down the list, and if I'd made a mistake, he'd catch it just like that."[26]

Stanley had the ability to select effective executives, and he tended to hire people he knew. "A lot of the early people at HON were people he knew from church, the community, from activities here in town," Dick Stanley said. "He had confidence in them and they in him."[27]

That confidence was never more apparent than when Max Stanley hired Stanley M. Howe early in 1948. Stanley had been Howe's scoutmaster when Howe was just 12. The Monday after high school graduation, Howe began working summers at Stanley Engineering while he pursued his undergraduate engineering degree at Iowa State University

and completed an MBA at Harvard Business School. Passing up opportunities to work at prestigious companies, Howe accepted his mentor's invitation to join The Home-O-Nize Co. and became assistant to Art Dahl in the production division. He proved Stanley's faith in him by eventually succeeding Stanley as CEO.[28]

"I think it was Max Stanley's letter of recommendation that got me into the business school because that was in 1946, and with the returning veterans, they had more applicants than they could use," Howe said.

Somehow they let me in, and I was one of the youngest members. I went to school with returning generals and captains and people like that from the service.

When I graduated, I decided that instead of going with a company like General Electric and getting a narrow, one department type silo, I'd go with a small company and get wide experience, and then I would go to a big company. Fifty years later, I retired from the same small company.[29]

The Corn Picker Fiasco

When John Deere did not renew its contract for the combine pick-up attachment in 1948, The Home-O-Nize Co. had to search for new sources of outside manufacturing income. That search led to an agreement with Associated Manufacturers Inc. of Waterloo, Iowa, to manufacture its corn picker for the 1949 crop year. The corn picker was designed to attach to the front of a tractor. "You'd drive your tractor in, pull the lever back, and it locked on. Then you'd go pick your corn," Lyle McCullough explained. "It pulled the corn up on either side of the engine. Then it had elevators up off of the picker snouts and it dropped the corn into a wagon behind the tractor."[30]

Stanley and Dahl went to Waterloo in July 1948 to sign the $450,000 contract—an amount that would exceed total 1948 revenues by more than $30,000—expecting the company now could work itself out of its financial problems. As it turned out, just the opposite happened.[31]

For the remainder of the summer and fall of 1948, the crew at the Oak Street plant in Muscatine set up the parts fabrication and assembly lines to prepare for corn picker production. Stanley praised all the members for their hard work in getting the plant ready and in making trial units in time for a December demonstration.[32]

"I was buying bearings and oil seals and snap rings and tires and wheels and roller chain—everything it took to make this corn picker," McCullough remembered. "We had a heckuva stock that we bought for this contract."[33]

Officials of Associated Manufacturers and The Home-O-Nize Co. and the president of Muscatine Bank and Trust witnessed the demonstration. McCullough recalled the scene. "When they had the

initial trial for the machine, they took it down to Fredonia, a little town near Columbus Junction, to a farm that had some standing corn. The picker made about 850 feet down the row and broke down."[34]

That moment captured the essence of the whole corn picker debacle. The design had weaknesses. Moreover, Associated Manufacturers lacked adequate financing and didn't seem to have a dealer network that could have sold the number of machines The Home-O-Nize Co. had agreed to build.[35]

Home-O-Nize members worked hard to change the design and managed to build 38 corn pickers by the end of February 1949. That's when production stopped because the two companies were arguing over payment for design changes, and The Home-O-Nize Co.'s invoices were not being paid promptly. Some workers had to be idled during four months of negotiations, but under a modified contract, production resumed in July and August, and 83 units were built. During September, much of the corn picker operation was moved to newly leased Quonset huts on Sampson Street in south Muscatine.[36]

A promotional flyer for "The Iowa...a corn picker that is really different." The Home-O-Nize Co. produced the corn picker during 1949 on contract to Associated Manufacturers.

Production continued in September and October, and 145 more corn pickers were built.

Unfortunately, Associated Manufacturers was having a legal dispute with its main distributor, Omaha-based Irwin Equipment, over complaints about the performance of the machines. Stanley wrote on October 31, 1949, of the impact on The Home-O-Nize Co.: "Looks like corn picker sales for the year are through. Leaves us out on a limb. Drastic staff reductions needed."[37]

No more corn pickers were produced, and negotiations dragged on for 12 months before a settlement was reached and the two parties signed an agreement. The Home-O-Nize Co. was to be paid for all corn picker inventory and tooling within the previous 12 months. That didn't happen. Instead, Associated Manufacturers defaulted and went bankrupt. McCullough, who had scrambled in 1948 to buy hardware to build the corn pickers, now found his job was to get rid of it. "I traveled around to state fairs where all this machinery was on display, talked to the manufacturers and farmers who might buy the roller chain and things that they needed for their own repairs," McCullough said. "We finally got the inventory dwindled down until we got rid of it." In 1951 the company wrote off $52,500 in losses on the project.[38]

The Home-O-Nize Co. had taken the corn picker contract with Associated Manufacturers to work its way out of a deep financial hole, but instead that hole had grown deeper. Total sales in 1948 had been $419,700, generating net income of $39,900, but the picture after the disaster of 1949 was dismal—$322,900 in sales and a net loss of $29,700.[39]

"Revenues from contract work, principally Stampings, together with those from factoring accounts receivable on office products, did not cover expenses," Stanley wrote in the margin of the company's 1959 annual report. "Because Home-O-Nize lacked credit, suppliers were beginning to ship materials only on a COD basis." Then, with a touch of gallows humor, he added, "The Central State Bank, understandably, would not factor accounts receivable for corn pickers."[40]

Around town, rumors spread that the company would shut down soon. In that atmosphere, stock sales to the public were all but impossible, although the Hansons did buy one final block for

The Quonset huts on South Sampson Street in Muscatine were originally leased for manufacturing the Iowa Corn Picker. Later, The Prime-Mover Co. made its motorized construction wheelbarrows there.

$1,200. That was the limit of their investment, and Clem Hanson told Stanley, "Max, this is the last I can do." Stanley sensed Hanson was ready to quit.[41]

"I think it affected Dad more than Mom," James Hanson said. "He could be a worrier. Mom didn't worry very much. She had a very strong German constitution that was full of faith. She was a real rock. I think she helped keep everybody on a level keel. My Aunt Betty [Stanley] was the same way."[42]

Calling it quits was not something Stanley would do. "Too many people had invested in Home-O-Nize because they had confidence in me," Stanley said. "Even if I had reconciled myself to failure and personal loss, I could not let them down." Stanley was also motivated by a deeper conviction, grounded in his faith. To him, keeping the company going and supplying employment in his community was good Christian stewardship of the gifts that had been given to him,[43] so he did everything he could think of to pull the company out of its worsening financial crisis.

Fixing a Hole

The production for Stampings continued, although the generally soft economy in 1949 lowered the company's sales projections. The financial situation at The Home-O-Nize Co. was so tenuous that many times the company met payroll by the skin of its teeth. On Fridays, recalled Robert Carl, it wasn't unusual to be working on the line and see Fred Winn, office manager, keeping tally of the number of bottled gas hoods coming off the line. "Fred would get the tally, and he'd drive to Stampings' headquarters in Davenport with a bill," Carl said. "He'd get a check from Stampings in order to deposit it in time to meet the payroll. Then he'd race back to the Muscatine bank."[44]

The Home-O-Nize Co. secured supplementary contract work with some area firms. It made metal connectors for Peter Products, a local manufacturer that assembled movable walls for Johns-Manville. The Home-O-Nize Co. also supplied components to two area pump companies, Red Jacket and Carver Pump. In addition it built cabinets for Collins Radio, based in Cedar Rapids, and made a kitchen table that contained a fold-out ironing board for G. W. Timmerman.[45]

Toward the end of 1948, about half the steel The Home-O-Nize Co. had ordered from the Granite City Steel Company in 1946 finally arrived. In response to demand from the local Batterson's store, the company used the steel to manufacture a 66-inch-high steel utility cabinet, which it painted white for household use. "We found out that if we painted them that new office color of avocado green, we could sell them for $29 instead of $19," Howe said. "So we sort of got into office products unintentionally."[46]

Still, The Home-O-Nize Co. needed more capital in 1949, but the prospects didn't look promising. Stanley couldn't go to the banks, no public investors would buy more stock, and the company was doing as much work as it could find. With nowhere else to turn, Max Stanley appealed to his partners at Stanley Engineering to loan him money, offering his partnership interest as security. With funds from the engineering partnership, he bought stock worth $30,500 and made some loans to The Home-O-Nize Co. "That wasn't met with universal acclamation by the other partners," Dick Stanley recalled, "because they weren't as enthusiastic about HON as my father was."[47]

While some of his partners at Stanley Engineering criticized his ventures, Max Stanley eventually repaid the money borrowed from the engineering firm.[48]

The scramble for manufacturing contracts brought all sorts of business through The Home-O-Nize Co.'s door, including this hideaway ironing board.

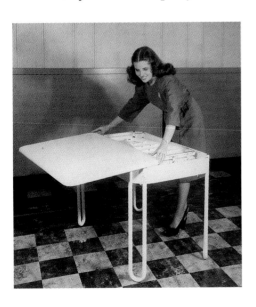  

A Prime Acquisition

Late in the difficult year of 1949, The Home-O-Nize Co. took a substantial step in the journey back from the brink. The revival came from an unexpected connection—Max Stanley's interest in the United World Federalists (UWF), which had begun two years earlier. Stanley's oldest son, David, had joined the Student Federalists while at the University of Iowa, and he introduced his father to the federalist idea of world peace. Through UWF, the elder Stanley had become acquainted with retired U.S. Army Gen. George Olmsted, an insurance executive from Des Moines who sat on the boards of the Equity Corporation of New York and the Bell Aircraft Corporation. Aware of Olmsted's financial expertise, Stanley discussed The Home-O-Nize Co.'s financial woes with him. To Stanley's surprise, a short time later Olmsted told him Bell wanted to sell one of its products, a motorized construction wheelbarrow called the Prime-Mover, and he asked whether The Home-O-Nize Co. might want to buy it.[49]

The half-ton capacity Prime-Mover Model 343 was commonly used on construction jobs to transport concrete to hard-to-reach sites. For Bell Aircraft, with its high overhead, the machine was not producing the anticipated level of profit, but Stanley appraised the opportunity and felt that The Home-O-Nize Co., with its lower production costs, could make it succeed. The Muscatine company's board approved the acquisition of the product line on February 20, 1950, and The Home-O-Nize Co. had its first wholly owned subsidiary.[50]

Bell's willingness to finance the deal made the acquisition particularly attractive. It loaned $125,000 to what was now called The Prime-Mover Co. to help purchase what Stanley described as "all patents, trademarks, tools, dies, fixtures, patterns, records, and sales materials as well as inventories of parts, accessories, and some finished Model 343s." That loan, plus another one directly to The Home-O-Nize Co. for $25,000, were to be repaid in full by 1957. Bell also was to

An ad in the *Muscatine Journal* for Batterson's department store urges consumers to buy Home-O-Nize's 66-inch utility cabinets.

BATTERSON'S
IS
PROUD TO PRESENT
To Our Friends
FOR IMMEDIATE DELIVERY
The New
HOME-O-NIZE
UTILITY CABINETS

Made in Muscatine by Muscatine People
and Offered by BATTERSON'S for Immediate Delivery
to the People of Muscatine!

THEY'RE HERE RIGHT NOW!

Extra Heavy 20 Gauge Steel—Gleaming White,
Porcelain Enamel Finish.

66 Inches High—26 Inches Wide—13 Inches Deep

IDEAL FOR STORING LINENS, DISHES,
CANNED FRUIT AND HUNDREDS OF OTHER
THINGS!

VERY SPECIALLY PRICED $19.85

Come in and See This
New Muscatine Product at
BATTERSON'S, Where You'll Find
Them for Immediate Delivery.

FURNITURE   THIRD FLOOR

BATTERSON'S

receive royalties on sales of Prime-Movers, parts, and accessories.[51]

During March and April of 1950, the Prime-Mover operation was moved from Buffalo, New York, to the Sampson Street Quonset huts in Muscatine. The purchase included enough parts for 540 units, which were built and sold by year's end. As that production was going on, Art Dahl and Dick Andrews designed a new model that was better suited to The Home-O-Nize Co.'s manufacturing operation and

had a carrying capacity of 1,500 pounds.[52] "The frames of the Model 343 were die-cast aluminum, which is fine for an aircraft company," Robert Carl explained. "But it's not so good for a sheet metal company. So they redesigned the Prime-Mover. It was called the Model 15."[53]

Dick Stanley recalled some of the testing of the new model during his summer vacation from Iowa State where he was studying engineering. "I remember hooking the thing up on a long radius

Max Stanley and the United World Federalists

FOR NEARLY 20 YEARS AFTER WORLD War II ended, Max Stanley was a major participant in the United World Federalists (UWF), a postwar world peace movement that advocated international government based on the federal system of the United States. Introduced to the organization in 1947 by his son David, who had joined the Student Federalists while he was at the University of Iowa, Stanley quickly embraced its goals. Late that year, he wrote in his journal, "Probably biggest news of the year is the Stanley family's all-out campaign for U.W.F."

Though Stanley and his son David may have been enthusiastic, Max's brother Art didn't support either the UWF or the idea of world government. It didn't help his attitude when FBI agents told him their agency was monitoring the UWF and asked him if Max Stanley was "a commie." Art assured them his progressive Republican brother was not at all subversive, but "the kind who gets involved in causes."

Undeterred by such opposition, Max Stanley quickly rose through the ranks of the organization. He was chosen president of the Iowa chapter in April 1950, just two years after joining. Six months later, he was elected to the National Executive Council and was promptly chosen its chairman. On June 16, 1954, his

50th birthday, he flew to Washington, D.C., to attend the national assembly of UWF; three days later, he was elected national president, serving until 1956. He held that office again from 1964 to 1966. He served as chairman of the Council of the World Association of World Federalists from 1958 to 1965. During his leadership, the UWF grew to 700 chapters with some 50,000 members.

While he was involved in the UWF, Stanley associated with some of the most influential people of the time: Norman Cousins, the editor of *Saturday Review*, whom he succeeded as UWF president; Oscar Hammerstein II, the lyricist; dramatist Robert Sherwood; labor leader Walter Reuther; Alan Cranston, who later was elected to the Senate from California; and George Olmsted, the insurance executive and retired general who had brought Stanley the Prime-Mover deal. In 1955, Stanley testified before a Senate subcommittee looking at revisions to the United Nations Charter. And he was invited to a White House conference, "Foreign Aspects of U.S. National Security," that included former presidents Eisenhower and Truman, Vice President Nixon, Illinois Governor Adlai Stevenson, Secretary of State John Foster Dulles, and Dulles' predecessor as secretary of state, Dean Acheson.[1]

arm so it would pivot at the center, so the machine would go around and around, and that was an endurance test. We had another hookup where we were trying out a cone clutch rather than a conventional leaf clutch." Early stages of production began in December, and dealers looked forward to placing orders for the Model 15 in early 1951.[54]

Prime-Mover's board of directors included two Bell representatives, George Olmsted and Harvey Gaylord, a Bell vice president. Stanley, Hanson,

and Miller completed the board. Its officers were Stanley, president; Hanson, vice president; and Fred Winn, secretary-treasurer. Dahl headed operations and sales as a vice president. With Dahl's new assignment, Stanley M. Howe took over the product design, industrial engineering, and production control functions for The Home-O-Nize Co. Howe had joined Home-O-Nize in the hopes of quickly gaining experience and responsibilities—and the company delivered.[55]

In the Clear

While the Prime-Mover activities occupied center stage in 1950, other aspects of The Home-O-Nize Co. made progress as well. Office products and

Above: In the summer of 1950, The Home-O-Nize Co. demonstrated the Bell Prime-Mover Model 343 outside one of the Quonset huts. Dick Stanley (with hand on hip and short sleeves) is third from right. Ralph Heckathorne is at far left, facing the the concrete buggy.

Left: As production of The Prime-Mover Co. was being moved to Muscatine in the spring of 1950, R. G. Ervin Jr. (left) of Bell Aircraft talks with Harold Barton (center) and Art Dahl, both of The Home-O-Nize Co.

Opposite: At the end of the assembly line, Stan McFadon (left) and Don Flake slip a shipping carton over a finished Model 38D combination file in 1950.

contract work together brought in $311,300 in revenue. A sales flyer for office products printed that year showed a lineup of 3-by-5 and 4-by-6 business card file boxes and eight models of file cabinets or combination file-and-storage cabinets. Contract revenue came from the Herman Nelson Division of American Air Filter, Red Jacket Pump, Carver Pump, and Collins Radio. The Home-O-Nize Co. also made its 400,000th bottled gas housing for Stampings. With the Korean War under way, the company also expected to procure contracts for the U.S. military.[56]

With much brighter prospects for the future, The Home-O-Nize Co. ended 1950 as a publicly owned corporation with 117 shareholders who together owned 24,030 shares. The Stanley family, who had faithfully invested so much money into the effort to keep the company going, owned 44 percent of the common stock. The once-ominous threat of financial ruin seemed to be in the past, as The Home-O-Nize Co. actually showed a profit of $10,500.[57]

True to the promise made in the company handbook, the profit-sharing program began in April of that year by distributing 25 percent of monthly profits to members. In that year's annual report, Max Stanley wrote, "This program has been well received, has increased efficiency of operation and hence, profits, and has improved the morale of the organization."[58]

Shareholders were displeased when they learned at the 1950 shareholders' meeting that The Home-O-Nize Co. would pay profit sharing to its members before any dividends would be paid,[59] but Howe said the rather unusual process was an important one. "The company paid profit sharing to everybody including the janitor—not just officers and managers," he said. "It started paying profit sharing before it ever paid a dividend to a shareholder, and I think that helped to make the company genuine."[60]

IN SUMMARY

THE FLEDGLING HOME-O-NIZE CO. took what work it could get. The company's first products, aluminum hoods for bottled gas canisters, were delivered in 1947. Eager to diversify, the company used scrap aluminum from the hoods to produce card file boxes, which sold well. Led by card file sales, The Home-O-Nize Co. still lost money in 1947, but stumbled into the office products niche that was destined to become its core business.

The company's future was still tenuous in 1948, a year that finally saw a tiny net profit of $39,900. That year The Home-O-Nize Co. set aside its dream of manufacturing kitchen cabinets. In 1948 cofounder Max Stanley hired young engineer and MBA Stanley M. Howe, who eventually succeeded Stanley as CEO.

The young Home-O-Nize Co. made a key acquisition in 1950, buying motorized wheelbarrow maker Prime-Mover from Bell Aircraft Corp. Thanks to The Prime-Mover Co.'s sales, The Home-O-Nize Co. actually showed a slim profit of $10,500 for 1950.

With the threat of financial ruin receding, the company ended the year with 117 relieved shareholders.

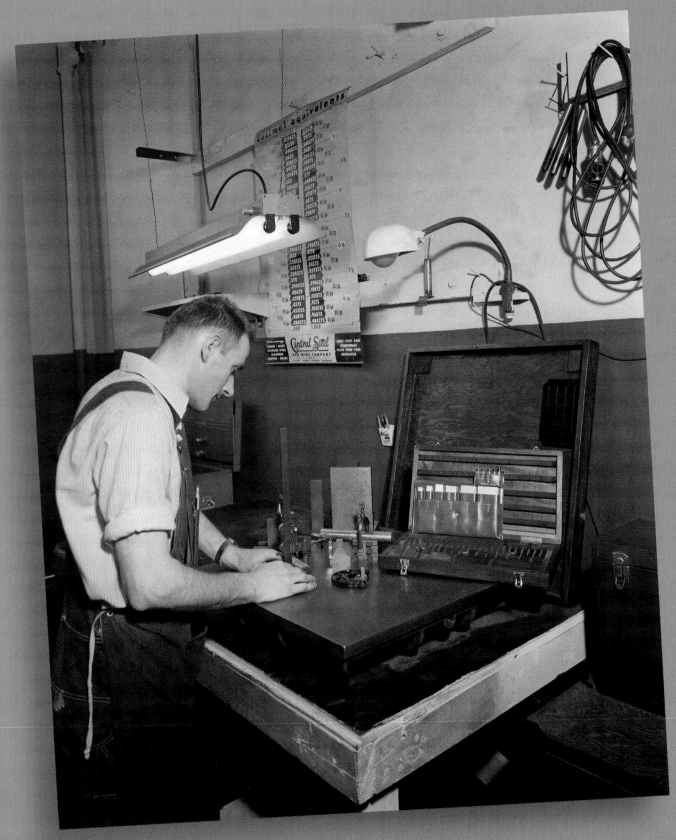

Much of the company's early equipment at the Oak Street plant was purchased used, but toolmakers such as Ervin Easterla (above) kept it operating smoothly. Once The Home-O-Nize Co. gained its financial feet, it would utilize some of the most advanced manufacturing methods and equipment in American industry.

CHAPTER THREE

Operation Independence

1951–1955

The 63 percent increase in our sales primarily represents increasing acceptance of our product throughout the country.

—The Home-O-Nize Co. 1955 Annual Report

THE HOME-O-NIZE CO. BEGAN the 1950s with great optimism. The company had earned a profit of more than $10,000 in 1950 and had acquired its first subsidiary, Prime-Mover, which it believed held substantial potential for growth. Moreover, The Home-O-Nize Co. had concluded that its future lay in office products.

One ominous cloud loomed on the horizon at the dawning of the company's otherwise promising future. The company still relied too heavily on contract work for other companies. The company was convinced, in Max Stanley's words, that "we could not attain our goals of greater sales volume and increased profitability as long as we were tied so firmly to contract work."[1]

To eliminate this obstacle, The Home-O-Nize Co. launched Operation Independence, a five-year, three-pronged effort to expand the office products business, grow the Prime-Mover subsidiary, and at least for the short term, assume more contract work to help fuel the two core enterprises.

Macro-Management

As the company moved to develop its own products, Home-O-Nize members were granted more autonomy. Max Stanley was known for his ability to choose effective executives who needed little oversight and who worked for the benefit of the company.[2]

Such devotion to the overall good of the company pervaded the organization. Dick Stanley recalled a summer job at The Home-O-Nize Co. during his school years. "Leonard Luedtka was my boss in the storeroom," he said. "Someone had checked out a shovel, and in the process of using it, he'd broken the handle. Leonard was really giving him what-for because he'd broken that handle and that was extra cost to the company."[3]

From the company's earliest days, it needed independent leaders, because the three founders divided their time between the company they had created and other enterprises. "I adopted a rather loose style of management, with the intention of allowing executives to develop their full capabilities," Max Stanley wrote. This created "a results-oriented style of management that would contribute significantly to the effectiveness of the decision-making process at all levels right up to the present day."[4]

Stanley cited evidence of that effectiveness among the company's earliest hires and among

The Unifile, popular at home or office, remained a steady seller for more than 30 years after its introduction in 1953. Its Unilock mechanism secured all drawers and doors from one lock.

those who joined just before and during Operation Independence. Members of the construction crew who had renovated the Oak Street plant in 1946 had risen to positions of significant authority by the mid-1950s. Ray Shellabarger, for example, was the assistant to Louis York, who was superintendent at the Oak Street plant during the 1950s. Lyle McCullough, member number four, was the purchasing agent for steel. Thanks to McCullough's self-proclaimed "scrounge" ability, the Home-O-Nize plant never shut down for lack of steel, despite the postwar shortage.[5]

Stanley M. Howe and Rex Bennett also accepted challenging roles under Stanley's relaxed leadership style. Bennett was hired from J. I. Case in the mid-1950s to head plant engineering, including much of the production responsibility. Over the years, he worked through a number of top management assignments. Howe had risen to vice president of production with broad responsibilities and eventually succeeded Stanley.[6]

With leaders such as these, The Home-O-Nize Co. plunged into Operation Independence, broadening its product line, strengthening marketing efforts, and increasing production capacity and efficiency.

Growing the Office

The Home-O-Nize Co. introduced a number of designs for office products, adding substantially to the 12 items it offered in 1951. In 1952, the company introduced two- and four-drawer nonsuspension file cabinets that used many of the same components that had been developed for the combination cabinets of earlier years. In addition, Stanley M. Howe designed a bookcase line in a

Production took on a new dimension in 1953 with extensive cost-reduction efforts that affected everything from product design to final production. Assembly lines were shifted to reduce material handling. For example, when sheet metal became available, it was cut into smaller pieces, which were made into components. Working at this station (from left) are Clarence Nolan Jr. (partially obscured by the shears), Bill Brendel, and Leonard Luedtka.

Fortitude in the Face of Disasters

EARLY IN OPERATION INDEPENDENCE, The Home-O-Nize Co. suffered through several near disasters, compelling Max Stanley to headline a page in the 1951 annual report, "Frustrations." In December 1951, a fire destroyed the contents of the Sampson Street Quonset huts, stopping work for three weeks. As if that weren't enough, The Home-O-Nize Co. twice had to contend with Mississippi River floods that sent water into the Oak Street plant in April of 1951 and 1952, halting production both times.[1] "The water backed up from the river into Mad Creek behind the Oak Street building," Clem Hanson recalled. Water rose three feet deep, in spite of the sandbagging. "Access to the entrance was by boat and a plank bridge."[2]

Stanley M. Howe recalled a worker trying to spear a fish off the shipping dock.[3] These disasters could have crippled the young company, but it showed fortitude and resilience—qualities that would serve it well in the face of future challenges.

The Model 30 office bookcases were available with or without sliding glass doors. With the addition of a drop-down shelf, the standard bookcase became a mimeograph stand.

variety of heights and depths with open, steel, or glass doors. That year The Home-O-Nize Co. also introduced the Model 30D duplicator cabinet—a bookcase with a foldaway shelf that cantilevered off one end.[7]

By 1953, the office product line had more than tripled to 42 items, and product development focused on improved combination cabinets, now called Unifiles. The name Unifile derived from its Unilock feature; by turning a key in the main handle, the door and all drawers within were locked or unlocked thanks to a unique design that linked hidden plungers to all the drawers.[8]

The line expanded in 1954 when The Home-O-Nize Co. made its first office products acquisition, buying the Essington Company, which made garment racks and costumers (stands with hooks on which to hang garments). It also expanded its own line with more drawers, sizes, and locking options; however, the biggest development of the year came when Stanley and Howe heeded the recommendation of their sales manager, Bill Hammon, to develop full-suspension filing cabinets.[9]

The full-suspension filing cabinets, called the Model 200 series, came in a variety of sizes and "filled a gap in the offerings of the industry," according to Stanley. Although constructed with high-quality materials and workmanship, they carried a less expensive price tag than other high-quality office products.

"One of the reasons for the low cost was we made our own drawer pulls and label holders and thumb latches. Other companies bought those," Howe said. "We made our own nylon rollers and really pioneered the change from ball bearing rollers to nylon rollers, which were quieter and one-tenth of the cost. We also made our own rivets to attach the rollers to the cradles." The sturdy, completely re-engineered files also featured side wall stiffeners and full-bottom trays. In later years, the nylon rollers became the industry standard.[10]

The Model 200 series was quite popular, and the company's leaders were encouraged to offer more office furniture. Thus, The Home-O-Nize Co. began what Stanley later described as "the transition from specialty office products to basic office furniture."[11] Before Operation Independence ended, the company had introduced its first single-pedestal desk, for example. With a Panelyte laminated top and "hairpin" legs, the desks were shipped as components and assembled with the pedestal on either the right or left—or both sides if desired. Matching tables were available. Well before home offices were fashionable, The Home-O-Nize Co. offered the Home Suite, with a single-pedestal desk and cabinets available in pastel colors.[12]

By 1955, The Home-O-Nize Co.'s office inventory had expanded to 93 items, and office sales accounted for 64 percent of the company's $1.64 million revenue (compared to 19 percent of 1951's $589,000 sales).[13]

Only a few years into Operation Independence, The Home-O-Nize Co.'s leaders had little doubt that office products should be their core business. "Expansion of business in this market appeared to be the best way to break away from contract work completely," Stanley wrote.[14] Moreover, because manufacturing office products required the same kind of equipment as manufacturing kitchen cabinets, the equipment The Home-O-Nize Co. had originally installed was no longer sitting idle.[15]

Smart Decisions

Encouraged by the Model 200's success in the early 1950s, the company's leaders made a strategic decision to compete in what is known as the "middle market" for office equipment, and that positioning has characterized much of the company's product line for half a century. Senior management felt that The Home-O-Nize Co. could not compete with premium manufacturers such as Steelcase, Shaw-Walker, and Corry Jamestown because it did not have the depth of product, nor could it afford huge advertising budgets. In making that decision, The Home-O-Nize Co. committed itself to expanding product lines and ensuring it was price-competitive with middle-market companies like Allsteel and Cole. The company's leaders never considered entering the lowest segment of the market.[16]

Beginning as early as 1952, The Home-O-Nize Co. also stepped up advertising and sales activities, directing ads to dealers through trade publications. By 1955 the company had greatly strengthened its sales organization by adding manufacturers' representatives who were experienced in selling office equipment. These changes in the sales structure began with Hammon as sales manager and continued after 1954 with Bill Duval.[17]

With so much attention to its image during this period, leaders of The Home-O-Nize Co. came to realize that the company's name and logo did not send the appropriate branding message to customers for office products. After much discussion, they decided not to change the company name but to simplify the identity of the office products portion through creation of The H-O-N Division.

"We found the dealers were calling us 'Hon,'" Howe recalled. "So we decided that if they wanted to call it Hon, we would. And so we did." The transition to HON INDUSTRIES and its largest operating entity, The HON Company, had begun.[18]

During the early years of Operation Independence, the company added more machines, shifted assembly lines to increase efficiency, cut back some contract work, and moved the Prime-Mover work to the Sampson Street Quonset huts. As Operation Independence wound down, the company invested

On the nonsuspension line in 1952, Kenneth Doak (center), Hubert Higgins (left), and Whitey Olson (right) work on four-drawer files, which The Home-O-Nize Co. had just introduced.

Opposite: The automatic drawer welder, which cost a hefty $16,000 in 1955, paid for itself within a year after installation because it added so much production capacity.

Right: Engineers at The Home-O-Nize Co. made many design changes that improved the capacity and safety of Prime-Mover material-handling equipment.

in more sophisticated machines, such as its first automatic drawer welder in 1955, that sped up production and ensured uniformity of product.[19]

Production took on a new dimension in 1953 with extensive cost-reduction efforts that affected everything from product design to final production. Under Howe's supervision, new products were designed and existing ones redesigned to cut labor and use interchangeable parts whenever possible. Assembly lines were shifted to reduce material handling, work flow was controlled more tightly, and purchasing was adjusted—all to achieve greater profitability without raising prices. At the end of 1953, efficiency had increased by 18 percent in the production of office equipment. The program expanded to include Prime-Mover in 1954.[20]

Prime-Mover Moves Slowly

In contrast to H-O-N, the office furniture division of The Home-O-Nize Co., Prime-Mover progressed slowly during Operation Independence, but it emerged as a solid entity, contributing positively to the overall enterprise. Prime-Mover's overhead stayed low, and the parent company provided wide support, from administration to production, under the direction of Art Dahl.

The construction industry responded well to the Model 15's introduction in 1951, buying 621 of them, but then construction sales stagnated, and no other markets were suited to the product. Moreover, most of the distributors The Home-O-Nize Co.

had inherited from Bell Aircraft were better suited to industrial markets than to construction, so Prime-Mover set about modernizing both its product mix and distribution network. It explored other construction products, such as masonry saws and concrete finishers, but backed away from them because of strong competition in those areas.[21]

As Operation Independence closed, Stanley reflected that the company "had succeeded in stabilizing" Prime-Mover, although it was "smaller than we had hoped."[22]

Continuing Contract Work

Contract work—which had prompted Operation Independence—continued to provide substantial income, although a decreasing percentage of the company's overall profits. Charts in each annual report marked the progress of "our products" versus "other contracts." The balance shifted from 65 percent contract work in 1951 to 83 percent Home-O-Nize products by 1956. Gradually, Stampings came to rely on The Home-O-Nize Co. for all its manufacturing, and that relationship continued after Operation Independence. As part of its contract with the Herman Nelson Division of American Air Filter, The Home-O-Nize Co. made steel storage cabinets for schoolrooms, leading to development of cabinets for office use. The company also made some signs for the Red Jacket Pump Company in 1955 and did small manufacturing jobs for other civilian companies.[23]

The relationship with Bell Aircraft led to a multi-year contract to manufacture engine nacelle fairings for B-47 bombers. Most of that manufacturing was done at the Oak Street plant, with assembly in the Sampson Street Quonset huts. The company also did some work for the military as a subcontractor to Magic Chef and to General Motors.[24]

Operation Success

During Operation Independence, officers and employees became true members of The Home-O-Nize Co. through several means of participation, some of which had been in place since the early years. Participatory committees established in the 1940s enabled members to decide on policies, plan activities, ensure workplace safety, and provide input on benefits such as health coverage. Face-to-face meetings between management and members, which began in 1949, gradually evolved into other forms of communication, including a newsletter called *Notes* that John Van Lent, the company's first personnel director, began publishing monthly in 1947. Members also shared in the company's fortunes: through profit sharing, which began in 1949 and evolved into a split between profit sharing and each member's profit-sharing retirement trust account (begun in 1960); through

stock purchases, which were made possible from the earliest years; and through stock dividends. The company began to pay quarterly dividends on common stock in 1955—$1 for each share in the first and second quarters and $1.50 in the third and fourth. This began a remarkable string of uninterrupted quarterly dividends continuing into 2004.[25]

Though total revenues climbed during the years of Operation Independence, from $589,000 in 1951 to $1.64 million in 1955, net income had to rise from a $5,000 deficit in 1951 to reach just less than $75,000 in 1955. Though the extreme financial pressures of the start-up years were past, the company clearly needed capital to fund growth.[26]

The Home-O-Nize Co. was, in fact, on the verge of acquiring new plant space in Muscatine. It needed more quality production space, and it wanted to phase out the Quonset huts. In 1956, it began leasing a 43,000-square-foot plant east of Muscatine on old Highway 61 (now Iowa Highway 22) and moved its Sampson Street operations there. The new plant

---

When Esther McCormick retired in 1974 (below), after more than 20 years with the company, she took more than her rocking chair with her. The company's profit-sharing retirement trust, begun in 1960, helped build financial security for her retirement. Early in her career, Esther inspected Unifiles (left), which were introduced in 1953.

was called the Geneva plant, after the name of the township, a creek, and a nearby schoolhouse. The company planned to use the plant for manufacturing Prime-Movers, costumers, and the contract work for Bell Aircraft.[27]

Even before Operation Independence officially ended in 1955, the strategy had clearly worked. In 1951, nearly two-thirds of The Home-O-Nize Co.'s sales came from contract work. By 1956 that figure had dropped to about one-fifth and would continue ratcheting downward. Meanwhile, in 1953 the company achieved the $1 million in sales milestone and

In 1953 The Home-O-Nize Co. leased the Dora Building on Mississippi Drive to warehouse products awaiting shipment. From left, Stan Tackenburg and Clarence Lick prepare a load for shipment.

more than doubled that amount by 1956. All in all, according to Stanley, the company had succeeded in making "a transition from what was primarily a job shop doing contract work...to a manufacturer of its own product lines."[28]

IN SUMMARY

THE HOME-O-NIZE CO. BEGAN THE 1950s with great optimism. But one cloud remained; the company still relied too heavily on contract work for other companies.

To eliminate this Achilles' heel, The Home-O-Nize Co. launched Operation Independence, an ambitious five-year effort to grow its own products. By 1953 the office products line had more than tripled to 42 items, including a bookcase line designed by Stanley M. Howe. The Home-O-Nize Co. also stepped up advertising and sales activities. By 1955 the company had greatly strengthened its sales organization as well.

The company's production shifted from 65 percent contract work in 1951 to 83 percent Home-O-Nize products by 1956. Total revenues climbed during the years of Operation Independence from $589,000 in 1951 to $1.64 million in 1955, but the struggle was not yet over. Net income was a deficit of $5,000 in 1951 and climbed just short of $75,000 in 1955.

Still, Operation Independence had succeeded in transforming The Home-O-Nize Co. from a job shop to a manufacturer of its own product lines.

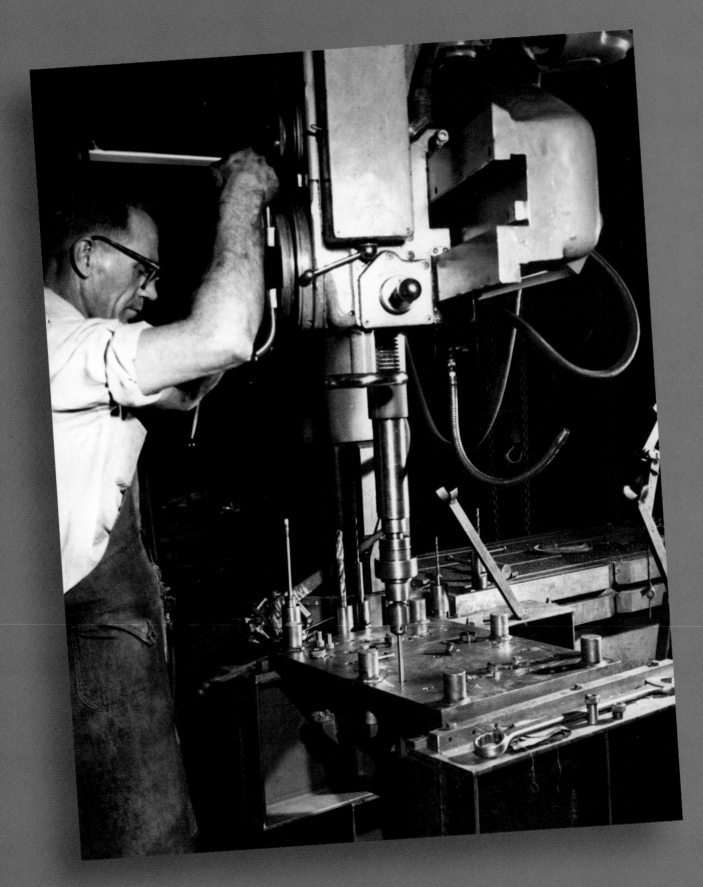

Member Floyd Payne operates a drill press at The Prime-Mover Co.

CHAPTER FOUR

Internal Growth

1956–1965

Largely by our own efforts, we were going to work toward greater market penetration in our businesses by expanding the sales of our office furniture and Prime-Movers, raising the productivity of our manufacturing, improving the quality of our products, and strengthening our financial position.

—Max Stanley

THROUGH OPERATION Independence, The Home-O-Nize Co. had eliminated its early reliance on contract manufacturing as a primary source of income. Then in 1956 the company embarked on a new mission, this one called Operation Bootstrap.

Operation Bootstrap was a ten-year effort to achieve a different kind of independence—an independence that would make this company stand out from the competition. Whether or not The Home-O-Nize Co. had boots, let alone straps, depended on its ability to develop and sell products; therefore, the first task was to expand its lines of office furniture and material-handling equipment. Next it focused on new products by developing them internally, looking for companies to acquire, and attempting to import techniques from other companies. In addition, sales at The Prime-Mover Co. had reached a plateau, so The Home-O-Nize Co. sought to add to The Prime-Mover Co.'s construction equipment base with new industrial products.[1]

A Multitude of New Products

As it had during Operation Independence, The Home-O-Nize Co. set strict criteria for new products; they had to be easy and economical to manufacture, suitable to existing production processes, and acceptable to the market. A proposed product had to clear a thorough analysis of production costs and potential profitability. To ensure quality, the company set up inspection procedures for parts and finished products and developed special machines to stress-test the office furniture. It even tested packaging materials in order to reduce possible product damage incurred during shipment.

Following these stringent requirements, the company's H-O-N Division (office supplies and furniture) was able to add a number of new products during Operation Bootstrap. Though its merchandise was not strikingly different from its middle-market competitors', the quality was better, and it cost less, thanks to innovative changes in design and manufacturing. New products included cash boxes (1958); the 310 and 410 lines of suspension files (in 1958 and 1960, respectively); the Honor line (modified H-O-N desks, files, and bookcases) in brighter colors for classrooms (1959); Convaire desks, credenzas, and tables (1960); the VS (Very Special) line of higher-end furnishings (1962); the Million line of modular desks (1959); and the 50 series of desks and related pieces (1965).

In the early 1960s, The Home-O-Nize Co. marketed a lower cost line of office furnishings under the Luxco brand.

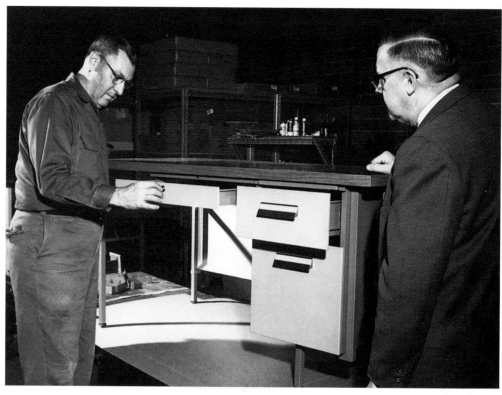

Right: A desk from the Million line gets a thorough examination from assembler Raleigh Rieke (left) and Stub Fillingham, Geneva plant superintendent. Drawer fronts and modesty panels took on bright colors through the use of vinyl cladding.

Below: The Home-O-Nize Co. purchased Luxco in 1960 mainly for its seating products. Luxco produced chairs, stools, and machine stands.

The Million desk was a popular one; founder Clem Hanson himself worked at one for the remainder of his years at The Home-O-Nize Co. "He had one of the first examples of the Million desk line," said James Hanson. "The line had an architectural sort of design that people liked a lot. It was the bridge between the credenza and the desk unit, all very contemporary. It had a laminate finish—a break away from the wood and steel desks. I still have that desk. It has lasted that long. It's quite a testament."[2]

After the success of the Million line of desks, The H-O-N Division realized that chairs should be a major product offering too, and in 1961 it purchased Luxco Inc., producer of chairs, stools, and machine stands. Initially, H-O-N intended to keep the Luxco operation in LaCrosse, Wisconsin,

where it was based, but by October 1962 it decided to move all production to the Geneva plant in Muscatine.[3]

The H-O-N Division was on a learning curve when it came to the chair business. After marketing the chairs under the Luxco brand for a while, H-O-N saw a need to sell them with the H-O-N label. It didn't take long for them to upgrade the quality of Luxco's chairs and bear the H-O-N label.[4] After a few years, H-O-N had become an expert in chairs and in 1966 introduced a contemporary chair line of its own.

Compared to internal development and acquisitions, imports proved the most disappointing way to diversify. In 1956, after meeting with Edgar Shannon, owner of Shannonvue, based in Sussex, England, Max Stanley agreed to import Shannon-

vue's line of shallow-drawer index card files. While the company strongly promoted the products and customers were satisfied, the Shannonvue line sold poorly because, as Stanley wrote later, "our distribution system—manufacturers' representatives and dealers—was neither qualified nor eager to sell systems. Their forte was furniture, and sales of Shannonvue products required a systems approach." The effort ended in 1961 after five years.[5]

Stanley also visited several German and Swedish companies and tried to reach export agreements with them for The Prime-Mover Co. He arranged to import Tremix concrete vibrators from a Swedish manufacturer from 1961 to 1965. Negotiations with another Swedish company, BT Cooperative (later BT Industries), ended without a deal. The Prime-Mover Co. in the early 1960s developed and marketed P-24 and P-45 pallet trucks and S-25 and S-45 skid trucks in competition with the Swedes. The relationship with BT would prove important in later years.[6]

Meanwhile, The Prime-Mover Co. introduced an impressive array of internally developed construction products, thanks in large part to Waldo Rodler, who became chief engineer in 1955. These included spin-offs of the Model 15A; a line of masonry tenders, which handled small pallets of brick or tile on construction projects and were similar in function to a fork lift; and 3,000-pound-capacity riding-type concrete wheelbarrows called the M-30 and the M-30A.

The Prime-Mover Co. also began expanding beyond the construction market into the industrial market. The F-40 utility vehicle, introduced in 1958, was a flatbed truck used for carrying materials or people. Improved models soon followed, but sales were sluggish, and the company was unwilling to commit to new products, though several—such as a three-wheeled golf cart and a three-wheeled mail carrier truck—were developed and tested. Meanwhile, Art Dahl rebuilt and refocused The Prime-Mover Co.'s distributor network. Production—after several frustrating attempts at contracting out portions of it—was brought entirely in-house.[7]

Rising in the Middle Market

The H-O-N Division's products were targeted at the middle market, "where the buyers expected sturdy, functional, and economical products without costly frills," as Max Stanley's biographer wrote.[8]

In the mid-1950s, H-O-N, like other office furniture manufacturers, sold directly to dealers through its territory managers or manufacturers' representatives. That approach changed in 1957 when, at Sales Manager Bill Duval's suggestion, The H-O-N Division took the revolutionary step of selling through wholesalers.

"It was an important shift and unique in the industry," said Howe. "Getting us into wholesaling was Bill's major accomplishment."[9]

The Home-O-Nize Co. member Harold McKamey operates a roll-forming machine to form drawer sides.

The Home-O-Nize Co. was committed to safety in all of its operations. Here, a Muscatine Fire Department instructor (right) involves workers from Oak Street Plant 1 in fire safety training. From left are Stratton "Stub" Fillingham, John Schmoldt, Howard Wagner, Francis White, George Butler, Harry Fuhlman, Jerry Grace, Howard Ziegenhorn, and Gerald Hetzler.

The new approach made it easier for customers to buy the company's products. Because H-O-N's production costs were so low, it was able to offer discounts that wholesalers were accustomed to—something that other middle-market office furniture companies tried to emulate with only limited success. Selling through wholesalers gave The H-O-N Division an edge in the middle market and opened a new channel to smaller dealers, who now could get quicker access to nearby warehouses.

"We gradually developed enough product line that we were selling office furniture to every major wholesaler of office furniture in the United States," Howe said. "That gave an availability to the dealers across the country that no other manufacturer had. By 1959 H-O-N had products in warehouses in New York, Philadelphia, Denver, Seattle, San Francisco, and Los Angeles. By 1965, The Home-O-Nize Co. was selling to about 75 wholesalers.[10]

H-O-N also focused its advertising on office equipment dealers through such magazines as *Office Appliances*, *Geyer's Dealer's Topics*, and *Modern Office Procedures*, as well as exhibiting its wares at trade shows operated by the National Stationers and Office Equipment Association, the National Office Furniture Association, the National Business Show, and at exhibitions of school furnishings.[11]

Meanwhile, The H-O-N Division found a way to diversify its market further—by making private-label products for Sears, Roebuck & Company. Sears gave The H-O-N Division another channel to reach the important small- and home-business markets. The partnership took root in 1963, when John Van Lent learned that Sears' Midwestern supplier of files could not keep up with demand. The next year H-O-N entered into an agreement in which Sears would sell H-O-N–made files and combination cabinets that were "different in design and construction from...the H-O-N trade name." Over the years, the volume of business grew, as did the list of products sold through Sears.[12]

"At the time, Sears was the largest distributor of office furniture because it had so many branches," said Howe, adding that the account came at a fortuitous time. "We had just expanded and put in another production line, so it really helped us put the file production line to use and moved us ahead," he said.[13]

More Space, Better Productivity

The Home-O-Nize Co. soon outgrew its original production space at the Oak Street plant and embarked on a wave of expansion, building new plants and warehouses that would cover three lots across from the original Oak Street plant. At the same time, The Home-O-Nize Co. was able to lower the cost of production and improve efficiency—cornerstones of its success and future growth.

The first new building, called Oak Street Building Number 2, was a 28,800-square-foot warehouse attached to the original plant. It opened in 1959 and could receive packaged furniture from the original plant via conveyor belt, reducing transportation and labor costs. The additional storage space allowed The H-O-N Division to support growing sales by housing more finished goods on-site.

Longer production runs, which lowered production cost, were also possible because now there was storage space for the finished goods.

Oak Street Building Number 3 followed the next year. The 5,500-square-foot facility was built to receive, store, and process coiled steel. Coiled steel was less expensive than flat-sheet steel and reduced the cost of the basic material in H-O-N's products. The coiled steel was unrolled and straightened to be cut to size and shape. Also, removing steel storage and shearing from Building Number 1 made more room for manufacturing and lowered production costs.

The largest facility constructed during that time was the 55,000-square-foot Oak Street Building Number 4, which was finished in 1963. The giant warehouse encompassed Building Number 3 and

Building Number 3's special steel-cutting equipment enabled The Home-O-Nize Co. to buy less expensive coiled steel.

Completed in 1959, the Building Number 2 addition to the Oak Street plant provided warehouse space for packaged furniture. The furniture was received by conveyor belt from Building Number 1, which reduced transportation and labor costs.

took up most of the block across Oak Street to the west of the original plant. Building Number 4 changed the company's entire production process by allowing the conversion of Building Number 2 from warehouse space to desk manufacture. At the same time, Building Number 1 could now be fully devoted to manufacturing files, combination cabinets, and bookcases. A conveyor belt was constructed over Oak Street to move product from the plant to the new warehouse, and finished product was loaded from the warehouse directly onto boxcars, thanks to new railroad sidings. This saved The H-O-N Division both time and money.

The company's 1964 annual report boasted rising productivity due to "greater utilization of expanded production facilities." That rising produc-

Dismantling a press break at the Oak Street plant required hard work. From left are Lyle Bigelow, Gerald Hetzler, and Bud Barton.

tivity contributed to rising sales, and in 1965 the company purchased yet more land, this time east of Oak Street Buildings 1 and 2, where a new facility would be devoted to file manufacturing. (When completed, the new plant rolled out a file every 40 seconds.) Also in 1965, the company broke ground for Building 5, a 75,900-square-foot facility that would encompass two stories of factory and an office mezzanine. The first floor of Building 5 was to be used for steel storage, fabrication of parts, and cabinet welding; the second floor was to be used for assembling, painting, and packing cabinets.[14]

The Geneva plant's role also changed during Operation Bootstrap. The Sampson Street plant and Quonset huts were shut down, and in 1956 The Prime-Mover Co.'s operations moved to the Geneva plant, as did the manufacture of B-47 aircraft fairings. (The contract work was phased out completely over the decade.) In 1957 small goods production (card files, etc.) moved to Geneva, and the product offering expanded to include card cabinets and cash boxes. After The Home-O-Nize Co. acquired Luxco in

The Home-O-Nize Co. maintained a stellar safety record, earning a Certificate of Meritorious Achievement in 1962 from the Industrial Safety Administration of Iowa. Hal Kent (right), of the Des Moines office of the National Safety Council, presents the award to Max Collins.

1961, its H-O-N Division added 18,000 square feet to the Geneva plant, where H-O-N began making chairs, stools, and machine stands.[15]

The overall effect of the new buildings and plant expansions was far-reaching. The company had more space for production lines to replace the manufacture-on-demand job-shop work it had been performing under contract. Production runs could be lengthened, which in turn lowered setup costs and raised manufacturing efficiency. As the company bought—or sometimes developed its own—more modern equipment, productivity also improved. More warehouse space allowed the company to house all the new product it was producing. Improved material handling and better access to transportation also increased efficiency and raised productivity. At the same time, product designers and production engineers worked together to use common parts where possible. They also avoided special colors and designs, thus further increasing efficiency. The end result of all this was a lean operation that spurred sales to new heights. Moreover, all of the buildings made a positive contribution to the Muscatine community by the improvement of declining neighborhoods, as in the case of the Oak Street Building Number 2, and in the creation of new job opportunities. Ironically, Glatstein's Junkyard, the property that had once been a treasure trove for spare parts and had figuratively held the company together, was now forever integrated into Oak Street Building Number 2.[16]

The space was a boon to production. Stanley M. Howe recalled reaching a production milestone. "I remember when we got the labor for a file cabinet down to one hour. It took years to do it," Howe said. "We had a party up at the Plantation (an elegant supper club) in the Quad Cities, and virtually everybody was there. It was the biggest celebration I remember."[17]

Strong Leadership

As the company's production facilities grew more sophisticated and the number of members increased, the management hierarchy also needed to evolve. During Operation Bootstrap, the production force more than tripled from 167 to 521. At the beginning of that period, ten people reported directly to Stanley M. Howe as vice president of production. By 1965, just four production managers reported to him, thanks to another layer of management that relieved some of Howe's burden: Phil Temple, vice president of product engineering; Rex Bennett, vice president of manufacturing services; Louis

At the packout station of the file assembly line, Don Flake (left) assembles a drawer as Louie York, plant superintendent, stands ready to help. At right, Esther McCormick examines a completed unit.

Fifteen-year members gathered for a photo in 1961. From left are Bud Barton, Lyle McCullough, and founders Wood Miller, Max Stanley, and Clem Hanson.

York, plant manager at Oak Street; Stratton "Stub" Fillingham, plant superintendent at Geneva; and Max Collins, vice president of personnel.[18]

Howe, meanwhile, was rising in the senior managerial ranks. In 1961 he was promoted to executive vice president and chief operating officer, which gave Max Stanley more time for policy and planning. Then in 1964, C. M. Stanley was elected chairman of the board and passed the presidential reins to Howe, who "had been fulfilling most of the functions of president for a number of years," Stanley noted. Stanley kept his post as chief executive officer.[19]

As the company grew, the board of directors was evolving also. At the beginning of the 1950s, the board consisted of the three founders plus two Muscatine businessmen, Carl Umlandt and Kenneth Fairall. Max Stanley was the only founder involved in the company's day-to-day operations. Clem Hanson remained on the board, but Wood

Miller left in 1958. "Hanson and I were distressed at the loss of an original partner," Stanley wrote, "but we recognized that Miller would be happier doing industrial design work in his own company."

When Miller retired, three new directors were elected—Stanley M. Howe and Bill Duval from inside the company, plus George Olmsted, who had been instrumental in The Home-O-Nize Co.'s purchase of The Prime-Mover Co. from Bell Aircraft. In 1959 Fairall left and was replaced by John Latta, an office furniture wholesaler and retailer from Cedar Falls, Iowa. Latta gave the board its first customer and supply-chain point of view. Olmsted resigned in

Wood Miller's Legacy

WHEN H. WOOD MILLER RETIRED from The Home-O-Nize Co.'s board of directors in 1958, he ended nearly all association with the company he helped found 15 years earlier. Except for continuing as a shareholder, his only connection with the company was to take an occasional industrial design assignment.

Max Stanley and Clem Hanson, the two other founders, were understandably distressed about Miller's departure, but they knew he wanted to spend more time doing industrial design work for his own company. Miller had founded the Davenport-based H. Wood Miller Design Company in the 1930s and had worked on designs for everything from fountain pens to kitchen stoves to locomotives.

Two years after retiring from The Home-O-Nize Co.'s board, Miller joined Sears Manufacturing Company in Davenport to create its engineering department. He was chief engineer and vice president of engineering for the manufacturer of tractor components and accessories until his retirement in 1975. Several of his designs were still in use 20 years after his retirement.[1]

Earlier, Miller had taught in the Davenport school system and at the Davenport Art Gallery, predecessor of the Figge Museum of Art. He was a graduate of the Chicago Institute of Art, where he had studied design and had been elected to the Kappa Alpha Phi honorary society.[2]

In the second issue of *The Home-O-Nizer* newsletter, Miller explained how he differentiated between styling and design: "Styling is a matter mainly of appearance—an attractive outside shape or covering device. Design, on the other hand, goes a great deal deeper into the problem. I choose to work from the design angle and thereby take into consideration every part of the product inside and outside. This method permits control over such features as easy accessibility for servicing, improved operation, and economy of space—oftentimes very important aspects from the consumer's viewpoint, and the dealer's too."[3]

Wood Miller died in 1994 at age 93. He was preceded in death by his wife of 55 years, the former Irma Marie Berg. The Millers had a daughter, Joanne, and a son, Jerry.

"When Miller left the board," Max Stanley wrote, "we paid tribute to the role that he had played in the early days of Home-O-Nize. Without his interest and imagination, we might never have been enthused about the manufacture of kitchen cabinets and appliances, and Home-O-Nize might never have been born."[4]

1961 and was replaced by James Delaney, a partner in a Chicago accounting firm, who brought corporate finance experience to the board. When Duval left in 1963, he was replaced first by Max Stanley's elder son David (who soon resigned due to the demands of his legal practice and his duties as an Iowa legislator) and then in 1964 by Max Stanley's other son, Dick, who was vice president and secretary of Stanley Engineering.

In 1965 Umlandt died, and Delaney resigned from the board. Their replacements were Albert Hinkle, a businessman from Cedar Rapids, Iowa, who had done consulting work for The Home-O-Nize Co., and Clarence Ager, who represented

Muscatine's business community. Thus in 1965, the board was made up of two men from inside the company—Max Stanley and Howe—and five from outside—Hanson, Latta, Dick Stanley, Ager, and Hinkle.[20]

Dick Stanley recalled that The Home-O-Nize Co. was "ahead of the curve in its governance practices," for it included outside board members well before it became standard practice. "From the very early days, Dad went out to find people to bring on the board who would bring points of view that were different from the managers of the company," he

recalled, "people who were strong enough to challenge and test management recommendations. That has proven to be a very good thing for HON."[21]

Being a Member

Under the board's watchful eye, the management team developed policies and procedures that provided more and more benefits for the company's members. The Home-O-Nize Co.'s leaders realized that its people were the company's greatest strength, for as Max Stanley acknowledged, "We had no lead in technology and no entrenched market position."[22] To attract and retain the caliber of talent that would help it grow and flourish, The Home-O-Nize Co. paid its members competitively, advanced them for a job well done, and developed personnel policies that went above and beyond the norm. The company also

The Home-O-Nize Co. members could buy company stock at below market prices. Pictured is a 1958 certificate for common stock.

The Stanley Foundation

MAX AND ELIZABETH "BETTY" STANLEY started the Stanley Foundation in 1956 to seek "a secure peace with freedom and justice, built on world citizenship and effective global governance."[1]

Since becoming involved in the United World Federalists, a post–World War II world peace movement, Stanley had pursued the elusive goal of a peaceful world community while managing two businesses. By the mid-1950s, he believed The Home-O-Nize Co. and Stanley Engineering had reached a point where he could turn more of his attention toward world peace.

Money was still tight in the Stanley family after Max had invested so much of his personal funds into The Home-O-Nize Co., so he and Betty began the foundation on a shoestring: $250 in cash and 160 shares of The Home-O-Nize Co. common stock, then worth $10 a share. (In later years, Stanley would say that HON INDUSTRIES "made the money that let us endow and provide the support for the Stanley Foundation." By his death in 1984, the foundation had assets of about $20 million.)[2]

The foundation's first board of directors consisted of Max and Betty Stanley and their three children, David, Dick, and Jane. Dick Stanley recalled that by the mid- to late 1960s, the foundation "started to take a significant share of my father's time. During the last ten, maybe 15, years of his life, the foundation became his primary area of attention."[3]

The work of the foundation began slowly. The first policy conference, "Strategy for Peace," occurred in 1960. Future conferences annually brought together sometimes 100 or more world experts on the year's given theme, often at a rural retreat outside New York or Washington, D.C. The first United Nations of the Next Decade conference was held five years later.

Project Enrichment, the foundation's first global education program, began in 1971 in the Muscatine school system. Three years later, the foundation began publishing the monthly *World Press Review*, a magazine that digested the work of foreign journalists and reported both the news in their countries and their perceptions of the United States. *Common Ground*, a weekly radio program on world affairs, was first aired in 1980.

From these beginnings, the Stanley Foundation in 2003 provided programs in global governance, U.S. foreign policy, global education, and media.[4]

That the Stanley Foundation was actively involved in world governments was evidenced by the fact that international leaders from the 1960s to the 1980s knew its founder on a first-name basis.

offered group production incentives to plant workers, thus promoting teamwork, and management received bonuses based on company performance.[23]

Moreover, plant members benefited from cash profit sharing, the profit-sharing retirement program (begun in 1960), and stock purchases. The profit-sharing plan in 1965, for example, paid the equivalent of 6.25 weeks' pay, distributing a cash payment in June and December and allocating the remaining half of the total payout to the member's individual retirement account. The Home-O-Nize Co. encouraged members to become stockholders by offering stock at below-market price. Starting in 1961, the company even loaned members money with which to purchase shares, allowing everyone in the company to reap the financial rewards of success. Members could borrow up to $600 to buy ten shares. Later, the company offered members a payroll deduction plan to help them buy stock.[24]

Members' fringe benefits improved over the ten years of Operation Bootstrap. Paid holidays increased from six days in 1955 to seven and a half days in 1965 (the half day on Christmas Eve). In 1955 members earned two weeks' paid vacation after one year. By 1965, members earned an extra half-day of vacation for every year beyond the first, up to four weeks after 19 years. The Home-O-Nize Co. continued to offer health and life insurance, with members and the company sharing premium costs equally.

Clearly, The Home-O-Nize Co. cared for its members, treating them more like family members than employees. When the company's insurance carrier increased premiums in December 1960, for example, management appointed a committee to find comparable coverage at a lower price. In addition, the company offered flu shots to members as early as 1962.[25]

As the company's workforce and facilities grew, communication lines evolved as well. The one large meeting for virtually every member was broken into a series of smaller meetings. Then Howe and Collins began conducting a series of quarterly meetings, choosing a cross section of about a dozen members with whom to meet for a short presentation and question-and-answer sessions.

Occasional open houses enabled members to show their friends and families the products they made and the work they performed. Open houses also helped recruit new members.

"We would sit around a table and talk at what we called two-way meetings," Howe said. "We never had their immediate bosses present. They could ask questions and talk freely."[26]

The company also published an internal newsletter called *On Target* to communicate to employees.

Even as the company grew, Max Stanley and Stanley M. Howe maintained an open-door policy, and the work environment was relaxed enough to allow for the occasional practical joke. Ken Meyerholz, who started with The Home-O-Nize Co. in 1963 and later became a vice president of The HON Company, recalled the story of how Max Stanley's open-door policy had an unintended outcome. "Our maintenance supervisor decided to nail Max's door shut," Meyerholz said. "They found out a few minutes later that Max was inside the office, but he took it in stride. He was a great gentleman, no doubt about it."[27]

The first annual recognition dinner for members was held on April 26, 1956, to honor those members with five or more years of service. The company held special dinners for members who had completed one year of service. The Activities Committee planned annual celebrations, such as picnics, Christmas parties, and basketball and baseball league teams.[28]

Also during the Bootstrap years, The Home-O-Nize Co. began directing more attention to its role as corporate citizen. Since its founding, The Home-O-Nize Co. had sought legal counsel to monitor its decisions, and during Operation Bootstrap it wrote standard-practice instructions to help guide officers and supervisors in legal and ethical matters. In its hometown of Muscatine, the company took an active role in the United Way and other charities, and it began developing policies on philanthropy that eventually led to the formation in 1985 of the HON INDUSTRIES Charitable Foundation. Meanwhile, in 1956, Max and Betty Stanley created the Stanley Foundation, which grew from Stanley's participation in the United World Federalists.[29]

Dollars and Sense

During Operation Bootstrap, the company's finances improved as well, thanks in large part to Secretary-Treasurer Fred Winn.

Winn had more than his share of obstacles to overcome. In 1956, The Home-O-Nize Co. reported about $500,000 in debt—and payments of nearly $300,000 were due within 12 months. The company owed more than $100,000 each to the Central State Bank of Muscatine and to Bell Aircraft. The

We've Grown a Lot in

20 YEARS

Since our beginning 20 years ago we have shown a steady growth in size, products and services.

For this healthy growth we thank our members —those dedicated men and women who have given their time and effort for the benefit of their company and the community.

DIVISIONS OF

THE HOME-O-NIZE CO.
Muscatine, Iowa

Home-O-Nize Co. was cash poor; it had more than $800,000 in assets in 1956, but slightly less than $24,000 of that was cash.

Despite such liabilities, sales were strong, and the workforce was dedicated and innovative. Winn set in motion a transition from the crisis management of the company's early years to financial management based on planning and more sophisticated use of credit. It started with a factoring agreement with the William Iselin Company of New York City in which Iselin made short-term loans to The Home-O-Nize Co. against its accounts receivable. The Iselin firm also granted The Home-O-Nize Co. a $200,000 term loan. The result was promising. By 1958 The Home-O-Nize Co. was able to keep up a payment schedule with its creditors and had almost paid off the $100,000 it owed to Bell Aircraft.[30]

As The Home-O-Nize Co. expanded its plant and warehouse space to keep up with growing sales, it needed to take its financing to the next level. The company sold $125,000 worth of convertible subordinated debentures to help finance construction of Oak Street Building 3, and other loans from Central State Bank and Iselin helped finance additional construction. Max Stanley observed that "these ad hoc arrangements kept our head above water, . . . [but] it seemed that we were scurrying around much of the time trying to arrange debt financing on rather short maturities." The Home-O-Nize Co. sold its common stock, but in those days the stock was "was still regarded as very speculative," Stanley said. What The Home-O-Nize Co. needed was long-term financing.

The company found what it was looking for in the insurance industry. After unsuccessful attempts to secure a long-term loan from Iowa-based insurance companies, The Home-O-Nize Co. turned to Prudential Insurance Company in Minneapolis,

"We've grown a lot in 20 years," read an ad in *the Muscatine Journal* in 1965 that celebrated The Home-O-Nize Co.'s 20-year anniversary.

Minnesota. In 1962 Prudential issued the company a 15-year loan for $1 million. "This financing and the increased earnings of 1962 give the company the strongest cash position it has ever enjoyed," that year's annual report proclaimed.

Before the year ended, The Home-O-Nize Co. had paid off its loans from Central State Bank and Iselin and still had plenty left over for working capital and plant expansion. The relationship between The Home-O-Nize Co. and Prudential was a lasting one. As Max Stanley observed, "Our arrangements with Prudential brought to The Home-O-Nize Co. the kind of financial security implied in that company's 'Rock of Gibraltar' advertisements," but that was not the only good news. Despite the maneuvering over finances, The Home-O-Nize Co.'s sales had risen from $2.78 million in 1956 to $10.96 million in 1965, and net income had climbed from $103,000 to $766,000.[31]

Shareholders who had the fortitude to hang on during this period received their reward. The common stock split 10-for-1 in 1957 and 5-for-1 in 1962, and the market value of the stock increased sixfold (adjusted for splits and stock dividends)

from 1956 to 1965. The string of quarterly dividends begun in 1955 continued. An investor who bought a share for $100 in 1955 received $170.99 in dividends over the next ten years.[32]

Another important event in The Home-O-Nize Co.'s financial health was its 1961 decision to insist on earning a return of 25 percent pretax on all assets employed. "A lot of companies have some such requirement for investments in manufacturing equipment or tooling or whatnot," said Howe, "but we took the position that you couldn't tell one dollar from another. It was important to earn a return on what you spent, whether it be for office buildings or airplanes or sales programs. A lot of companies spend money on items they can't possibly earn a return on—huge fancy office buildings, for example. Our corporate office building cost only $4 a square foot. That had something to do with trying to earn a return on dollars invested."[33]

By any measuring stick, Operation Bootstrap had been a resounding success, but the accomplishments of the 1950s and 1960s would seem small when compared to The Home-O-Nize Co.'s next surge of growth.

In Summary

AFTER THE SUCCESS OF OPERATION Independence, The Home-O-Nize Co. in 1956 embarked on a new mission, Operation Bootstrap.

This was a ten-year effort to achieve a branding identity to stand out from the competition. First, the company would expand its lines of office furniture and material-handling equipment. Next, The Home-O-Nize Co. would roll out new products through internal development, acquisitions, and importing lines from other companies.

The Home-O-Nize Co.'s H-O-N Division, producing office supplies and furniture, was able to launch a number of new products during Operation Bootstrap. In addition, The H-O-N

Division manufactured private-label products for Sears, Roebuck & Co.

The Home-O-Nize Co.'s production facilities and roster of members grew. During Operation Bootstrap, the company's production force more than tripled from 167 to 521.

Wood Miller retired in 1958. Meanwhile, Stanley M. Howe was rising steadily through the senior managerial ranks. In 1961 he was promoted to executive vice president and chief operating officer, which gave Max Stanley time for policy and planning.

In 1964 Stanley was elected chairman of the board. He passed the presidential reins to Howe. Meanwhile, Stanley kept his post as chief executive officer.

Stanley M. Howe (left) and Max Stanley discuss business inside the room that housed HON INDUSTRIES' early computer. The early technology was so large that it occupied an entire room.

CHAPTER FIVE

Leaps and Bounds

1966–1972

The progress of your company in the past has not been left to chance. It is the result of policies that promote growth and prepare for it in advance.

—Max Stanley and Stanley M. Howe, 1969

FROM 1966 TO 1972, THE company that began as Home-O-Nize with the idea of manufacturing kitchen cabinets jettisoned that vestige of its past. Its name changed, its organizational structure was updated, and its operation expanded across the continent as it matured into a dominant player in the office furniture market.

And it *grew!*

By any measure, the company that began as Home-O-Nize and became HON INDUSTRIES Inc. performed extremely well. Sales grew from $10.96 million in 1965 to $49.32 million in 1972. Net income nearly quadrupled from $766,000 to $3.03 million. Shareholders' equity ballooned from $3.08 million to $14.43 million, and return on shareholders' equity averaged 20 percent. Retained earnings grew more than fivefold from $1.76 million in 1965 to $10 million in 1972. Total assets climbed by more than $25 million from $5.43 million to $30.76 million, while the total workforce grew from 521 to 1,871.[1]

Max Stanley and Stanley M. Howe realized that the name Home-O-Nize, with its logo showing musical notes inside the capital O, no longer represented the company's identity. The transition had begun in the 1950s with the abbreviation H-O-N to identify the company's office products division—an abbreviation that dealers quickly shortened to one syllable, "HON." The office products divi-

sion officially became The HON Company in 1967.[2]

Within three years, after much debate among the management team and a contest among members (who submitted 190 suggested new names), HON INDUSTRIES Inc. emerged as the winner, and that has been the parent company's official name since 1968.[3]

Stanley and Howe were the driving forces behind HON INDUSTRIES' astounding growth. They put in place a research and development program that continually filled the pipeline of products. They also emphasized market research, product design, and engineering and constantly reassessed the company's plant, manpower, and management requirements. Extensive job training also promoted growth.

The HON Company

Throughout the late 1960s and early 1970s, The HON Company, HON INDUSTRIES' office products division, broadened its line of office furniture in the middle market, offering new products for both the high- and low-end markets.

The HON Company introduced the W Series of desk chairs in 1969.

This made the company more attractive to dealers and wholesalers, who preferred to deal with only a few companies to fill out their product array. The HON Company also ventured into the premium-quality segment of the office furniture market, first through internal development and, when opportunities arose, through acquisition.

The HON Company's growth in the office furniture industry benefited from a demographic shift in the American workforce. As the white-collar workforce expanded, so did the need for desks, chairs, and other office equipment. HON INDUSTRIES' 1967 annual report noted that the office equipment industry was "growing at a faster rate than the American economy."[4]

The HON Company continually replenished its pipeline of new products. In the late 1960s, the company introduced new lines of conventional furniture—desks, chairs, storage cabinets, and furniture for reception areas—as well as furnishings with contemporary styling—sleek-lined desks, desks with returns, credenzas, chairs, tables, cabi-nets, and machine and typing stands. In 1968 the company launched nine major products, including contemporary desks and conference tables and a fire-insulated file. It also offered three modifications of existing products, including the completely redesigned and restyled W series of executive, secretarial, and side chairs.[5]

In the 1970s, The HON Company explored new directions, with mixed results, but even when a venture did not work out as planned, the company learned from the experience. The HON Company's management took a new approach that established the company in the premium market but also gave it traction in another market: the "open-office" approach to office design. As offices needed to

HON INDUSTRIES expanded beyond its traditional base in the middle market during the late 1960s and early 1970s, combining new capabilities to produce attractive furniture for reception areas.

become more flexible and more efficient in their use of space, open-plan furniture designs became increasingly popular. To take advantage of this growing segment, The HON Company in 1971 introduced Environ 1. Environ 1 was made up of moveable wall partitions (in 15 different sizes and a variety of colors and textures) from which cabinets, shelves, and desk surfaces could be attached to create a system of "wall-hung" furniture. It included drawers, tub files, and electrical accessories.[6]

The HON Company made another attempt to branch out from its traditional strengths by purchasing the patent for an electric file in 1964. Four years later, after significant improvements to the original design, the electric file hit the market. It consisted of a series of file shelves that rotated via an electric motor, much like clothing at the dry cleaner's rotates on racks. Despite the electric file's merits as a space and time saver, the product never took off. Only a few units were sold, ranging in price from $3,400 to $6,200. The HON Company stopped marketing the electric file in 1972.[7]

The experience with the electric file substantiated the idea that marketing and distribution were as important as the products themselves. In the late 1960s and early 1970s, the evolution of The HON Company's marketing and distribution channels helped it grow into a national player. In the late 1960s, Edward Jones, vice president of The HON Company, led the company's transition from manufacturers' representatives to distribution through a direct sales force. The company also began selling through multiple channels, which stabilized its sales effort. Its direct sales force called on office furniture dealers all over the country, sold to office furniture wholesalers, and targeted the home market with private-label products sold at Sears. With multiple ways for its products to reach customers, The HON Company's sales were more resistant to fluctuations in any one market segment.

The HON Company's relationship with Sears was a win-win situation. For four consecutive years,

starting in 1967, Sears honored the company with its "Vendor of the Year" award. In a company bulletin, Stanley M. Howe explained that the award was "Sears' way of acknowledging our excellence in performance, which is superior when measured against the performance of the many other firms who supply them with product."[8]

The HON Company was also improving its national distribution system. In 1967 it began a strategy to manufacture goods near regional marketplaces rather than centralizing production in Muscatine, buying a 61,700-square-foot building on 25 acres at Cedartown, Georgia (about 60 miles outside Atlanta). The site became the company's first distribution center outside of Muscatine and gave The HON Company a home base in the Southeast, which reduced transportation costs for shipping and helped the company give better service to customers in the Sun Belt states. As a result, sales in the Southeast doubled within two years.[9]

Then in 1969, The HON Company opened a service-distribution center in Fresno, California. The acquisitions of Holga Metal Products in 1971 and Corry Jamestown Corporation the next year provided similar bases for distribution in Southern California and the Northeast. In addition, Corry Jamestown's showrooms in Chicago and New York were major boosts to marketing.[10]

The electric file conserved floor space and lowered filing costs, but it did not fit The HON Company's distribution channels. It was abandoned in 1972, four years after it was introduced.

easosoni

At the national sales meeting in 1967, manufacturers' representatives Ernie Stewart, far left, and Bob Cleary, far right, received recognition for their service with The HON Company from Chairman C. M. Stanley, standing, as President Stanley Howe looked on. Stewart represented HON in Dallas, Texas, for 13 years, and Cleary handled sales from Winnetka, Illinois, for 12 years.

The HON Company's Domain

As sales increased with the introduction of new products and better distribution, plant and office facilities in Muscatine and Cedartown expanded by more than 400,000 square feet from 1966 to 1972.

In 1966 Building Number 5 at Muscatine's Oak Street plant was completed. The two-story, 75,900-square-foot building contained a high-speed file production department, a receiving and processing area for steel, and 4,800 square feet of office space. With an eye on future expansion, The HON Company bought the 50,000-square-foot Hawkeye Button Company property on the east side of Orange Street in Muscatine where it had been leasing 17,000 square feet. The old structure was razed in 1969 to make way for Building Number 6, which was linked to the Building Number 4 warehouse via a conveyor and to Building Number 5 with a bridge that crossed the street between the two buildings.[11]

Part of the Cedartown building was also remodeled and equipped for manufacturing vertical files. Rex Bennett, The HON Company's vice president of manufacturing services, moved to Georgia to oversee the remodeling, which was completed on time and under budget in the spring of 1969.[12] A 42,200-square-foot Cedartown Building Number 2 was finished in January 1970, and in Muscatine, Building Number 6 was expanded with a two-story, 57,200-square-foot finished goods warehouse. Power conveyors overhead linked it to the Oak Street Building Number 1 warehouse.[13]

The HON Company's facilities in Muscatine were becoming a veritable showcase of manufacturing efficiency, and still the company kept enlarging its footprint. In 1973 the 92,400-square-foot Oak Street Building Number 7 came on-line for manufacturing larger, more complex desks, credenzas, laminated particle board tops (which had previously been outsourced), and all chairs that did not need painting. Opening that second chair operation freed space in Building Number 2, where simpler, lower-priced desks were manufactured.[14]

Prime-Mover

Once The HON Company had moved most of its production out of the Geneva plant, The Prime-Mover Co. came into its own. In contrast to how The HON Company evolved, The Prime-Mover Co. stayed close to home, developing new products and marketing and distributing from its base in Muscatine.

That's not to say The Prime-Mover Co. didn't change with the times. Beginning in 1966, it strengthened its position in the industrial market,

at the same time lessening its dependence on the more limited construction-equipment market. This was achieved by introducing a variety of battery-powered material-handling trucks, each of which satisfied a need that wasn't being fulfilled by major fork-truck manufacturers. Spurred by the desire to reduce labor costs and conform to new clean air requirements, the electric industrial truck market was growing rapidly.

The first electric truck, the PE-40, debuted in late 1965. It was a walking-type, low-lift pallet truck with a 4,000-pound capacity. Over the next six years, The Prime-Mover Co. developed and sold 13 different electric trucks for the industrial market,

Left: Under construction in 1972, Building Number 7 added 92,400 square feet to the Muscatine Oak Street plant. The plant manufactured complex desks, credenzas, and related case goods. It also manufactured laminated particle board tops, which previously had been outsourced, and all chairs that did not need painting.

Below left: The plant at Cedartown, Georgia, started production in 1969, and an addition was built shortly thereafter. The Cedartown plant served the southeastern United States.

Below right: The craftsmen who produce The HON Company's traditional office furniture pay special attention to style details, fit, and finish. This laminate desk and return was produced at the Oak Street plant.

including stacker and order-selector trucks with 2,000- to 6,000-pound capacities in a variety of lift heights. Some models were of the walking type while others were of the stand-on rider type.

During that time, The Prime-Mover Co. introduced just one unit for the construction market, the L-32 mason tender, which transported bricks and blocks. Prime-Mover's construction equipment sales continued growing, however, for its products were important to controlling the cost of handling concrete and bricks. The Prime-Mover Co.

also offered excellent help to dealers with their sales efforts and ensured prompt delivery of parts and service information.[15]

In 1967 a 36,000-square-foot addition to the east end of the Geneva plant provided new truck

By the early 1970s, the Prime-Mover company offered a variety of types and models to suit a wide range of industrial, commerical, and warehousing applications.

docks and more space for manufacturing The Prime-Mover Co.'s electric material handlers and The HON Company's small goods, chairs, and stands.

By the end of 1972, The Prime-Mover Co.'s sales had increased by 250 percent over 1965's figures, and it was no longer dependent on the construction industry.

Holga: A Good Fit

Prime-Mover launched HON INDUSTRIES into manufacturing material-handling equipment, and the subsidiary became a profitable contributor to the corporation's bottom line. In the office equipment industry, though, the most successful acquisition of three, according to Stanley, had been Luxco, the chair and stand manufacturer that HON INDUSTRIES acquired in 1961. Even that was a qualified success, Stanley reasoned, because the company spent several years developing appealing designs and learning to produce and market chairs efficiently. The other two acquisitions fared worse, and HON INDUSTRIES soon discontinued the Essington Company's costumer and garment racks and R.J.R. Industries' wooden partitions.[16]

HON INDUSTRIES learned from its mistakes, however, and examined future acquisitions with a more critical eye. HON INDUSTRIES wanted to diversify into new products and markets, but experience had shown that it should probably acquire an entire company—personnel, facilities, and all—rather than simply a product design and inventory. HON INDUSTRIES targeted companies whose products could be marketed through its existing office furniture and material-handling distribution systems. Because the company intended to grow nationally, it considered companies that would add to its manufacturing capability in the East and West, particularly businesses in the premium, open-office systems, and custom-made furniture markets.

HON INDUSTRIES did not actively seek out companies to acquire, but a number of businesses flew into the company's radar in the late 1960s and early 1970s. Not until 1971 did it find a match with Holga Metal Products, based in Van Nuys, California.

Holga's product line was very similar to that of The HON Company. It manufactured desks, credenzas, suspension files, shelf files, and storage cabinets. Though it didn't manufacture chairs, it brought other assets to its new parent: blueprint storage cabinets and drafting desks and more importantly a foothold in the lucrative Southern California market. This, according to Stanley, was "a substantial market in which we have had limited penetration."[17]

Holga marketed through a network of dealers in western states, with direct sales to major industrial accounts in greater Los Angeles. Its four-year net sales averaged about $2.4 million—about one-tenth of HON INDUSTRIES' sales volume in 1970. HON INDUSTRIES planned to operate Holga as an independent division under the direction of Holga's president, James Arthur. The division would also sell The HON Company's products out of a distribution center in one of its buildings.[18]

When HON INDUSTRIES acquired Holga, Holga's production facilities were in poor shape, but Arthur, with HON INDUSTRIES' backing, set about changing the plant layout to improve production, lower costs, and raise product quality. By installing roller conveyors, rerouting some overhead conveyors, and knocking out walls, he streamlined the flow of desk and case-goods manufacturing.

Holga's manufacturing was located in buildings near the airport in Van Nuys, California.

Fun Facts about Holga

A CLASSIC MOVIE BUFF WHO VISITS ONE of the 1920s-vintage airplane hangars at the Holga Metal Products plant near the Van Nuys, California, airport may get a slight feeling of *déjà vu* when viewing the hangar from a certain angle. The feeling might grow stronger on a foggy night under certain lighting conditions. Wheel an old DC-3 in front of the hangar, place a man and woman in trench coats in front of it, and play a few bars of "As Time Goes By," and that movie buff almost certainly will recognize it as the scene in *Casablanca,* when Humphrey Bogart tells Claude Rains, "Louie, this could be the beginning of a beautiful friendship."

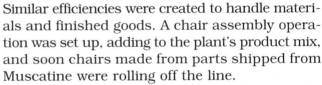

Not many manufacturing plants have been part of a movie set, but Holga can make that claim to fame, according to Tom Head, vice president and general manager of Holga. What's more, that photogenic hangar isn't Holga's only link to the Hollywood film industry, according to Head.

In the late 1940s, shortly after Holga was founded, while it was still making aviation-related products, a young woman was hired as an assembler. She considered the job a way to pay her bills as she was trying to break into the movies. She got that break. A few short years later, the world would know her as Marilyn Monroe.

In addition to its ties to Tinseltown, Holga has other stories to tell—like how the name of the Holga company is really a mistake. According to Head, the company's founder wanted to name his new company after his wife, but after he had filled out some forms, the clerk in the county courthouse misread his handwriting and named the company "Holga" instead of "Helga."[1]

Similar efficiencies were created to handle materials and finished goods. A chair assembly operation was set up, adding to the plant's product mix, and soon chairs made from parts shipped from Muscatine were rolling off the line.

By the end of 1972, Holga's sales had risen by half a million dollars. Stanley attributed much of the company's turnaround to Arthur. "He was close to everything at Holga," Stanley wrote, "and his aggressiveness and enthusiasm stimulated morale. Arthur's performance underlined the crucial importance of the continuity of competent management to the success of any acquisition."[19]

Holga expanded the range of HON INDUSTRIES' products— such as the blueprint cabinet pictured—that were not in The HON Company's line.

Corry Jamestown: Premium-Quality Furniture

The HON Company had just entered the premium-quality open-office systems market with the Environ 1 line when it learned that Corry Jamestown Corporation was up for sale. After careful scrutiny, HON INDUSTRIES acquired Corry Jamestown Corporation in May 1972 and pulled the plug on Environ 1.[20]

Based in Corry, Pennsylvania, Corry Jamestown was a nationally recognized manufacturer of premium-quality metal and custom-made office furniture. Corry was widely recognized for its expertise in designing and fabricating metal. It operated its own fleet of trucks, which added efficiency to its distribution, and sold to large national accounts. For instance, Corry furnished the new corporate headquarters of Deere & Company in Moline, Illinois.

Founded in 1920 by David A. Hilstrom, Corry Jamestown had been purchased in 1968 by the Singer Company, which planned to pair Corry's products with its adding and calculating machines, but the idea fell through because the marketing of the two products proved too different. When HON INDUSTRIES bought it, Corry manufactured six

Right: Rex Bennett (left), vice president of manufacturing, talks with Stanley M. Howe, president. In the early 1970s, Bennett spent about 40 percent of his time at Corry Jamestown to introduce better production methods at the recently acquired company.

Below right: The Corry Jamestown acquisition included this substantial manufacturing facility. The property included an attractive corporate headquarters (seen at right) and a large parcel of land across the highway.

Below: The Corry Jamestown Doric desk with modular return.

series of desks with credenzas, five series of chairs, and a full complement of case goods, but its sales had slipped by $5 million during the Singer years to $13.8 million in 1971, and it had recorded a $179,000 loss for the year.[21]

Bricks, Mortar, and Computers

Early in 1970, HON INDUSTRIES purchased an old building at 414 East Third Street across from Muscatine County's stately 19th-century courthouse and hired Stanley Consultants to redesign it for office space. The remodeling was completed within the year, and the site became the headquarters for both HON INDUSTRIES and The HON Company. Remodeling an existing building rather than constructing a new one "permitted deferment for several years of earlier plans to construct a new office building at a cost at least four times greater," Stanley and Howe told shareholders in 1970.[22]

In July 1968, HON INDUSTRIES jumped into the information age when it installed its first computer, a Honeywell 120, on the second floor of Oak Street Building Number 1. The computer was so large (as all computers were in those days) that it took up an entire room. Because HON INDUSTRIES had prepared for computers for several years, the transition went smoothly. Though it was "not without headaches," Stanley and Howe told shareholders, its speedy installation was "the envy of many companies."[23]

At first the pioneer computer—which handled payroll, accounting, order processing, inventory control, and management information—seemed to meet all of the company's needs, but soon its memory was filled to capacity, and in the fall of 1969 The HON Company upgraded to a Model 125. In 1971 the company installed a Honeywell 115/2 mainframe and tripled the memory with a Honeywell 2200 only a year later. The Honeywell 2200 was at least four times faster and had three times the memory of HON INDUSTRIES' first computer. It also stored information on disks, which were more durable than tapes. As HON INDUSTRIES' hardware and software became more sophisticated, the computer staff went from 13 people in 1968 to six in 1972.[24]

HON INDUSTRIES' automated processing equipment handled thousands of tons of coiled steel each year.

The Leadership

Striving to digest two acquisitions in such a short time, HON INDUSTRIES restructured. As the parent company, HON INDUSTRIES maintained a comparatively small corporate staff that provided finance, accounting, human resources, data processing, and planning services for the entire organization. Key leadership at HON INDUSTRIES included Max Stanley, chairman; Stanley M. Howe,

Above inset: By 1970 HON INDUSTRIES was in dire need of office space. It bought a sound, if somewhat unsightly, three-story building across the street from the stately Muscatine County Courthouse.

Above: Remodeled, the site became the headquarters for HON INDUSTRIES and The HON Company, providing 15,000 square feet of office space.

Right: Art Dahl, Ed Jones, and Robert Putnam in the HON INDUSTRIES board room in 1971. At the time, Dahl was dividing his time between The Prime-Mover Co. and HON INDUSTRIES. Jones was vice president of sales, and Putnam was vice president of systems and data processing.

Above: During a meeting in 1970, three HON INDUSTRIES executives inspect the features of a desk drawer: (from left) Leo Hooks, a former Corry Jamestown executive who was instrumental in the Corry acquisition; Phil Temple, vice president of product engineering; and Ralph Beals, manager of the Oak Street plant.

Right: Clifton Reeves inspects a finished chair at the Geneva plant. After plant expansions in the late 1960s and early 1970s, the chair operation at the Geneva plant specialized in only those lines that needed painting.

The operating divisions—The HON Company, The Prime-Mover Co., Holga Metal Products, and Corry Jamestown—became separate profit centers and operated semiautonomously. Each was responsible for manufacturing and marketing its product line, and each was expected to be self-sufficient and responsible for its profitability. Howe was president of both The HON Company and Corry Jamestown; Gene Waddell was vice president and general manager of The Prime-Mover Co.; and James Arthur was president of Holga.[25]

Meanwhile, HON INDUSTRIES' board of directors was growing stronger too, with eight of the ten directors from outside the company. In 1972 the board consisted of J. Harold Bragg, vice president of Lennox Industries and general manager of Marshalltown Division; William Cory, CPA of his own accounting firm; Clem Hanson, chairman of his advertising agency and a HON INDUSTRIES founder; Albert Hinkle, former partner at Ernst & Ernst; Ralph Hofstad, manager of the Agriculture Service division of Land O'Lakes; Stanley M. Howe, president of HON INDUSTRIES; Austin Hunt Jr., corporate director of manufacturing at the J. E. Baker Company; Dr. Dan Throop Smith, professor at the Harvard University Business School; Max Stanley, chairman of HON INDUSTRIES; and Dick Stanley, president of Stanley Consultants.

Member Satisfaction

HON INDUSTRIES members who owned stock saw substantial returns on their investment dur-

president; Art Dahl, senior vice president; Max Collins, vice president of personnel; Robert Putnam, vice president of systems and data processing; Fred Winn, secretary-treasurer; Maurice Jones, head of plant engineering; Clare Patterson, head of manufacturing research; Robert Carl, assistant to the president; Kermit Cook, assistant secretary and assistant treasurer; and Mary Ann Stange, Collins' assistant.

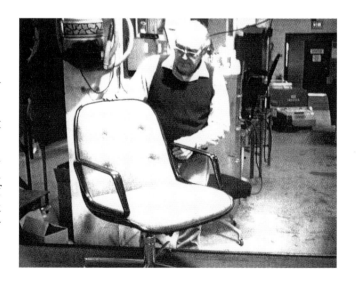

Member Vern Greer (left), from the seating assembly line, discusses features of a new unit with Clare Patterson (center), who headed HON INDUSTRIES' manufacturing research, and Cliff Brown, a manager in the seating group.

ing this period. In addition to payment of quarterly dividends, common stock was split 3-for-1 in 1968 and 2-for-1 in 1969. Due to the stock splits, 100 shares of stock in 1967 had turned into 600 shares by the end of 1972.[26]

Members saw improvements in benefits during the period as well. Paid holidays were increased to nine and one-half days each year, and by 1972 the company was paying 75 percent of members' insurance premiums. HON INDUSTRIES contributed more than $4.8 million to the profit-sharing and retirement plan from 1966 to 1972; the total fund exceeded $6 million in 1972. Before 1967 member contributions to the retirement fund had been mandatory, but that practice was discontinued, and The HON Company raised its contribution from 2 to 4 percent of members' pay.[27]

IN SUMMARY

FROM 1966 TO 1972, THE COMPANY that began as Home-O-Nize changed its name, updated its structure, and expanded its operations across the continent.

Home-O-Nize became HON INDUSTRIES Inc. in 1966, maturing into a dominant player in the office furniture market.

Its office products division officially became The HON Company in 1966. In contrast to how The HON Company evolved, The Prime-Mover Co. stayed close to its home base in Muscatine, Iowa.

In 1971 HON INDUSTRIES acquired Holga Metal Products of Van Nuys, California. Holga manufactured desks, credenzas, files, and stor-age cabinets. The move gave HON INDUSTRIES a foothold in the lucrative Southern California market. In 1972 HON INDUSTRIES acquired Corry Jamestown Corporation, a respected Pennsylvania manufacturer of custom-made office furniture.

By that time, HON INDUSTRIES' operating divisions—The HON Company, The Prime-Mover Co., Holga Metal Products, and Corry Jamestown—were separate profit centers operating semiautonomously.

The company's total sales grew from $10.96 million in 1965 to $49.32 million in 1972. In the same period, HON INDUSTRIES' workforce grew from 521 to 1,871.

The HON Company exhibited its latest products, including the M Series upholstered office chairs, at the National Stationers and Office Equipment Association's 1979 trade show.

CHAPTER SIX

More Significant Growth

1973–1980

The management of HON INDUSTRIES feels we have every reason to be optimistic about the future of the company, and confident that the management philosophies which have served us so well will continue to do so.

—Max Stanley and Stanley M. Howe, 1977

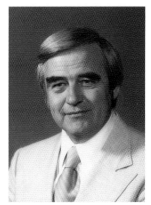

THE DECADE OF THE SEVEN-ties presented difficult challenges to the American economy and to businesses in every sector. The beginnings of the Watergate scandal, the growing conflict in Vietnam, and the often violent opposition to the civil rights movement had already soured the country's mood. Then in 1973, Egypt and Syria launched a massive offensive against Israel.[1]

Following weeks of desperate fighting, the United States airlifted $2 billion in aid to Israel to counter the Soviet Union's support of the Arab nations. Incensed, the Organization of Petroleum Exporting Countries (OPEC) united behind Saudi Arabia on October 20, 1973, in a complete embargo of oil shipments to the United States.[2]

The resulting energy crisis forced conservation to the top of the national agenda, and the economy tossed and turned in a swirl of inflation and recession.[3] From 1973 to 1974, consumer prices rose 12.2 percent and continued to rise until 1978.[4]

Despite severe economic challenges, HON INDUSTRIES continued to prosper during the 1970s. A steady rise in the number of office workers contributed to this prosperity. From the mid-1970s to the mid-1980s, the white-collar workforce was growing at a compound annual rate of 3 percent, and this trend prompted a spike in office construction and a growing need for office furnishings. Moreover, office managers were trying to cre-

ate attractive, well-organized environments to improve efficiency and productivity.[5] Through The HON Company, Corry Jamestown, and Holga, HON INDUSTRIES offered one of the broadest lines of office furniture in the nation.

At the same time, HON INDUS-TRIES maintained conservative financing that gave it a solid foundation for growth even while paying quarterly dividends to shareholders. From 1973 to 1980, the company was able to expand and improve product lines, enlarge and add facilities, and acquire valuable companies, despite the vagaries of the national economy.[6]

The Leanest Manufacturing

Even as early as the 1950s and 1960s, HON INDUSTRIES had been installing "elements of efficient mass production for which Japanese industry later gained fame," wrote James Soltow, coauthor of *The HON Story,* and the company's manufacturing grew more efficient over time.

Edward Jones was the first chief operating officer of The HON Company after its reorganization in 1973. He was promoted to president in 1977 and retired two years later, although he remained a part-time senior vice president of HON INDUSTRIES.

By 1976 all of The Prime-Mover Co. had moved into a newly built plant and office building in Muscatine. From left are Howard Worst, HON INDUSTRIES advertising department; Gene Waddell, general manager; George Dunker, customer service manager; Roy Hansen, sales manager; and Merv Comfort, plant superintendent.

"Vertical integration was a basic element of the HON system of mass production," Soltow wrote. "Instead of just assembling components produced by other firms, HON workers, starting with coils of steel and other basic materials, performed virtually all the manufacturing operation needed to turn out finished products. The people at HON...had the manufacturing know-how to devise ways to improve the quality and lower the costs of almost every component that went into a HON product."[7]

The HON Company installed modern, labor-saving equipment in every plant, and product engineers and manufacturing worked together to refine designs that simplified manufacturing. To reduce handling costs, material flowed through production processes over the shortest possible distance. The HON Company also minimized scrap, combined operations where possible, and kept inventory low. The result was a lean manufacturing machine that produced high-quality products at a lower cost—savings that it passed on to customers.

As Rex Bennett explained, "We were always looking for a better way. We met once a week and just brainstormed. One idea bred another. That's essentially the way we put in so many of the manufacturing ideas that made HON a success."[8]

Success created a need for more manufacturing capacity, and The HON Company expanded from its original Muscatine Oak Street plant as though by centrifugal force. In 1973 The HON Company purchased one block of Fourth Street from the city and built a 31,400-square-foot addition that joined all of The HON Company's manufacturing into one plant. The next year, The HON Company began leasing a 60,000-square-foot warehouse for finished goods. It also improved the plant's railroad and shipping flow by purchasing all the land along Third Street from Orange to Poplar, plus a nearby alley.

When Muscatine-based Huttig Manufacturing shut down operations in 1974, HON INDUSTRIES bought the company's 260,000 square feet of office, manufacturing, and warehouse buildings and its seven acres of land, annexing it to the Oak Street plant. In 1978 the main Huttig building became The HON Company's Oak Street plant Number 2, where it made wood office furniture. The next year, the former Huttig office building across the street became The HON Company's new headquarters.

The Prime-Mover Co. was changing, too. In 1975 it moved out of the Geneva plant and into a newly constructed plant and office in Muscatine. The 150,000-square-foot facility enlarged The Prime-Mover Co.'s production capacity by two-and-a-half times and helped make it more self-sufficient.[9]

The Geneva plant, meanwhile, was converted to chair manufacturing for The HON Company. "The old plant was making 500 chairs a week, and after we upgraded it, it made 5,000 chairs a week," said Ken Meyerholz, who oversaw the conversion. Meyerholz noted that in 2003 from the same building the Geneva plant consistently provided 41,000 chairs a week. "Back in the early days, inventory was not something we worried about," he explained. "So the first thing you did as an engineer when you laid out production was put in your main aisles to accommodate the flow of product, and then you put racks down each side of the aisles filled with raw material. Today none of those racks exist. We used to keep six months of raw materials on hand, and today we have two-and-a-half to three days' worth."[10]

Still, The HON Company's manufacturing methods were on the cutting edge. Unlike many of its competitors, The HON Company made all the chair components at its own plant, including the chrome plating, tubing, foam cushions, plywood parts, and chair bases. A two-story addition in 1980 to the Geneva plant doubled its size to meet demand for chairs.[11]

Meanwhile, Stanley and Howe's strategy to manufacture and distribute in regional markets was proving an effective way to get product to customers. That's why in 1973 the plant in Cedartown, Georgia, was expanded by 95,000 square feet. This doubled the plant's size and added another filing cabinet production line. In 1980 an even larger addition of 114,300 square feet added space for making files and desks.

To help jolt sales in the Northeast, in 1974 The HON Company began leasing a 200,000-square-

Below right: In 1976 the governor of Virginia officiated at the opening of The HON Company plant in Richmond. From left are Rex Bennett, who led the plant's start-up; plant member Carroll Waller; Stanley M. Howe; Governor Mills Godwin; and Edward Jones.

Below left: To place production closer to markets in the Northeast, in 1974 The HON Company began leasing a 200,000-square-foot plant near Richmond. A slump in the office furniture market during the latter half of that year slowed its opening, but the first production line for files started work in late 1975.

Above: In 1974 HON INDUSTRIES acquired Norman Bates Inc., an Anaheim, California, manufacturer of quality wood office furniture.

Right: At Norman Bates Inc., laminated components are glued under high pressure and elevated on a clamp carrier.

foot plant near Richmond, Virginia. Five years later, a 67,900-square-foot addition was completed, and The HON Company's eastern distribution operation moved from New Jersey to Virginia.[12]

A Wooden Leg

Until the early 1970s, most office furniture companies specialized in either metal or wood furniture, and The HON Company, with its sturdy line of metal desks, tables, and chairs, was no exception. However, Max Stanley and Stanley M. Howe did not want to limit the company to metal office furniture. Their decision to diversify gained further justificiation when the energy shortage caused steel prices—the basic raw material of The

HON Company's office furniture—to spike. In 1974 alone, the cost of steel rose 60 percent.[13]

In 1974 HON INDUSTRIES made its first acquisition in wood office furniture when it bought Norman Bates Inc., based in Anaheim, California. Norman Bates Inc. was a two-year-old manufacturer of high-quality, contemporary wood furniture for the premium market—a comparable market to Corry Jamestown's upscale metal furniture. The company's 75-member workforce built desks, bookcases, chairs, tables, and made-to-order furniture

inside a modern 55,000-square-foot plant. In 1974 the company had sales of about $1 million. The company was named after its founder, who became executive vice president of HON INDUSTRIES' Norman Bates division.[14]

HON INDUSTRIES further expanded its presence in wood in April 1977 when it bought Murphy-Miller Co., based in Owensboro, Kentucky, from Kroehler Manufacturing. Founded in 1945 (a year after The Home-O-Nize Co. was incorporated), Murphy-Miller Co. employed 400 people in a

Right: Murphy-Miller Co. executives tour the drying yard at the plant with Denny Waterman, vice president of sales for The HON Company. From left are Dan Lauterwasser, product manager; Walt Connor, general manager; Waterman; and Harold Nall, customer service manager.

Below: In 1977 HON INDUSTRIES acquired Murphy-Miller Co. of Owensboro, Kentucky, to gain entry into the wood seating market. It was consolidated into The HON Company as a wholly owned subsidiary because its products were so compatible with The HON Company's lines.

270,000-square-foot plant when HON INDUS-TRIES acquired it to diversify into wood seating. It became a wholly owned subsidiary of The HON Company because the two companies' products were so compatible.[15]

Norman Bates Inc. and Murphy-Miller Co. showed The HON Company the basics of manufacturing and selling wood furniture, and in 1978 The HON Company began producing its own wood desks.

Stanley M. Howe explained the importance of being a national player offering a broad line of office furniture.

In our mission statement, we said that HON would manufacture and sell a broad line of metal and wood office furniture nationally on an open basis through dealers, wholesalers, and other compatible channels. That mission statement really had a lot of meaning because in the early years, wooden furniture manufacturers were completely separate from metal. Companies were specialized.

They might be a wood chair company or a metal chair company or a metal file company. So to have one company make a broad line of products of both metal and wood was rather unique.

Selling on an open basis like we did was unique, too. Many of the companies at that time were regional rather than national, and, in fact, it was common for the larger manufacturers to have a separate higher price list for different parts of the United States because the freight costs were an additional expense.[16]

New Furniture

HON INDUSTRIES now had five furniture companies: The HON Company served the broad middle market where competitive pricing and product

Holga's 100 and 200 Series shell chairs were introduced in 1978.

Members at the Norman Bates plant work in 1978 to keep production at levels to meet customer demand.

availability were vital; Corry Jamestown specialized in premium furniture requested by office interior designers and architects; Holga Metal Products served the West Coast with a wide variety of metal office furniture and related products; Norman Bates gave HON INDUSTRIES a position in the premium wood furniture market; while Murphy-Miller Co. added wood furniture to The HON Company's middle market selection. By 1976 The HON Company had become the second-largest metal office furniture manufacturer with more people buying HON files that year than any other brand. Two years later, HON INDUSTRIES' combined office furniture sales ranked second among all U.S. office furniture manufacturers.[17]

HON INDUSTRIES' leaders had long recognized that new products were the company's lifeblood,

and its subsidiaries developed a constant stream of desks, files, panels, bookcases, and chairs in a variety of styles, sizes, colors, and price ranges.

The HON Company introduced two lines of shell-type chairs and four lines of files in 1975. Two years later the company rolled out new metal desks, chairs, and economy-priced lateral files. Thirty models of Murphy-Miller Co. chairs were also modified and improved. Late in the decade, The HON Company rounded out its product offering with wooden desks and chairs. It also added new models of nonsuspension files, steel chairs, compact wooden desks for smaller offices, and colorful bolster-back chairs.

Meanwhile, Holga, led by Jim Arthur, was growing more than twice as fast as the West Coast metal furniture market it served. During the decade, Holga added several series of shell chairs, "soft-look" chairs (plush chairs with soft, rounded corners), and lateral files. When Arthur retired in 1977, Rex Bennett took over Holga's leadership. By 1980 Holga's selection included metal desks, chairs, traditional office files, specialty files and cabinets, drafting furniture, and other products specific to West Coast industry needs.

The Norman Bates division revamped its furniture line with innovative new designs for both executive and general office use. The company added several series of wood desks, bookcases, and chairs, including upholstered wooden chairs and the Modillion series of desks and bookcases. In 1980 the division introduced a new desk series called Avatar that quickly became a best-seller.

Corry Jamestown introduced chairs, lateral files, and partitions, touted as "movable walls with a permanent look."

Hiebert: Open-Plan Office Systems

Previously, in 1971, The HON Company had tried unsuccessfully to gain a foothold in the open-plan office systems furniture market with Environ 1 but abandoned the line after acquiring Corry Jamestown. Corry Jamestown was slowly building a position in systems furniture, but HON INDUSTRIES was eager to take advantage of the rapidly growing market. In 1980 it finally gained the strong position in office systems furniture it had been seeking when it bought Hiebert Inc., based in Carson, California. Hiebert was arguably the premiere wood systems manufacturer in the country at that time. In fact, Norman Bates Inc. had been trying to emulate Hiebert's products.

Hiebert's products were distributed nationally and were well received by the design community and major corporate clients such as Mobile Oil, Equitable Trust Center, Pillsbury, and Levi Strauss. Office designers and architects often specified which manufacturers should supply a corporation's office furniture. The corporation would negotiate directly

An employee of Norman Bates Inc. assembles office furniture.

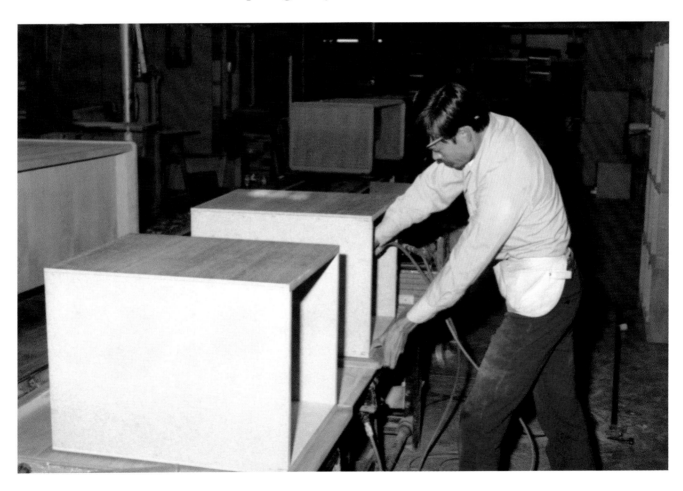

with the manufacturer for product specifications and price. Hiebert specialized in this type of sale, which added another facet to HON INDUSTRIES' diverse operations. Hiebert also strengthened HON INDUSTRIES' position in wood furniture.

Jay Simmons, who had turned around the struggling company after he purchased it in 1965, continued as president of Hiebert, which became a subsidiary of HON INDUSTRIES. Late in 1980, Hiebert moved its 750 employees into a 361,000-square-foot office and manufacturing facility that doubled its production capacity. HON INDUSTRIES would continue to expand its position in the systems segment with acquisitions in the 1980s.[18]

Prime-Mover Primes Up

The Prime-Mover Co., supported by the widespread need to reduce material-handling costs, had earned a reputation for high-performance products, excellent engineering, and exceptional service training. The Prime-Mover Co. continued emphasizing industrial products over construction, introducing more sophisticated models of battery-powered pallet trucks that offered greater speed and higher lifts. With the oil shortage and the material-handling industry's new emphasis on clean air, market conditions in the 1970s were ideal for The Prime-Mover Co.'s electric trucks. At the same time, it built a reputation for service by ensuring that replacement parts were readily available and by providing service training.

To help grow the business, The Prime-Mover Co. concentrated on finding and meeting specialized needs and emphasized quality, ease of operation, and service. The company designed trucks

By 1980, the Prime-Mover line had been expanded to include more than a dozen industrial material-handling lift trucks, such as the PE/HT rider pallet carrier, and a selection of construction machines, such as the LD-50 front-end loader.

specifically for narrow aisles, for example, along with trucks that moved pallet loads at ground level for relocation, dock handling, and truck loading.[19]

The Prime-Mover Co. continued to manufacture its motorized wheelbarrows for handling concrete and masonry products. Though these products were well received, the company looked for other niches in the construction market. As the energy crisis eased in the late 1970s, it was able to expand with forklifts designed for rough terrain and gasoline- and diesel-powered front-end loaders.[20]

Like the furniture operations of HON INDUSTRIES, The Prime-Mover Co. looked to grow through acquisition. In 1980 it entered the agricultural market by acquiring Oakes Manufacturing, based in Oakes, North Dakota. Oakes was a two-year-old manufacturer of skid steer loaders used primarily by farmers. The small, highly maneuverable skid steer loaders, with capacities ranging from 600 to 1,200 pounds, complemented The Prime-Mover Co.'s front-end loader line. What's more, the loaders were versatile enough for agricultural, industrial, and construction markets, thanks to a removable loader bucket that could be replaced with an array of attachments.[21]

Marketing and Distribution

HON INDUSTRIES' overall distribution philosophy was to make it as easy as possible to buy HON products. With that in mind, The HON Company's strategically located distribution centers sold to thousands of office equipment dealers, hundreds of wholesalers, and a number of major retail chains, including Sears. As a result of this well-balanced marketing program, The HON Company reached nearly every segment of industrial, financial, commercial, educational, and home markets. HON INDUSTRIES' premium-quality divisions marketed through select dealers and wholesalers and

By 1980, The HON Company truck fleet was delivering product in 46 states.

exhibited their products at trade shows, galleries, and showrooms.

To better serve different markets, HON INDUS-TRIES periodically revised its complex marketing and distribution systems. In 1975, for example, it expanded Norman Bates' reach by using Corry Jamestown—with its dedicated fleet of trucks and showrooms in Chicago and New York—to market and distribute Bates' wood furniture nationwide. Corry Jamestown also improved productivity and delivery time and redesigned its Chicago showroom to attract architects, space planners, and designers who influenced purchases of premium office furniture. Norman Bates added sales representatives, and Holga expanded its dealer network and improved distribution in Washington, Oregon, Idaho, and Alaska. Meanwhile, The HON Company added wholesalers, expanded sales territories, and launched its own nationwide fleet of trucks.

Management

Since the 1960s, Max Stanley as chairman and Stanley M. Howe as president had worked as a highly efficient management team. In the 1970s, Stanley began disengaging from HON INDUSTRIES and from Stanley Consultants to focus more of his time on the Stanley Foundation, philanthropy, and his own writing. In 1977 he began recording his recollections, interviewing veteran HON Company employees, and scouring company records to write *The HON Story.* He published *Managing Global Problems,* his second book on world peace, in 1979. In the meantime, Howe took over much of the responsibility for HON INDUSTRIES and in 1979 was named its chief executive officer.[22]

The significant expansion of the 1970s brought other changes in The HON Company's management structure. Arthur Dahl, who had proven his talents in both management and manufacturing, became senior vice president of HON INDUSTRIES. One of the company's first employees, Secretary-Treasurer Frederick Winn, retired in 1976 after 31 years of service. That same year, Robert Carl became corporate secretary.

Susan Cradick, who had been with the company since 1966, became Howe's new assistant. "He always amazed me," Cradick said. "He had a great sense of humor. He used to joke that he had to get my coffee in the morning." Cradick also remembered Howe as an ethical, moral man—unselfish and unpretentious. "He had an open-door policy," she said. "Anybody in the plant who wanted to come in and talk to him could, and many did. And in those years, he often went to the plants and greeted people by name. The workers always looked forward to seeing him come through. They had great respect for him."[23]

Cradick told another story that illustrated Howe's character. Before HON INDUSTRIES bought its own corporate aircraft fleet, it shared a fleet with Stanley Consultants. The fleet flew with both a pilot and copilot for its president and for Stanley M. Howe but only one pilot for everybody else. "Mr. Howe said his life wasn't any more important than the next guy's," Cradick remembered. "He said that if they flew with two pilots for him, they'd have to fly with two pilots for everybody. And so that's what they did."[24]

At The HON Company, in 1973 Edward Jones, who had joined the company in 1963 as a sales manager, became executive vice president and the company's first chief operating officer. Four years later, having further proven his abilities, he was promoted to president. During his tenure, Jones spearheaded much of The HON Company's successful sales and marketing strategies. In 1979 he transferred to the parent company as senior vice president of HON INDUSTRIES. J. Harold Bragg, who had been on the HON INDUSTRIES board, succeeded Jones as interim president of The HON Company when Jones retired in 1980.

The senior management in 1980 of HON INDUSTRIES' other subsidiaries included Harold Bragg, pulling double duty as president of Murphy-Miller Co. and The HON Company; Samuel Clarke as president of Corry Jamestown; and John Stewart, who succeeded Rex Bennett as president of Holga when Bennett retired in 1980.

Member Relations

In the meantime, HON INDUSTRIES continued its policy of treating members at all levels with fairness and dignity. HON INDUSTRIES worked hard to give members new job opportunities, job security, and above-average compensation and benefits, including stock ownership and profit sharing. It also began a management development program to identify and train potential managers from within the company and encouraged members to pursue internal training programs and promotions.[25]

At all HON INDUSTRIES divisions, the line between managers and plant employees was deliberately blurred; even the policy of reserved parking spaces for officers was abolished. As a case in point, in 1978 workers at Norman Bates voted to decertify their carpenters union, preferring HON INDUSTRIES' oversight and protection to the union's.

When all of HON INDUSTRIES had resided in Muscatine, it had been easier to maintain personal relationships among members. It wasn't uncommon for Max Stanley and Stanley M. Howe to greet the plant workers by name, but with thousands of

Officers of HON INDUSTRIES included, from left, Max Collins, vice president of personnel; Arthur Dahl, senior vice president; Stanley M. Howe, president; Herbert Williamson, vice president of planning; and Fred Winn, secretary and treasurer.

members in facilities across the map, that kind of camaraderie became harder to achieve.

Nevertheless, HON INDUSTRIES limited the size of its plants so managers could maintain close personal contact with members. It also encouraged open communication. Management at each facility continued to hold regular group meetings to keep members informed and listen to their questions and comments. Every facility had company picnics, holiday parties, and recognition dinners. Wearing HON INDUSTRIES jerseys or T-shirts, members participated on a variety of athletic teams in their local communities.[26]

Still, no company is immune to some internal strife, and HON INDUSTRIES was no exception. Soon after the Richmond plant opened in 1975, The HON Company experimented by eliminating distinctions between hourly and salaried workers. Every member was paid weekly, and no one had to punch a clock. However, when supervisors asked plant members to account for their time away from work, resentment built, and the experiment was abandoned. That same year, a machinists union

In the early 1970s, Sales Manager Edward Jones (fifth from right) converses with Max Stanley during a sales meeting dinner.

strike idled Corry Jamestown for nine weeks. As Soltow explained, "Under previous ownership [at Corry Jamestown], a confrontational, 'we-they' style of relationships had evolved between management and the union." The strike ended with a wage and benefit adjustment of only three cents per hour more than the company had offered before the strike. When Corry's contract expired in 1978, workers again went on strike, this time for two weeks; in the end, they accepted the original pact worked out by the union negotiating committee and the company.[27]

A Good Corporate Citizen

From the company's founding, HON INDUSTRIES had been socially responsible, and it viewed that responsibility as a moral and ethical obligation. In the mid-1960s, the company had begun setting aside one percent of the previous year's pretax earnings to support charities and other community causes. It also offered college scholarship programs. Stanley and Howe led by example, supporting multiple community, educational, youth, health, and faith-related organizations. The HON

HON INDUSTRIES conducted its first formal strategic planning retreat in 1978. From left are Clare Patterson, vice president of manufacturing research; Don Holt, data processing manager; Robert Carl, corporate secretary; Gene Waddell, executive vice president of The Prime-Mover Co.; Max Collins, vice president of personnel; Herbert Williamson, vice president of planning; Richard Johnson, advertising manager; Stanley M. Howe, president; Max Stanley, chairman; Samuel Clarke, president of Corry Jamestown; Rex Bennett, president of Holga Metal Products; Don Swanson, controller; Maurice Jones, vice president of plant engineering; Gerald Rosen, general manager of the Norman Bates division; Art Dahl, senior vice president; John Axel, vice president of finance; and Bruce Jolly, treasurer.

Company was also an equal opportunity employer, and it ensured that members worked in a safe environment.[28]

What's more, HON INDUSTRIES was a leader in energy conservation thanks to a company-wide effort. A 1974 memo from Howe to members illustrates the company's dedication to being a responsible corporate citizen. "President Ford has reminded us that the energy shortage is still with us and of the need to continue to conserve energy," he wrote. "We can help by reducing fuel consumption during the heating season....I encourage you to also look for other ways to reduce our energy requirements."[29]

Members did look for other ways and formed an internal energy conservation committee. By 1977 the company had substantially reduced its use of natural gas while concurrently increasing production by 20 percent.[30]

A Record of Growth

In *The HON Story*, Max Stanley dubbed the chapters covering the mid-1970s to the mid-1980s

A three-story atrium greeted visitors at the new headquarters of The HON Company on Oak Street in downtown Muscatine. The building was completed in 1980.

"Another Surge of Growth." That seems a modest understatement for a period when sales rose from $71.1 million in 1973 to $201.9 million in 1980 and profits climbed from $4.6 million to $15.2 million. HON INDUSTRIES had grown sufficiently to make *Fortune* magazine's list of the top 1,000 industrial companies based on its 1976 sales, debuting with a ranking of 980 by sales and 684 in total net income.

HON INDUSTRIES ranked much higher in its value to investors. From among the 1,000 top industrials that year, the company was ranked 78th in return on stockholders' equity, 46th in ten-year growth of earnings per share, and 23rd in its ten-year growth rate for total return to investors.[31] In subsequent years, HON INDUSTRIES advanced its ranking on *Fortune*'s list.

To finance its growth during the 1960s and early 1970s, the company had borrowed from the Prudential Insurance Company and established a line of credit with its bank, the Northern Trust

Company of Chicago. By 1974, however, with growing retained earnings and manageable long-term debt (and in the face of rising interest rates), HON INDUSTRIES relied mostly on its own cash and a new funding source, industrial revenue bonds.

While HON INDUSTRIES made no public stock offerings during this period, members had three opportunities to purchase common stock through payroll deductions at 90 percent of the market price. They took full advantage of those opportunities. All shareholders saw their investments grow through stock splits—two-for-one in 1973, three-for-two in 1977, and two-for-one in 1979. HON INDUSTRIES delivered its 100th consecutive quarterly dividend on common stock in March 1980.

HON INDUSTRIES emerged from the difficult decade of the 1970s stronger and more diverse than ever. In 1980 the company boasted 3,300 members, 12 manufacturing plants, and offices, showrooms, and distribution centers in nine states. HON INDUSTRIES not only outperformed the office furniture and material-handling markets and gained a bigger piece of the overall market pie, it also served a variety of market segments that allowed it to survive market weaknesses in certain sectors. That diversity would prove especially beneficial in coming years.

IN SUMMARY

THE 1970S PRESENTED CHALLENGES to the American economy and to businesses in every sector. Despite a floundering economy, HON INDUSTRIES prospered. A steady rise in the number of American office workers also contributed to HON INDUSTRIES' prosperity. At the same time, HON INDUSTRIES maintained conservative financing that gave the company a solid foundation for growth, even while paying continuous quarterly dividends to shareholders.

Meanwhile, the company's furniture manufacturing methods remained on the cutting edge, enabling it to produce quality furniture at competitive prices.

By 1977 HON INDUSTRIES operated five furniture companies: The HON Company, Corry Jamestown, Holga Metal Products, Norman Bates Inc., and Murphy-Miller Co.

In the 1970s, co-founder Max Stanley began disengaging from his long career at HON INDUSTRIES to focus on philanthropy. In the meantime, Stanley M. Howe took over much of the responsibility for running The HON Company and in 1979 was named chief executive officer of HON INDUSTRIES.

Marking 40 years since the incorporation of HON INDUSTRIES, the company's founders, Clem Hanson, left, Wood Miller, and Max Stanley gathered in early 1984. In less than a year, the brothers-in-law Stanley and Hanson had died.

CHAPTER SEVEN

How to Grow by Leaps and Bounds

1981–1988

We feel confident about the future because of our people, our products, our markets, and our loyal customers.

—Stanley M. Howe, 1987

THE ELECTION OF RONALD REAGAN to the presidency in 1980 heralded enormous changes in the United States, including less governmental control in the marketplace, increased consumer spending, and some new limitations on organized labor. While a new social strand of self-motivated professionals called "yuppies" would capitalize on the burgeoning Reaganomics opportunities, others wouldn't be quite so fortunate. A recession in the early 1980s slowed many businesses, and though consumer spending soared throughout the decade, financial woes struck many individuals and companies following the collapse of savings and loan institutions and the "Black Monday" stock market crash of October 1987.

Many companies were acquired or folded altogether during this time, but HON INDUSTRIES continued to be a model of business success. The office furniture industry continued to grow in the 1980s, thanks to new designs and products, office construction growth, and a rise in the number of white-collar workers. In 1981 industry sales were close to $4 billion and experts predicted sales would reach $13 billion by the end of the decade.

Throughout the 1980s, HON INDUSTRIES maintained a strong position in both metal and wood office furniture, offering many types of both choices to a wide array of customers at all price levels. To build upon that strength, the furniture companies introduced new products each year that capitalized on emerging trends. At the same time, HON INDUSTRIES provided for future growth by significantly expanding and modernizing its manufacturing and distribution systems. While much of corporate America engaged in a rash of acquisitions, often of entities far outside the industries they knew and understood, HON INDUSTRIES made strategic acquisitions that strengthened its core competencies.

The company also got more attention from Wall Street. In August 1983, HON INDUSTRIES was listed on Nasdaq Exchange. Then in 1986 it made *Fortune* magazine's prestigious list of the 500 largest industrial corporations in the United States, debuting at 478th in sales volume, 80th in average return to investors during the preceding ten years, and 51st in net income as a percent of shareholders' equity.

Heatilator: The Third Diversity

HON INDUSTRIES found the "third diversity" it had been seeking in 1981 when it acquired the Heatilator Fireplace Division of Vega Industries. Most of Heatilator's sales came from home contractors

C. Maxwell Stanley, HON INDUSTRIES' chairman and founder, died of a heart attack at age 80 in 1984.

and builders buying fireplaces in bulk, but the company also sold to home remodelers and do-it-yourself homeowners.[1]

The acquisition raised more than a few eyebrows, as fireplaces seemed a far cry from office furniture, but as Stanley M. Howe explained years later, "Manufacturing-wise, they're the same. They're just metal boxes. We had a lot of know-how for metal box manufacturing. We sold Heatilator on that idea and greatly improved their efficiency."[2]

"The manufacturing processes were very similar for file cabinets and fireplaces," said Phillip Hecht, who joined Heatilator in 1974 and later became its vice president for member and community relations.[3]

Based in Des Moines, Iowa, with plants in Mount Pleasant and Centerville, Iowa, Heatilator became a wholly owned subsidiary of HON INDUSTRIES, which consolidated the operation into the 293,000-square-foot plant, closed and sold the other properties, and updated production methods. Robert Day stayed as president until his retirement in 1985 and was succeeded by Robert Burns.[4]

Below left: Heatilator's open-end fireplace and other models in the Designer Series reached a market not previously served.

Below right: In 1986 Heatilator introduced its 46-inch fireplace, which gave homeowners the look of a large, old-fashioned masonry fireplace at a fraction of the cost.

Heatilator had a rich history. The first Heatilator was produced during the waning years of the Great Depression and soon became one of the "best-known brand names in fabricated metal fireplaces," according to James Soltow, coauthor of *The HON Story.*

During the 1960s, Heatilator's zero-clearance fireplaces became immensely popular because they could be installed on or against combustible surfaces such as wood floors or walls. This made installing them easier and less expensive. Sales increased because more people could afford to have a fireplace in their homes. Heatilator's sales shot up again as a result of the oil crisis of the 1970s when wood-burning stoves grew more popular.[5]

There was some early trepidation among Heatilator employees about being acquired, but fears were soon laid to rest when people learned more about HON INDUSTRIES. "It became evident after people started digging for information about HON INDUSTRIES that we had the good luck of being linked up with a very high-quality, value-based organization," said Hecht. "We realized that HON INDUSTRIES' people were here to fix things; they were here to join with us and seek ways to make improvements. That participatory style was refreshing."[6]

Because of the homebuilding slump of the late 1970s, Heatilator was in some financial difficulty when HON INDUSTRIES acquired it. Heatilator had also lost touch with the market. In the late 1970s and early 1980s, it had a limited product line.[7]

Heatilator's History

LIKE HON INDUSTRIES, THE COMPANY that eventually became Heatilator spent several years discovering the product line that would propel its success—and several more years settling on a name.

The company began in 1917 as a cloth dying business in Syracuse, New York. Because it imported dyes from Germany, the advent of World War I soon closed that business. During the war, one of the founding partners sold commodes part-time and persuaded some investors to back him in starting a factory to manufacture them. That resulted in the Chemical Toilet Corporation, which opened a plant in suburban Liverpool, New York, in 1919. Two years later, the company shifted production from chemical toilets to steel septic tanks. In 1925 the company returned to Syracuse.

Wanting to diversify, in 1927 the company started making oil storage tanks and manufactured its first fireplace, branding it "Heatilator." The early model had design problems, but the addition of a down-draft shelf in 1929 resolved them. The redesigned fireplace was named the Mark C, and it remained in production until 1995.

Over the next 35 years, the company changed its name twice—to San-Equip Inc. in 1930 and Vega Industries in 1955. It added production plants in Chicago and Chattanooga, Tennessee, and built fireplaces in Salt Lake City from 1952 to 1963.

Along the way, in 1946 the company developed the first factory-built fireplace system, eliminating the need for masonry construction, and in 1955 it introduced the "uni-bilt" fireplace, which began the zero-clearance product line. The next step in that technology came in 1972 with the zero-clearance heat-circulating fireplace.

In 1965 Vega Industries moved its fireplace manufacturing operations from Chicago and Chattanooga to Mount Pleasant, Iowa, adding a second plant in Centerville, Iowa, a few years later. It moved its corporate headquarters from Syracuse to Des Moines in 1978.

Although the company's product had been known as Heatilator since 1927, the name was not official until 1981, when HON INDUSTRIES purchased it from Vega Industries and named it Heatilator Inc.[1]

Stanley M. Howe got involved in improving specific areas of Heatilator by forming ten task forces consisting of Heatilator and The HON Company managers. For example, Heatilator worked closely with The HON Company's manufacturing experts to apply what later became known as "just in time" manufacturing methods, which greatly reduced material-handling costs while increasing efficiency. One task force put the fabrication equipment right into the assembly line, made the piece, and then immediately assembled it onto the product. Another task force drove down scrap. Yet another devised a sales strategy for Southern markets to take some of the seasonality out of the business.[8]

"The company needed turning around," Howe said more than 20 years later. "They had two plants and their corporate office was clear off in Des Moines. So we closed the Centerville, Iowa, plant and consolidated everything at Mount Pleasant, including the management. That really improved efficiency."[9]

Heatilator's product development had fallen behind the times, but engineers quickly got to work and developed a new energy-efficient zero-clearance model, the BF36, which debuted at the National Association of Home Builders show in 1982. The next year it introduced a competitively priced model to supplement its Advantage premium-priced fireplace. In 1985 the company came out with a fireplace-stove unit and a designer series of fireplaces that included a see-through model.

Heatilator diversified in 1985 with the purchase of Arrow Tualatin, which manufactured fireplace

Shown here are Heatilator members proudly wearing their customized T-shirts awarded them for their efforts to enhance teamwork by their suggestions or excellence on the job.

inserts and wood-burning stoves at its 32,000-square-foot plant in Tualatin, Oregon. In 1988 the company moved Arrow's production to Mount Pleasant, thus reducing manufacturing and national distribution costs.[10]

Later in the decade, Heatilator introduced wood stoves and fireplace inserts that met the Environmental Protection Agency's new emissions standards. It also introduced a variety of fireplace models and chimneys that captured the attention of builders, architects, and interior designers.

Corry Gets Bigger

Seeking a stronger position in the upscale contract and office systems markets, HON INDUSTRIES in 1982 merged Holga and Norman Bates into Corry Jamestown, creating its third national office furniture company (along with Hiebert and The HON Company). Corry Jamestown now marketed Norman Bates and Holga products through its established national marketing and distribution system. Samuel Clarke continued as Corry Jamestown's president.[11]

The restructured Corry Jamestown marketed Corry Jamestown and Holga labels to the medium and high-end segments of the office furniture market. In the early 1980s, it introduced new models of open-plan systems—including motorized electronic computer furniture—as well as complete lines of wood and metal furniture in a wide selection of colors and fabrics.

In 1985 Corry Jamestown showrooms began offering computer-aided design (CAD) systems that produced scale drawings of installations to make it easier for office designers to envision their plans and order the furniture. Also that year, Corry moved its headquarters to Irving, Texas, which was more accessible to the design community and corporate customers. The move also gave it closer access to Sun Belt markets, where HON INDUSTRIES wanted to grow.[12]

Rishel Brings More Woodwork

Meanwhile, in 1982, HON INDUSTRIES bought J. K. Rishel Furniture Company. Based in Williamsport, Pennsylvania, Rishel was founded in 1857 and had evolved into a highly respected manufacturer of wood furniture. Known for its meticulous craftsmanship, Rishel made wood furniture for U.S. government agencies and made office furniture on contract for other companies. The deal included a 229,000-square-foot manufacturing, warehouse, and office facility on 6.5 acres in Williamsport and

Right: Rishel executive office furniture had long been a favorite of the federal government. By 1982 it was so well-established in Washington, D.C., that a Rishel desk was used on the sound-stage where members of Congress videotaped messages to be televised to constituents in their home districts.

Below: HON Company's 68000 Series modular office furniture combined a sleek style and practicality.

Rishel's Rich History

FOR NEARLY 150 YEARS, FURNITURE manufacturing had been part of Williamsport's industrial scene—an outgrowth of a lumber boom in that part of Pennsylvania that began in the 1850s and thrived for about 50 years.

Rishel had two origins. The furniture manufacturing *building* started in 1883 as John A. Otto and Sons, a furniture factory and planing mill.

The *company*, J. K. Rishel, was founded in the late 1860s in nearby Hughesville, Pennsylvania, by James Laird as either a case goods manufacturer or planing mill (accounts differ). Within a few years, Laird sold the business to his son John and son-in-law J. K. Rishel, a dentist. Then in 1878 John Laird sold his share to Rishel. By 1897 the company was manufacturing chamber suites, bureaus, and chiffoniers in oak, mahogany, bird's-eye maple, and birch.

In November 1899, Rishel bought the Otto Furniture Company in Williamsport and moved his company's offices there. The company was incorporated in 1900 as the J. K. Rishel Furniture Company with plants in Williamsport and Hughesville. Its line had expanded to include matching dining room suites in repro-

ductions of historical furniture styles such as Queen Anne, Chippendale, Italian Renaissance, and French Provincial. Its home furnishing lines included Arts and Crafts bedroom suites, Swiss-Austrian dining room suites, and mission style items.

Rishel's ability as a marketer fueled the company's growth. The company exhibited at the 1895 American Furniture Manufacturers Exposition in New York. Soon it had a permanent "wareroom" in the New York Furniture Exchange and showrooms in Philadelphia, Boston, and Columbus, Ohio. Salespeople traveled from store to store with photos of the Rishel line. As early as 1909 the company published an annual catalog.

Although Rishel's early 20th-century home furnishings still remain objects of admiration to some antique furniture enthusiasts, it was the high-quality office furniture that debuted in 1918 that led to its becoming part of HON INDUSTRIES. The office furniture manufactured at Rishel's Williamsport plant appeared in such distinguished buildings as the White House, the U.S. House of Representatives, numerous American embassies around the world, and offices and board rooms of prominent corporations.[1]

a 169,000-square-foot plant on 50 acres in Louisburg, North Carolina.

HON INDUSTRIES consolidated Rishel's production in Williamsport and integrated the Louisburg plant into Hiebert to supplement Hiebert's presence on the West Coast. Rishel became a HON INDUSTRIES subsidiary in 1984 with Richard Mellish as president.

By the time Vincent Burns succeeded Mellish in 1988, Rishel was well established as a HON INDUSTRIES subsidiary, offering traditional and contemporary executive desks, secretarial work stations, bookcases, cabinets, storage units, office and conference tables, computer-support furni-

ture, and modular office systems. Rishel also made furniture on contract and even manufactured furniture for The HON Company, including an executive series of walnut and mahogany furniture. In addition, Rishel made traditional and Danish modern bedroom furniture for the U.S. Armed Forces Family Housing Program.

CorryHiebert

Hiebert, specializing in premium-quality wood office and systems furniture, introduced some innovative designs in the early 1980s, including chairs with removable arms, mobile pedestals (file

As testament to the new market presence of CorryHeibert, soon after their merger in 1986, these Prism modules were installed at Chicago's Water Tower.

drawers with wheels that fit neatly under desks), and conference tables, among others.

In the mid-1980s, Hiebert's Carson and Louisburg plants underwent renovation, improving their production capabilities and their ability to service dealers and customers. Showrooms in New York, San Francisco, Denver, Houston, and Atlanta were key in Hiebert's marketing program; its redesigned Chicago showroom drew attention in 1984 by winning the prestigious American Society of Interior Designers' award for excellence in showroom design.[13]

Then in 1986, HON INDUSTRIES merged Corry Jamestown and Hiebert, forming CorryHiebert, to strengthen its position in the contract office furniture segment. It made sense to combine the two, for both companies' salesforces worked with architects, designers, and dealers to sell to corporate clients, and they maintained showrooms in many of the same cities. The new company was headquartered in Irving, Texas, and led by Nigel Ferrey. Under Ferrey's leadership, CorryHiebert improved manufacturing and product quality while reducing production costs. By 1988 the company had an administrative office in Carson, California, various plants, and ten showrooms strategically located across the country.[14]

Diversifying Further

HON INDUSTRIES continued to diversify in 1983 when it purchased 35 percent of Ring King Visibles, a 20-year-old Muscatine company that manufactured computer-related office products such as disk storage boxes and sound enclosures for printers. Originally, Ring King had been an outgrowth of a Muscatine office supply dealership founded by Byron and Martha Massey, but in 1972, after its sales skyrocketed from selling microfiche files, Ring King became a separate company. With the advent of personal computers and floppy disks, Ring King began manufacturing disk storage boxes, which were very successful, but by the early 1980s it was forced to maximize its debt load in order to grow.

For Ring King, the selling of stock to HON INDUSTRIES meant an infusion of funds at a critical time—a time when businesses were still in the early stages of bringing small computers into the workplace. For HON INDUSTRIES, the purchase presented an opportunity to expand into office equipment, something it had not done since it made aluminum card file boxes for the office. Craig Drake, grandson of the founders, was chairman

and president of the company; John Axel, HON INDUSTRIES' vice president of finance, became a member of its board.[15]

By 1988 HON INDUSTRIES had bought the remaining 65 percent of Ring King Visibles. As a HON INDUSTRIES subsidiary, Ring King acquired the sound-enclosure cover portion of Gates Acoustinet and the Quiet Print division of Zero Corporation, gaining a sizeable market share in sound enclosures for printers. By 1988 Ring King, still led by Craig Drake, had consolidated most of its manufacturing in Muscatine. Its main products were disk storage trays, sound enclosures, micrographic products, and workstation accessories.[16]

Continuing its office equipment diversification strategy, in 1987 HON INDUSTRIES created a new division called the XLM Company, led by Walter Grace, to manufacture a new style of filing cabinet for home offices. XLM marketed the prod-

Left: Data Defender accessories provided space-saving protection for diskettes of different sizes.

Below: To enhance the usefulness of XLM cabinets in the home office, accessories such as a desktop were added in 1988.

uct under the trade name Office Partners through mass merchandisers such as Wal-Mart and Kmart and catalog showrooms. Manufacturing was set up in Heatilator's Mount Pleasant plant. The product

was so well received that a second production shift began in late 1987. In 1988 XLM added four-drawer files, wood-grained finishes, and compatible hanging file folders.[17]

HON INDUSTRIES made another acquisition in 1986, buying the four-year-old Budget Panels Inc. (BPI) of Kent, Washington (BPI would later become Maxon). According to John Axel, Budget Panels had "carved a very substantial place" for itself in the lower-priced end of the systems market, for which The HON Company had no products. "Budget Panels filled a void in our product line," he said. Marketing its products to office furniture wholesalers and retailers, BPI had developed distribution channels that would make valuable contributions to The HON Company's position.

"We got into the panel business kind of late," explained Thomas Miller, who joined HON INDUSTRIES in 1987 and in 2003 was acting president of

Above: Ring King's Sound-write acoustical covers, left, reduced office noise from printers.

Below: Office Partners' hanging-file folders were marketed by XLM Company in a variety of package sizes.

Right: Many leading mass merchandisers such as Wal-Mart were XLM Company customers. James N. Vander Brug, right, vice president of sales and marketing for XLM, discusses a display of Office Partners file cabinets with Lonnie Neubauer, the Wal-Mart store manager in Muscatine, Iowa.

HON International. "That's why we decided to buy Budget Panels. If we were going to enter the business, we decided we'd enter a part of the market that we could understand since there were so many other high-end competitors."[18]

BPI founder Gary White became executive vice president of the new HON INDUSTRIES subsidiary, and founder Leslie White became vice president of administrative services. Robert Kroon was president.[19] By 1988 Budget Panels had become a leading company in budget-priced screens and wall panels. The company offered everything from simple room dividers to panels equipped for electrical components.

The HON Company

Since its formation, The HON Company had been the largest, most profitable subsidiary of HON INDUSTRIES, but The HON Company's leaders received something of a wake-up call when sales slowed and profits dropped as a result of the early 1980s recession. The company had enjoyed more than two decades of yearly growth, and suddenly managers realized the company was not immune to market fluctuations—that its infrastructure had not kept up with its rapid growth.

After J. Harold Bragg retired as interim president of The HON Company in 1983, Ronald L. Jones, who had been hired as executive vice president of The HON Company the previous year, became the new president of The HON Company. Jones didn't hesitate to put The HON Company back on track. He started by decentralizing the

The acquisition of BPI in the mid-1980s quickly gave HON INDUSTRIES a foothold in the lower-priced portion of the rapidly growing systems market.

management structure and giving more decision-making power to members who were in touch daily with the marketplace. He formed two operating groups, one for seating and one for case goods, and regional managers were given more power to make decisions based on their specific markets. Jones created business units that focused on meeting customer needs in specific market segments and reorganized marketing and distribution to better suit the company's broad range of products. Computers helped decentralize some of the company's administrative functions.

Throughout the decade, The HON Company maintained its dominant position in the middle market, coming out with new wood and metal seating, desks, and files in a variety of designs, styles, colors, and price ranges, but the company diversified beyond those traditional offerings, too. In 1982, after 30 months of planning, The HON Company created a Modular Systems Group and began offering furniture for open-office systems in the middle market.

Systems furniture required a different type of distribution than The HON Company was used to, so it hired specialized salespeople who devised a strategy for distributing systems furniture to the middle market. As more offices began using electronics, The HON Company introduced modular panel systems and special furniture and accessories designed for audio-visual equipment and personal computers. It also introduced a wood veneer line of traditional furniture (crafted by Rishel). When the commercial market for office furniture dipped in the early 1980s as a result of the recession, The HON Company diversified its customer base and began selling to the General Services Administration of the U.S. Government.

Jean Reynolds started her career with The HON Company in 1981, and later became president of HON INDUSTRIES' Maxon Furniture Group, formerly BPI. Reynolds remembered how the company's reputation preceded it with the government and how important the government contracts were on the tail end of the recession.

We started going after government business and won several single-award government contracts. Within 60 days of winning the contract, orders just began flooding into the company. The government

had not been happy with its prior contractors, and when they heard HON had a chance of bidding on the contract, they all stopped buying and waited for us to win. Then we were just inundated with orders. We had folding tables set up in the aisles around customer service and order processing. We had stacks of orders that were three feet deep. To keep up, people from all across the company got involved to learn how to process government orders.[20]

Ronald L. Jones left as The HON Company president in 1987 and was succeeded by Ed Shultz. That year, Thomas Miller joined The HON Company as vice president of marketing. It was around that time that The HON Company began building high-end office furniture for large companies on a contract basis in order to compete with companies like Steelcase and Hayworth. "The big companies had long since expanded into the contract segment of the market, which is the segment that sells to the very large corporations to outfit an office building or replace a whole floor of furniture," Miller said. "We were just beginning to nibble away at some of that market when I joined."[21]

Taking Care of Business

One reason for HON INDUSTRIES' success was its willingness to invest in the future. The company installed the latest, most efficient machines and implemented preventative measures to ensure its equipment stayed in prime working condition. It also expanded production capacity by adding plant space and building new production lines.

Early in 1981, for example, The HON Company enlarged the Oak Street complex in Muscatine with 39,000 square feet of warehouse space. When completed, the L-shaped addition covered a part of Third Street that The HON Company had acquired in 1980 and, by means of a computer-controlled conveyor system, linked with two other warehouses to form an efficient finished-goods storage facility.[22]

Also in 1981, HON INDUSTRIES executives at last gained the substantial foothold they had been seeking in the fast-growing Southern California market, acquiring a closed-down Firestone Tire & Rubber plant at South Gate. Rex Bennett came out of retirement in the spring of 1981 to manage the 53-year-old property.

Above: In 1981 The HON Company acquired the closed Firestone Tire & Rubber plant in South Gate, California, giving the company a major facility in the Los Angeles market.

Inset: The white-roofed area at the upper-left portion of the South Gate facility was used by The HON Company.

The facility was huge—measuring more than 1.6 million square feet on 52 acres—and encompassed more space than The HON Company needed, so it quickly set up a distribution center there and saw a substantial increase in dealer business as a result. By the next spring, suspension files were rolling off the plant's assembly line, marking The HON Company's first manufacturing on the West Coast. Parts of the property were sold and leased in 1982, and in 1984 a second, more flexible line began producing nonsuspension files, lateral files, desks, and bookcases.[23]

In 1982 The HON Company's Modular Systems Group launched an open furniture line; late in the year it improved its manufacturing operations by moving from leased property into The Prime-Mover Co. plant. In 1987 the Modular Systems Group plant doubled in size.[24]

To increase its competitive presence in the fast-growing southwestern region, in 1985 The HON Company bought a 65-acre site in Sulphur Springs, Texas, where it built a plant and distribution center for metal case goods.[25]

In 1988 the company had manufacturing facilities in Muscatine, Iowa, where it was headquartered, and in Virginia, North Carolina, Georgia, Kentucky, Texas, and California. It also had showrooms in New York, Chicago, Los Angeles, and Muscatine.

Prime-Mover Moves On

Meanwhile, The Prime-Mover Co., led by L. Gene Waddell, who was promoted to president in 1981, broadened its market reach by adding new models and modifying existing ones. Weak demand for construction equipment in the early 1980s hurt The Prime-Mover Co.'s sales, but the sales and marketing staff promoted more aggressively, and by the time the market rebounded in mid-decade, The Prime-Mover Co. was well positioned to compete. Jack Michaels, who later became chairman and CEO of HON INDUSTRIES, was at J. I. Case in the mid-1980s and remembered The Prime-Mover Co. as being a "good competitor.... They were well respected," he said. "They had good products, good people."[26]

Concentrating on industrial trucks designed for narrow aisles, The Prime-Mover Co. combined the best features of several models of reach trucks. It introduced a low-lift warehouse transporter in 1983 and a 3,000-pound capacity narrow-aisle lift truck two years later. For the construction market, it introduced a 50-horsepower loader and a 4,000-pound rough-terrain forklift. It also redesigned four skid-steer models to handle bulk materials and added a compact skid-steer for farm use. In 1985 The Prime-Mover Co. redesigned the 1,300-pound capacity skid-steer, and in 1987 the company expanded its manufacturing space by 50 percent to accommodate future growth.

Despite The Prime-Mover Co.'s sound position, its products were far different from the rest of HON INDUSTRIES' offerings, and as The HON Company solidified its position in office furniture, that fact became increasingly apparent. HON INDUSTRIES did not specialize in material-handling equipment and was not dedicating the resources The Prime-Mover Co. deserved to help it grow. Thus in 1988 HON INDUSTRIES cut the last tie to its Home-O-Nize days when it sold The Prime-Mover Co. to Sweden-based BT Industries, from which The Prime-Mover Co. had imported concrete vibrators in the early 1960s. "The decision to sell Prime-Mover was not an easy one," Howe said. "The people in that organization have been outstanding members of HON INDUSTRIES. The final decision... was based on the belief that our shareholders would benefit from the sale and the people of Prime Mover would become a part of an outstanding, worldwide materials handling equipment company."[27]

Indeed, the sale earned HON INDUSTRIES $8.3 million in after-tax gains, and BT signed a long-term contract to lease the Muscatine plant from HON INDUSTRIES. Over the nearly four decades that The Prime-Mover Co. had been a part of HON INDUSTRIES, it had grown from one product—the construction-site concrete wheelbarrow—to a manufacturer of many specialized types of material-handling and construction equipment.[28]

By the mid-1980s, a growing number of specialized lift trucks enabled Prime-Mover to gain marketshare in narrow-aisle material-handling warehouse equipment.

In Memory: Max Stanley and Clem Hanson

The people of HON INDUSTRIES were saddened on September 20, 1984, with the unexpected death of C. Maxwell Stanley at 80 years of age. Stanley died at Bellevue Hospital in New York City after suffering a heart attack while in the editor's office at *World Press Review*, the magazine of the Stanley Foundation. The news of his death stunned Muscatine. "It was quite an emotional time in Muscatine," one former executive of The HON Company said, "especially for old-time employees of the [Stanley] companies."

Stanley was so well respected in the community that the mayor of Muscatine ordered flags on public buildings flown at half-staff for four days. Expressions of condolence came from around the globe: from foreign diplomats praising his work for world peace, from recipients of his philanthropy, from fellow Iowa Hawkeye fans, and from people whose lives he had touched. At his memorial service in Muscatine's Wesley United Methodist Church, Congressman Jim Leach read a message from Javier Perez de Cuellar, then secretary-general of the United Nations, who praised Stanley for his long support of the principles and

objectives of the United Nations. The Stanley Foundation's conferences were called, "a great—indeed unique—contribution to promoting international cooperation."[29]

Although Stanley's numerous obituaries included his achievements as founder of HON INDUSTRIES and Stanley Consultants, they began with his work for world peace. United Press International called him an "internationalist with grand dreams and ideas."[30]

The stories from fellow Muscatine citizens touched his family, for they told of how he helped with people's medical bills, mortgages, and college tuition. "We all heard for the first time of the many acts of kindness he had done," said Mary Jo Stanley, wife of Dick Stanley.[31]

After Max Stanley's death, Stanley M. Howe, who had been president and chief executive officer of HON INDUSTRIES, was named chairman of the board.

In 1985, a year after Stanley's death, the HON INDUSTRIES family was saddened again, this time by the death of cofounder Clement T. Hanson. It was in Hanson's backyard in Moline, Illinois, where Stanley and Hanson sat that Sunday afternoon in 1943 discussing the idea that blossomed into HON INDUSTRIES.

In 1944, around the same time Hanson became the marketing officer for The Home-O-Nize Co., he founded his own advertising agency, the Clem T. Hanson Company. "That was his primary job," Hanson's son James said, "just like Max's primary job was running Stanley Engineering. In

---

Third from left, Elizabeth Stanley, Dorothy Dahl, Dennis Wolfs, Coralee Wolfs, Art Dahl, C. M. Stanley, and Max Collins join the Banjo Buddies music group at a member recognition dinner in the early 1980s.

Community Giving

FROM ITS EARLIEST DAYS, HON INDUSTRIES knew it had a responsibility to be a good corporate citizen, and it backed that realization with action. In 1947, even while it struggled to find profitable products to manufacture, the company established committees (one of which was Civic Affairs) that encouraged members' involvement in charities and other community matters. It had long been part of HON INDUSTRIES culture to encourage members to volunteer in their community while the company itself was allocating 1 percent of pretax profits for charitable causes.[1]

In 1985 HON INDUSTRIES formalized its philanthropic efforts by forming the HON INDUSTRIES Charitable Foundation to administer its corporate giving program, with Stanley M. Howe, Mike Derry, and Max Collins as trustees. Like the Corporate Gift Committee before it, "the Foundation's goal is to give primarily to programs and organizations that benefit our members, the communities in which they live, and the educational institutions that they and their children attend," according to Susan Cradick, who became the Foundation's secretary and treasurer in 1999.[2]

Foundation board member Jeff Fick said, "We're much more likely to contribute money to nonprofits when members actively participate."[3]

"HON INDUSTRIES," Fick continued, "funds a competitive scholarship program for members' children and gives approximately $250,000 annually to new and renewed applicants to further their education."[4]

"Our Foundation focuses on projects that serve the communities where our members live and work, that benefit families and children, and that support education. Whether supporting a small town volunteer fire department, a high school athletic field, a city library or hospital, or supporting Big Brothers and Big Sisters, our Foundation continues the philanthropy started by its founders so many years ago."[5]

those early years, his advertising company was the advertising arm of The Home-O-Nize Co.; all those ads and brochures and sales sheets came from Clem's agency."[32]

Perhaps Hanson's most lasting contribution to the company was the way he treated every employee like a member. "Clem Hanson added the excitement to the enterprise that kept people working and enthusiastic long after the company might otherwise have closed its doors," wrote James Soltow, coauthor of *The HON Story*. "He helped tide it over until better times finally arrived."[33]

While Hanson focused on his agency for the previous two decades, he remained an active member of the HON INDUSTRIES board. When he retired in 1964, HON INDUSTRIES named him director emeritus—the only director to receive that honor—a title he held until his death. In 1966, when he reached age 65, he retired as CEO of the advertising agency, turning the reins over to his son

James. In retirement, James Hanson said, Clem worked in support of a number of charities. "The one that made him the happiest was the University of Iowa Foundation." Having attended Iowa on scholarship himself, Clem saw his work for the foundation as a way to help deserving future students. In addition to events in the Midwest, Clem and Sylvia Hanson hosted fundraisers for the foundation at their winter home in Florida. Because education was so important to him, his family formed a scholarship in his name. Each year three or four graduates of Moline High School receive a scholarship in Clem Hanson's name.[34]

HON INDUSTRIES experienced other transitions as key leaders retired. In 1981 HON INDUSTRIES Senior Vice President Arthur Dahl retired after 35 years with the company. He was succeeded by Michael Derry. Robert Carl retired as corporate secretary in 1988 after more than 40 years, many of them as right-hand man to Stanley M. Howe.[35]

Pioneer shareholders—those who had bought shares in the original Home-O-Nize Co.—received special recognition at HON INDUSTRIES' 1981 shareholders meeting.

Member and Customer Relations

HON INDUSTRIES continued to carry on its basic objective to be a good place to work—to treat its members with "fairness and dignity." Members were given opportunities to grow through company-sponsored training programs and seminars, for example, and HON INDUSTRIES offered programs that helped pay for college classes.

When the recession of the early 1980s reduced orders, the company took an extraordinary step to prevent layoffs—reducing all members' work hours (and pay) by 10 percent. "All of these people are tied into one overall profit-sharing program from which they have benefited during the years of growth and prosperity," Howe explained in a company-wide memo. "We are now expecting all to share in the current adversity."[36]

Beginning Monday morning, April 5, 1982, the normal workweek was reduced to 36 hours for most members. Howe also implored members to "severely restrict and control expenditures of all kinds." By early September the company's situation had improved enough that the work-sharing plan was discontinued, and pay and workweeks were returned to a 40-hour basis, though Howe asked that "cost reduction efforts . . . be continued."[37]

Good Press

Amid all these developments, HON INDUSTRIES had some very good years financially. Net sales doubled from $266.9 million in 1981 to $532.5 million in 1988. At the same time, net income rose from $19.1 million to $35.3 million.[38]

By the time HON INDUSTRIES made the *Fortune* 500 list in 1986, it had already been attracting attention in some of the nation's elite business circles. HON INDUSTRIES had the 26th best ten-year dividend growth rate in 1982, according to *Dun's Business Month.* The National Association of Investment Clubs rated HON INDUSTRIES' 1982 and 1983 annual reports "Best in its Industry," and *Financial World* magazine gave both annual reports a Merit Award. Corry Jamestown's 1000 Series executive desk, 3600 Series chair, and QQ Series seating won design awards, and Hiebert's Chicago showroom earned the American Society of Interior Designers' award for excellence of showroom design.

"The secret to what we have done is the ability to make good, valued products very efficiently," Richard Johnson, corporate planning and advertising manager, told *Business Record* in 1986. "We are certainly one of the most efficient manufacturers in the office furniture business."[39]

In Summary

THE 1980S SAW LESS GOVERNMENTAL control in the U.S. marketplace and increased consumer spending. Throughout the 1980s, HON INDUSTRIES maintained a strong position in metal and wood office furniture, offering both choices to a wide array of customers at all price levels.

HON INDUSTRIES raised eyebrows in 1981 when it acquired the Heatilator Fireplace Division of Vega Industries. The acquisition was not as far from the core business as it may have first appeared.

In 1982 HON INDUSTRIES merged Holga and Norman Bates into Corry Jamestown, eyeing a stronger position in the upscale contract and office systems markets. Then in 1986, HON INDUSTRIES merged Corry Jamestown and Hiebert, forming CorryHiebert, to strengthen its position in the contract office furniture segment.

The members of HON INDUSTRIES were saddened on September 20, 1984, by the unexpected death of cofounder C. Maxwell Stanley. In 1985, the HON INDUSTRIES family was again shaken, this time by the death of Clement T. Hanson, cofounder with Max Stanley of The Home-O-Nize Co.

HON INDUSTRIES saw good financial results in the 1980s. It also attracted attention in furniture industry circles.

In 1996 Stanley M. Howe, right, stepped down as chairman of HON INDUSTRIES and became chairman emeritus. He was succeeded by Jack Michaels, left, who joined The HON Company as president in 1990.

CHAPTER EIGHT

The Race for Improvement
1989–1996

Business, in my mind, is all about people. Some people say that's the soft side; I say it's the most important side.

—Jack Michaels, chairman and CEO, 2003

HON INDUSTRIES USHERED IN a new era of leadership in 1990 when Jack Michaels, at the age of 53, joined the company as a director and president. The following year, he was promoted to CEO, and in 1996 he became chairman of the board when Stanley M. Howe was named chairman emeritus.

Michaels brought to the job an impressive history of leadership in operations, manufacturing, and marketing. Most recently he had been president and CEO of Hussmann Corporation, a commercial refrigerator manufacturer with 8,000 employees and more than $800 million in sales. He also served in leadership roles at International Harvester and J. I. Case.

Howe recruited Michaels to help reinvent the company. An outside consultant for HON INDUSTRIES had contacted Michaels while he was at Hussmann, and initially Michaels had no interest in switching jobs. This changed, however, after Howe flew to St. Louis to talk with him; Michaels became intrigued with Howe's description of the company's culture and values. "We spent a lot of time getting to know each other, understanding who we were," Michaels said. "We're really good friends, and he was and still is a strong mentor to me. But the thing that really intrigued me about joining HON was its philosophy of being all about the people. Business,

in my mind, is all about people. Some people say that's the soft side; I say it's the most important side."[1]

By all accounts, Jack Michaels was committed to that basic principle of treating people with respect and fairness on which the company was founded. Jeff Fick, vice president of member and community relations, described an incident that illustrates this.

A member called Jack and was upset about his shift assignment. He'd been asked to work second shift and wanted to work first shift. Jack was on vacation, but when he called in for his messages, he dropped what he was doing and called the member back. Then he was back on the phone with me asking me to help resolve the matter.

That's the kind of tone he sets—that everyone in the organization is important. It's not that he wants to make everyone feel *important; he helps them recognize that they* are *important, and he does that by his actions. He's insistent that management recognizes that we're not always right*

The striking grain pattern of the custom directors table, seen from overhead, illustrated the quality craftmanship of Gunlocke fine wood furnishings.

and that at times we need to reexamine a decision and make sure we're doing the right thing.[2]

Lessons Learned

Michaels' first years at HON INDUSTRIES were a baptism by fire. For years, the company had enjoyed sustained growth, in part because the nation's white-collar workforce was growing so rapidly; office space was springing up everywhere, and businesses needed furniture to fill it. December 1990, though, brought a dramatic drop in orders for new office furniture. Industry shipments from January to September 1991 were 9 percent less than a year earlier, according to the Business and Institutional Furniture Manufacturers' Association. At HON INDUSTRIES, net sales for the first two quarters of the year were down 16.6 percent, and net income fell a staggering 45 percent from 1990 levels. The company responded by reducing costs, increasing efficiency, and speeding the introduction of new products. At the same time, it invested in product development, support for customer service, and distribution programs—all of which

improved its position when the economy turned around. As a result, sales in the second half of 1991 were down only a fraction of a percent from 1990 levels.[3]

While a weak economy was to blame for the the 1991 hit, in 1995 HON INDUSTRIES fell short of its predictions for sales and earnings growth because the office furniture industry had turned into a competitive battlefield. Pricing had become "aggressive," according to the *Muscatine Journal.* The market environment had become "generally hostile." The industry had been undergoing fundamental structural changes, the result of "a rapid and unprecedented level of consolidation." Making matters worse, major office furniture customers in the budget segment significantly cut their inventories. HON INDUSTRIES responded to the intense competition by investing more in updated sales tools and advertising.[4]

In 1991 and especially in 1995, HON INDUSTRIES was able to recover quickly thanks to swift

Member Michael Frank at work in the plant.

Member Janet Hazen.

action from Howe and Michaels. As a result, the company emerged stronger than ever.

In the 1992 report to stockholders, Howe and Michaels said global business was demanding "greater value, better service, and higher quality." American industries were "using new ways, new products, and new services" to contain costs, increase market share, and bring about "greater output by fewer people." Growth of the white-collar workforce had slowed. Meanwhile, because customers at all levels were choosing value over image, high-end furniture manufacturers began encroaching on The HON Company's hold on the middle market. Many companies were acquired or closed their doors altogether. HON INDUSTRIES being more astute than much of the competition, saw the industry moving toward "fewer, stronger, and more aggressive competitors"—and it was determined to be one of the survivors.[5]

Rapid Continuous Improvement

To do so, HON INDUSTRIES' leaders knew the company had to change; the company needed to become more efficient, productive, and responsive. Thus all of the HON INDUSTRIES' subsidiaries

began a "Lean Conversion" through a method called Rapid Continuous Improvement, or RCI. As the 1992 annual report stated, "The race for improvement has no finish line at HON INDUSTRIES."[6]

RCI was based on the Japanese *kaizen* system. "We wanted to make sure we kept our efforts kind of secret from our competitors, so we didn't want to use the word *kaizen*," explained Thomas Hammer, who joined HON INDUSTRIES in 1977 and later became vice president of continuous improvement.[7] The basic philosophy of *kaizen* was developed by Japanese engineers at Toyota who studied U.S. grocery stores to see how huge supermarkets with thousands of items turned over their inventory quickly and efficiently without maintaining huge warehouses of goods. Toyota applied what it had learned to the way inventory flowed across a production line and developed basic inventory-reduction principles.

The HON Company began implementing RCI in 1992 after teams of members from all operating companies developed a successful safety pro-

gram. Encouraged by that experience, management created more teams to focus on ways HON INDUSTRIES' units could improve manufacturing lead times, product development cycles, productivity, and waste reduction strategies.

Hammer explained how RCI changed his way of thinking.

As an industrial engineer, I thought it logical to add more capacity to our racks where we held the drawers for our vertical files. We'd hold about 300 drawers in a rack, and that wasn't enough capacity. So we spent a lot of time and money building a rack that would hold more. There were changeovers on the drawer welding machines, and we thought that if we had more storage space, we wouldn't have to shut the line down. We could change it and we'd still have drawers.

Well, in 1992, when we started our Lean Conversion, we discovered the complete opposite was true. We actually took the drawer racks completely out. We went from 300-plus drawers to four drawers, because it took four drawers per unit. That was an epiphany for me. The RCI philosophy

Members of The HON Company's plants developed a successful safety program that focused on ways the units could improve manufacturing lead times, product development cycles, productivity, and waste reduction strategies. Pictured is Mike Hazen.

was a complete 180-degree shift in the way we thought about doing things.[8]

To help train members in RCI, the company brought in former Toyota people from Japan. Hammer admitted that at first RCI seemed counterintuitive, and there was quite a bit of resistance to it. "We thought, 'We're profitable, so why change?' We didn't have very many different models of a product, and we had long changeovers between models. We didn't see the benefit of having a short changeover. We didn't understand that the real objective was to be more flexible, and it took a while to get there."[9]

Dave Burdakin, president of The HON Company, explained how, as general manager of the Geneva plant, he helped members overcome their resistance to RCI.

The original implementation of RCI at the Geneva plant did not go particularly well. We struggled for the first few months trying to apply new principles, and then we decided to let the RCI members have their own work areas. So the members worked as teams to do the layouts of their own assembly areas. We gave them a brief training on Toyota production system principles and let them utilize their experience and expertise in building chairs to design their own work space. That's what really got the whole RCI process going. It was very effective because members had a chance to impact their own work environment rather than having outsiders or consultants changing it.[10]

President Stan Askren noted that RCI was not a new concept for The HON Company. "Max Stanley and the other folks talked about the principle of always finding a better way," he said. "We simply brought in some tools to reinvent that, to take it to the next level—working with members and saying, 'We have an obligation and a responsibility to work to make things better.' And that means removing waste, increasing speed, improving quality, lowering cost, and taking better care of our customers. You take those tools with that culture and fold in the reciprocal rewards—the profit sharing, stock ownership, good communication, and avoidance of artificial class distinctions. That gives you a very powerful engine for continued regeneration and improvement."[11]

HON INDUSTRIES encouraged members to see the shop floor as a laboratory in which to experiment, to get personally involved in finding ways to eliminate waste in the manufacturing process. Throughout the organization, team members were taken off their regular jobs for a week to devote their time to problem solving. Each day they implemented solutions and executed them. Each day they presented their progress, and at the end of the week they shared the results.

HON INDUSTRIES has mastered the physical distribution of its broad and deep range of products through an operational infrastructure that includes manufacturing, logistics, and customer service. Pictured is member Brad Soukup.

The Gunlocke Company

IN 1902, FIVE WOODWORKERS FROM Manhattan launched their own furniture manufacturing company in a vacant factory in Wayland, New York. Led by William H. Gunlocke, the partners and a growing force of craftsmen turned out bedroom, library, and lounge chairs as well as rockers. Gunlocke gradually built a name in the area for chairs that combined creative design features with durability. The company also had a reputation for timely delivery of its finished products.

From the start Gunlocke designs employed a distinctive technique—steam-bent wood. In 1912 the plant set up a separate department to apply exact measures of moisture, heat, and pressure to bend wood to desired curves. The company is still one of few manufacturers to steam-bend wood rather than use cut-and-join methods.

In the late 1920s Gunlocke received from Western Electric Corp. its first large industrial office furniture contract. To fulfill that order, Gunlocke halted its household furniture operations. Through the 1930s the company increasingly gained industry and government contracts. Gunlocke added a line of school furniture in 1934. When Howard Gunlocke became president in 1937 upon his father's death, he increased the company's marketing visibility by placing company salespeople and manufacturing representatives in key buying centers around the country. To fill government contracts for chairs during World War II, the company adopted assembly-line manufacturing methods.

Gunlocke's support of the war effort attracted the attention of President Franklin D. Roosevelt, who purchased a Gunlocke chair for his Oval Office. That began a presidential tradition that lasted through Jimmy Carter. In one of the most famous presidential photos, in which John F. Kennedy works at his desk while his son "John-John" plays on the floor, the President is seated in the chair Gunlocke designed and hand-crafted to ease his chronic back pain.

Gunlocke made only chairs until 1972 when it added case goods, which would grow to be its largest division. In 2000 the company adopted manufacturing cells as the means of

An important aspect of RCI was the HON Member Proposal System in which members were given the opportunity to channel their suggestions for improvement. "I've always contended that the person doing the job eight to 12 hours a day knows more about that job than anyone else," said Michaels. "If they want to make improvements, whether it be for quality, productivity, or safety, management's role is to listen to them and then work with them to implement their ideas."[12]

Tony Hayden, vice president of The HON Company's seating business unit, explained how the system worked.

The members have to identify a current situation, whether it's a problem or opportunity. Then they need to provide at least four solutions and tell which one they think is best and why. Then the *person sits down with his or her supervisor, and if the supervisor agrees that the idea has merit, then the person has responsibility for implementation. They might not have the exact skills needed to implement the idea, but they have to be a part of the implementation.*

We give small rewards for ideas that are implemented, but the real reward comes with harnessing the member's creativity and making them a part of the process. Our members know how to do their jobs better than anyone else, and they know how to improve their jobs better than anyone else.[13]

RCI produced near immediate results. The HON Company's lead times were cut in half in 1993. "Dealers use these shorter lead times to get our product to end-users faster," the company production, reducing inventory and lead times significantly.

Prior to 1969, The Gunlocke Chair Company was privately managed. In 1969, new owners Sperry & Hutchinson Company changed the name to The Gunlocke Company. During the 1970s, the company focused its marketing toward interior designers who specialized in corporate offices. Shortly after

Kenneth Book became president in 1980, Gunlocke's executives bought the company from Sperry & Hutchinson.

In 1987 Gunlocke was purchased by Chicago Pacific Corporation. Two years later, Chicago Pacific's parent, The Maytag Corporation, sold that group of companies to LADD Furniture in North Carolina. A few months later, LADD sold Gunlocke to HON INDUSTRIES.

Even before the acquisition, the cultures of the two companies were remarkably similar. Gunlocke had long offered a generous array of benefits and amenities and embraced values similar to HON INDUSTRIES': "serve all stakeholders, integrity, delight the customer, empowerment and ownership, teamwork, continuous learning."[1]

Kennsignton—exquisitely crafted from cherry and select cherry and Cerejeira veneers enhanced with rich Clear Tech finish—exemplified Gunlocke's reputation for fine wood furnishings of value.

explained in its 1993 annual report. "This improves the dealers' profitability and strengthens relationships throughout the distribution channel."[14]

By 1995 RCI—combined with an 80/20 focus, which recognized that 80 percent of results came from 20 percent of customers, products, and services—continued to show significant results. The 1995 annual report read, "Inventory turnover improved. Return on beginning assets was increased. Days' sales in accounts receivables declined. Cash generated by operations increased."[15]

RCI was also applied to product development, distribution, and administrative processes. By 1996 defect rates and lost-time accidents were down by 90 percent, and lead times had dropped 60 percent since 1992. Customers were getting "feature-rich products and short delivery times" without price increases. These efficiencies by themselves did not

fuel earnings growth, but RCI did send more and better products to market, which fueled sales.[16]

With typical HON INDUSTRIES optimism, Michaels summed up the company's attitude concerning improvement. "We don't sit around saying the glass is half empty; we say the glass is half full. Still, it's only half full when it could be completely full. That's our challenge."[17]

Closing Doors and Opening New Ones

In October 1989 HON INDUSTRIES purchased The Gunlocke Company, an 87-year-old manufacturer of premium-quality wood office furniture. Gunlocke was highly regarded by architects and designers, and because of its history of profitable growth, management saw it as "an excellent long-term strategic fit." With headquarters in Avon, New

York, and a plant in Wayland, New York, Gunlocke made wood seating, tables, and case goods, often incorporating steam-bent wood into its designs.[18]

"In a lot of ways, Gunlocke is very similar to HON INDUSTRIES," said Gunlocke President Don Mead. "The role it plays in the community of Wayland, New York, is just as important as its commercial success. Gunlocke is a very important part of that community, and we have a very strong obligation to that area."[19]

That same year, The HON Company's senior management determined that CorryHiebert wasn't performing to expectations and thus restructured it. The former Holga plant in Van Nuys, California, was separated and revived as Holga, manufacturing metal case goods and selling them in the West. CorryHiebert's Carson, California, plant was closed, and Gunlocke took over production, marketing, and sales of its wood desks, seating, and systems furniture. For several years, CorryHiebert continued to manufacture premium-quality metal furniture at the plant in Corry, Pennsylvania, but in 1993, HON INDUSTRIES made the difficult decision to close the plant. Although the doors closed for the last time on December 17, 1993, one phone number remained in operation until all customer questions had been answered.[20]

"We had an image problem related to Hiebert," explained Bob Hayes, HON INDUSTRIES' vice president of business analysis and general auditor. "There were lawsuits surrounding a bad chemical in some of the finish that Hiebert used, and we never really fully recovered from that. It hurt the whole operation of CorryHiebert, and we finally just exited the business."[21]

In 1989, The HON Company opened a research and development building to cultivate new products and manufacturing processes. Two years later the center expanded to include all divisions of HON INDUSTRIES and was renamed the HON INDUSTRIES Development Center. Later it was dedicated as the Stanley M. Howe Technical Center in recognition of Howe's contributions to advancements in manufacturing and the use of alternative materials. By that time, the center housed designers, researchers, engineers, quality assurance laboratories, a pilot manufacturing facility, and environmental staff.[22]

"In terms of technology development, the driving factors in the office furniture business have to do with better functionality," said Pete Atherton, HON INDUSTRIES' chief technology officer. "Issues of weight, aesthetics, cost, durability, and the ability to manufacture it better are all equally important."[23]

On any given day, the creative members at the Technical Center might come up with as many as 20 ideas. "We have to save some of them for a later

The CorryHiebert Environments 20/20 freestanding desk system filled the need for more flexible and cost-effective furniture systems.

time, and some don't really fit," said Atherton. Typically the Technical Center worked on three major projects at one time.[24]

Tony Hayden described one of the revolutionary technologies that came out of the Technical Center.

Most chair products utilize plywood. Everybody in the industry uses plywood, and it's pretty expensive for what it is. Rather than using plywood in the backs and bases of the chairs, we developed a process called co-molding [short for compression molding]. This co-mold process utilizes wood waste from the construction industry. So instead of sending wood waste to a landfill, we have a couple of suppliers that have grind and

screen equipment that can process the wood waste to a certain size chip. We developed and built the technology to press those chips in with a resin to make a co-mold board. The board it makes is stronger than plywood. You can form it better, get more unique shapes, and it's barely 25 percent of the cost of traditional plywood. That cost savings gives us a huge competitive edge.[25]

Above: The Stanley M. Howe Technical Center houses designers, researchers, engineers, quality assurance laboratories, a pilot manufacturing facility, and environmental staff who develop new products and manufacturing processes.

Right: The HON Company purchased a plant in Winnsboro, South Carolina, in 1989 and equipped it to manufacture metal seating products for customers in the East and Southeast.

Expanding the Umbrella

In 1989, The HON Company took over Rishel's Williamsport, Pennsylvania, plant, although the facility continued to manufacture and market product under the Rishel brand for the federal government. Andrew Santulli, who had been vice president of manufacturing, was promoted to vice president and general manager. The HON Company also purchased a new plant in Winnsboro, South Carolina, and equipped it to manufacture metal seating products.[26]

In 1990 office file and furniture manufacturer XLM more than doubled its capacity to produce files for home offices with a new plant in Mount Pleasant, Iowa, and the remodeled office-production-warehouse facility in Avon that was acquired with the Gunlocke purchase. Then in April 1994, XLM was consolidated into The HON Company, which used the distribution channels to increase sales to retail and commercial office furniture dealers.[27]

Also in 1990, BPI (now Maxon) bought property in Salisbury, North Carolina, where it built a plant and distribution center to extend the company's competitive reach in the East and Southeast. The original Kent, Washington, plant could no longer keep up with demand, so BPI manufacturing engineers, marketers, and human resources experts developed a new concept of manufacturing, which they implemented at Salisbury and in new leased premises in Kent.[28]

At the end of 1991, HON INDUSTRIES created Chandler Attwood as a strategic business unit of BPI. It used a different production distribution model called "distributed manufacturing" to produce build-to-order office furniture for customers in large metropolitan markets. By late 1992, the pilot plant was operating in Kent, Washington. The next year Chandler Attwood expanded into Denver, Houston, Dallas, Atlanta, and San Jose, California, but unfortunately, the experiment proved disappointing. By the spring of 1996, Chandler Attwood was no more, and all of its operating sites had been closed.[29]

In January 1992, Ring King Visibles acquired the rubber band and glove business of Plymouth Rubber Company in Canton, Massachusetts. The products were imported from Asia and distributed from a California warehouse; other customer service and distribution was handled from Ring King's Muscatine headquarters. Then in 1996, HON INDUSTRIES sold Ring King Visibles to Esselte Corporation, a Swedish office products supplier, which continued to operate the company in Muscatine. "We realized that the distribution channel for Ring King's products was too different," explained Jerry Dittmer, who started in 1991 and

Right: As an experiment in distributed manufacturing— producing furniture-to-order for clients in the community where the plant was located— Chandler Attwood made products such as these Series 140 components in six metro areas.

Opposite: In 1992 BPI introduced People Furniture— computer furniture emphasizing ergonomics and affordability.

Counterclockwise from left: Heatilator Inc.'s T series wood-burning fireplace and its DV10 gas stove were successful launches in 1993; Heatilator's DOVRE DV400 stove put gas combustion inside an existing cast-iron stove in 1994; Versatile enough for use as an extraordinary room divider or the elegant base for a bar, the Pier from Heat-N-Glo beautifully delivered all of the advantages of a direct-vent fireplace.

later became chief financial officer of HON INDUS-TRIES. "They went to market differently from the rest of HON INDUSTRIES," he added. "Also, Ring King's main product was sound enclosures for printers. With the advent of laser printers, that product went by the wayside."[30]

"With Ring King in good hands," said Michaels, "we'll be able to concentrate our management

efforts and financial resources on growing our office furniture and hearth products subsidiaries."[31]

Late in 1993, Heatilator purchased the Dovre brand of cast-iron woodstoves and fireplaces from a Belgian company and began assembling and selling them from its Mount Pleasant plant. By combining Dovre cast-iron products with the Arrow brand of steel stoves and inserts, Heatilator became the only company to offer both cast-iron products and steel stoves and inserts.

Heatilator had been growing sufficiently since HON INDUSTRIES purchased it in 1981, but it was in a niche market, and Jack Michaels and HON INDUSTRIES' board of directors decided to make it larger through acquisition. Thus in 1996, Heatilator purchased Heat-N-Glo Fireplace Products, a private company in Savage, Minnesota, that manufactured fireplaces and gas hearth products. Combined, Heatilator and Heat-N-Glo became the leader in the North American market.

When looking to acquire companies, HON INDUSTRIES considered more than finances, products, and leadership. It also considered the company's culture. "We've declined to move forward with acquisitions where the company's culture was fundamentally at odds with ours, where there was not an employee-oriented culture," said Jeff Fick, who joined HON INDUSTRIES in 1994 and later became vice president of member and community relations. "The founders of Heat-N-Glo had values very similar to HON INDUSTRIES, values of openness, integrity, and appreciation for the people in their organization."[32]

Heat-N-Glo was founded in 1975 when brothers Ron Jr. and Dan Shimek built their first free-standing, wood-burning fireplace while tinkering in Ron's garage. They would soon become innovative leaders in the hearth industry. In 1987 their direct vent fireplace changed the industry forever by making possible unprecedented creativity in placement and design. Heat-N-Glo went on to produce the first multi-sided fireplace, a remote controlled fireplace, and Zone Heating, which increased the functionality and efficiency of gas fireplaces.

Heatilator and Heat-N-Glo continued to market their products through their existing channels and merged in July 1996 into Hearth Technologies Inc. Dan Shimek became president of the new enterprise.[33]

Askren explained the sense of ownership held by HON INDUSTRIES' division leaders. "HON's division presidents understand the business better than a corporate office could ever understand it because they're standing in the middle of it all the time. So a person gets this tremendous sense of ownership, of responsibility. It's not like this big machine where a person is just a cog. If the business does well,

everyone knows. And if it doesn't do well everyone knows, too, and each person is accountable."[34]

Askren joined The HON Company in 1992 as corporate vice president of human resources and in 2003 would become president of HON INDUSTRIES. He recalled what attracted him to the company.

I spent lots of time talking to Jack Michaels and Stan Howe and then other senior executives. I really probed hard trying to understand if this whole member culture thing was real or some sort of marketing fabrication. During a trip through Iowa, I had the chance to stay at a hotel in Muscatine and I asked people who worked there to tell me about HON INDUSTRIES. Every one of them talked about it being a great place to work. Every one of them talked about the strong member culture. It was clear that the culture was real.[35]

To support its commitment to change and Rapid Continuous Improvement, in January 1995, HON INDUSTRIES opened a Learning Center. Though headquartered in Muscatine, the Learning Center offered classes, training, and consulting across the United States to help members perform their jobs better.[36]

The company's facilities were also evolving. Oak Street plant Number 1 in Muscatine was des-

ignated Oak Steel plant, and Oak Street plant Number 2 became the Oak Laminate Plant. Warehouse space serving the Oak Steel and Oak Laminate plants was expanded. A 70,000-square-foot, one-story addition to The HON Company Systems Furniture plant in Muscatine provided more warehouse space for raw material storage and finished products. Finally, a new finishing system for lateral files went on-line at the Richmond plant. The system lowered freight costs, expanded manufacturing capacity for more models, and provided shorter delivery lead time.[37]

Family Vision

In the early 1990s, HON INDUSTRIES renewed its commitment to the six tenets in its Corporate Vision from the boardroom to the shop floor, from Muscatine to Van Nuys to Richmond. During this period of intensifying competition and economic turmoil, HON INDUSTRIES' leadership returned to these principles again and again, the members learned by example, and all in the HON INDUS-TRIES family benefited. Although the exact wording evolved, the central idea of each remained:

- Profitability—pursuing partnerships that are mutually profitable to the company, its customers, and its suppliers
- Economic soundness—protecting and increasing shareholders' equity through good financial management, ensuring flexibility to respond to marketplace conditions
- Sound growth—sustaining growth that can be financed from retained earnings plus prudent debt to benefit members, customers, suppliers, shareholders, and the public
- Customer focus—supplying safe products and high-quality, valuable services to end-users so both the company and its distributors make a fair profit

- Good workplace—providing a work culture and environment that attracts and retains members who are committed to the success of the company and themselves
- Corporate citizenship—acting responsibly as a company and as individuals to benefit every aspect of the community

At the same time, HON INDUSTRIES sought to build on its "pivotal strengths": "efficient manufacturing of quality products; product scope and coverage that are unsurpassed in the industry; effective use of multiple channels of distribution; and customer service that stresses complete, consistent, and rapid delivery." This back to basics strategy produced gratifying results in all aspects of the company.[38]

On a Roll

Because first-to-market products often earned better margins, HON INDUSTRIES' product designers, marketers, and manufacturing engineers worked together to bring new products to market as quickly as possible. By the mid-1990s, they were adept at using a process called "concurrent product development"—essentially doing all the product

The ComforTask chair, introduced in 1994 by The HON Company, adjusted for different tasks and operators and appealed to the commercial market.

End of an Era

I T SEEMS MORE THAN COINCIDENCE that the man who cofounded what became HON INDUSTRIES and the man who succeeded him share a name. Their lives have been intertwined in many ways.

Max Stanley, as scoutmaster of Boy Scout Troop 127 at the Wesley United Methodist Church in Muscatine, began mentoring Stanley M. Howe. Max also taught Howe in his Sunday school class.

Howe worked at the Stanley Engineering Company following high school graduation and during summer recesses while an engineering student at Iowa State University. After graduation, Howe often said that a letter Max Stanley wrote to the Harvard

Business School helped his admission among all the "generals and captains" entering graduate school after World War II. After graduating with an MBA, Howe returned to Muscatine and joined his mentor's new company in 1948.

Howe worked his way up the ladder at what became HON INDUSTRIES. He was promoted to vice president of production in 1954; elected to the board of directors in 1958; elevated to executive vice president in 1961; president in 1964; and chairman of the board from 1984 to 1996.

Howe departed as HON INDUSTRIES chairman in 1996 as the last leadership link to the company's pioneers.[1]

development processes at the same time rather than sequentially—to eliminate delays in bringing tested products to customers. It also cut costs.[39]

HON INDUSTRIES brought a number of successful products to the office furniture marketplace from 1989 to 1996, many with ergonomic designs. The ComforTask chair, for instance, was popular for features such as comfort adjustments and deep cushioning, yet it was priced in the lower range, which appealed to buyers in large commercial markets.

Meanwhile, BPI introduced a price-competitive "electrified" desk system that was compatible with other systems furniture. The system was designed for use with computers and other equipment. Other product innovations included Heatilator's modular gas fireplaces, which were popular with builders because they could be installed, cleaned, and maintained easily. The low-cost models were

upgraded with additional features, either in the field or from the factory.

Finally, Holga began specializing in the niche market for high-density storage, shelving, and mobile filing systems that maximized space for use in law offices, insurance companies, and hospitals. About the same time, Gunlocke began combining metal and wood to create attractive designs that incorporated the company's signature steam-bent wood features with the high-tech look of metal.

By 1996, more than 25 percent of HON INDUSTRIES' total sales came from products introduced in the preceding three years, spurred by the company's consistent ability to introduce new products and quickly bring them to market.

Despite lower residential housing starts in 1989, Heatilator's sales rose, partly due to the introduction of new products such as Fireside Furnishings accessories that included mantels and marble hearths. Meanwhile, Hearth & Home Technologies' products continued to meet the stringent requirements of the EPA, which was no easy feat.

"The cost of making the product increased dramatically as we complied with the Clean Air Act," said Mike DeRosier, vice president of marketing for the Quadra-Fire brand of Hearth & Home Technologies. "The companies that survived had to be better managed, better capitalized, and simply bet-

ter run." The regulatory changes decimated the industry; as a result, many of the more than 300 fireplace manufacturers folded or were acquired by other companies.[40]

With the arrival of Jack Michaels, who had extensive international business experience, HON INDUSTRIES looked more seriously at exports and in 1991 founded HON Export Limited to handle all sales beyond the United States and Canada. The next year it began to export products from several companies within HON INDUSTRIES to strategic overseas markets. By 1995 The HON Company's exports were "growing at four to five times the rates of U.S. office furniture exports in general," according to James F. O'Crowley III, who was appointed vice president of international in 1993. Late in 1996,

In 1994 The HON Company developed extensions of existing lines to update the look of its products and attract more customers. This 38000 Series desk was an example.

Above: Quick turnaround gave The HON Company a competitive edge on such products as this CONCENSYS line, which maximizes work space without compromising privacy.

Below: This Gunlocke Prism reception station incorporated design elements of related products.

superstores. In hearth products it was the primary supplier to dealers, builders, and consumers.[43]

Due to the roller coaster economy, HON INDUSTRIES, by some measures, experienced more difficulty in the early and mid-1990s than it had in some

the export staff moved from the Technical Center to the corporate headquarters led by Thomas Miller, vice president of marketing and international.[41]

Innovations were not restricted to the area of new product development, however. To improve customer service throughout its companies, in 1992 The HON Company began an order-entry system that coordinated everything from specifying production dates and ordering raw materials to preparing invoices. After production, it even tracked the order by truck and trailer number to the customer's door.[42]

By 1996 HON INDUSTRIES was ranked the number one or number two supplier to most national office products dealers, wholesalers, and

time. Net sales actually dropped
by 8.5 percent in 1991, and net
income tumbled by about 24 percent in both 1991 and 1995. Yet
HON INDUSTRIES' office furniture companies and its Heatilator
division consistently out-per-
formed their industries. In 1989,
for example, The HON Company's
net sales gained 13 percent over
1988—a full ten percent ahead
of its industry average. The next
year, Heatilator's sales increased
while its industry's sales fell 13
percent overall. It was a similar
story in 1996; while the industry grew between six and
seven percent, The
HON Company's
sales gained
11.8 percent.[44]

In the 1993 annual report, Howe and Michaels
attributed the company's performance and growth
to four factors: "new products and services, sales
in new markets, new sales through new ventures,
and, of course, increased sales to existing customers." With an ongoing goal of double-digit earnings growth each year, the company's leaders generally expected to generate 8 to 12 percent of that

Above and below: By the early 1990s, Holga had become adept
at helping business offices file a huge amount of information in
minimal floor space in Smart Space lateral files mounted on
tracks. It also brought files used daily to fingertip convenience
in credenzas and moveable pedestals. Shown above is the
Holga Smart Space, and at left, the 8000 Pedestal model.

growth from internal operations plus 4 to 5 percent "from the effective redeployment of free cash through acquisitions and share buyback."[45]

While the company had become a fixture on *Fortune* magazine's annual list of the 500 largest industrial corporations, HON's management noted, "Companies are included on the basis of annual net sales, but [we suggest] it is bottom-line performance that really distinguishes HON INDUSTRIES." For example, based on sales, the company climbed gradually from 462 on the 1991 list to 414 in 1993. However, during those three years, HON INDUSTRIES' profits always ranked in the mid-200s, and profits as a percent of sales consistently put the

Right: Designed by Ken Reinhard and inspired by the club chairs of an earlier era, the thoughtful design of Gunlocke's Napoli Chair made a completely updated statement in steam-bent European beech that was at home in contemporary environments.

Below: Member Janet Fry at work at one of HON INDUSTRIES' manufacturing plants.

company in the 130s. Even better, in 1993 the company ranked 33rd in profits as a percent of shareholders' equity, and it was the 30th best corporation in America in terms of profits as a percent of assets.[46]

Environment and Technology

By reacting intelligently to political realities, HON INDUSTRIES further strengthened its leadership position. Government environmental regulations tightened the reins on industry, but they also created opportunities for innovation. HON INDUSTRIES incorporated eco-friendly thinking into its manufacturing and shipping strategies. For example, by 1990 most of HON INDUSTRIES' plants used powder-coat and high-solid paints to minimize airborne emissions. The Geneva plant even won an Iowa Governor's Award for Waste Reduction that year for dramatically cutting emissions from its chrome-plating operation.

Recognizing that disposal of wood, cardboard, and paper waste took a heavy toll on both the environment and the company itself, HON INDUSTRIES obtained a 1990 grant from the Iowa Department of Natural Resources to identify ways to convert

HON INDUSTRIES incorporated eco-friendly thinking into its manufacturing strategies. Its facilities joined "Green Lights," a five-year EPA program to make industrial lighting more efficient. Shown here is member Craig Kennedy.

those materials into marketable products. Within a year, environmental and manufacturing engineers had developed a process for turning waste into pelletized fuel that could be burned in Heatilator's pellet stoves. By converting waste to pellet fuel, HON INDUSTRIES' Muscatine plants kept 6,000 tons of waste out of landfills and lowered disposal costs by $500,000 in 1991.

Two years later every HON INDUSTRIES facility joined "Green Lights," a five-year EPA program to make industrial lighting efficiently. The HON Company developed cleaner water-based stains for wood products and sent upholstery trimmings to a company that made automobile carpeting from them.[47]

Beyond this, BPI teams cut material expenses by using technology. Rather than buying costly panel assembly hardware, they fabricated it themselves at a fraction of the price. In addition, machine operators began placing routine restocking orders directly, which lowered the burden of administrative purchasing. Heatilator increased fireplace production by automating chimney pipe manufacturing.[48]

As always, these advances allowed all company members to share the wealth, a reflection of HON INDUSTRIES' intrinsic, core value system. To enable members to share in the growth and prosperity of the company, on December 29, 1991, all non-bargaining HON INDUSTRIES members became eligible for an Employee Stock Ownership Plan (ESOP) long-term retirement benefit called the HON INDUSTRIES Members' Company Ownership Plan. Over the following seven years, shares were allocated to participants based on eligible compensation. The company contributed about $2.7 million to the ESOP in 1992, and by 1996 its annual contribution had grown to $3.3 million.[49]

To reduce on-the-job injuries, in 1991 all operating companies adopted the HON INDUSTRIES Member Safety Program, which involved the implementation of 29 action steps within 18 months. "We are determined to make HON INDUSTRIES the model of safe and healthy work practices," Stanley M. Howe and Jack Michaels told investors.

After the first six months, lost-time accidents were down 67 percent on an annualized basis. Safety records continued to improve so that by the end of 1992, lost-time accidents were 61 percent below the previous year's, and recordable accidents declined 24 percent.[50]

Also in 1992, HON INDUSTRIES created a healthcare task force made up of members from across the country to help the company contain healthcare costs. It produced a plan for retirees and worked on one for members as well.[51]

In 1996 *Fortune* magazine chose HON INDUSTRIES as one of "America's most admired companies" based on a survey that measured financial soundness, product quality, ability to attract and retain talented people, community and environmental responsibility, and product value as a long-term investment. HON INDUSTRIES ranked in the top 50 percent of all companies and third among furniture companies.[52]

There was no question that HON INDUSTRIES had lived up to the values inherent in its Vision Statement—parlaying its success company-wide, from its many employee-members to the upper reaches of its management team.

In Summary

HON INDUSTRIES ENTERED A NEW era of leadership in 1990 when Jack Michaels, age 53, came aboard as president and a director. The next year Michaels became CEO. In 1996 Michaels was named chairman when Stanley M. Howe—ending an era—became chairman emeritus.

Howe had recruited Michaels to help reinvent the company, but Michaels' first years at HON INDUSTRIES were spent putting out fires. A 1991 sales slump sparked efforts to increase efficiency and speed the rollout of new products. Then in 1995, cutthroat industry pricing spurred HON INDUSTRIES to trim its workforce and boost advertising.

In 1992 HON INDUSTRIES began to implement Rapid Continuous Improvement (RCI), a disciplined plan to make the companies more efficient and responsive. The campaign worked.

Meanwhile, HON INDUSTRIES continued to make acquisitions. These included the 1989 purchase of The Gunlocke Company, manufacturer of premium office furniture, and purchase of Heat-N-Glo Fireplace Products.

Heatilator and Heat-N-Glo merged in 1996 to form a new unit, Hearth Technologies Inc.

In 1996, *Fortune* magazine chose HON INDUSTRIES as one of "America's most admired companies."

Office Solutions and Environments magazine ranked three HON INDUSTRIES brands among the top five manufacturers of filing cabinets.

CHAPTER NINE

Market Sector Leadership

1997–2003

We have the attitude that we're never satisfied with where we are today. We are always looking for ways to improve.

—*The HON Company President Dave Burdakin*

AT THE TURN OF THE MILLE-nium, under the leadership of Jack Michaels, HON INDUS-TRIES solidified its niche atop the office furniture and hearth products industries. Constantly developing and enhancing its products, stream-lining its manufacturing process, and improving its service to consumers, the company sharpened its focus on profits despite an industrywide eco-nomic downturn.

Steady growth in the white-collar workforce had always fueled demand for office furnishings. This dynamic was evident in high-end custom markets as well as consumer discount outlets, and The HON Company was particularly good at adapting its product line to market conditions.[1] By 1997 growth in office furniture sales was driven largely by the proliferation of small businesses and home offices. There were 23 million small firms in 1998 and some 40 million people doing at least some work at home—underlining the need for affordability in this fastest-growing market seg-ment.[2] The HON Company was optimistic about its broad selection of moderately priced products available through multiple distribution points—and a constantly expanding product base.[3]

Over the next few years, The HON Company focused on changes in the broad discount market. Technology, ergonomics, organizational restructur-ing, productivity, and job migration all affected fur-niture design. The company real-ized that "environments that once simply pushed people to work harder now aim to help them be more creative, more comfortable, more open, more human." The trend of ever changing work teams fostered open offices and systems that let people find their own paths to comfort and productivity. The HON Company confidently stated, "We are poised to take advantage of these trends."[4]

Acquisitions & Restructuring

In 1997 HON INDUSTRIES described itself as "the nation's largest manufacturer of value-priced office furniture and fourth largest office furniture manufacturer and marketer in North America." To accommodate such growth, The HON Company undertook a major expansion of its facilities. In 1997, the company renovated part of the Muscatine plant that it had leased to The Prime-Mover Co. to give the Systems Plant in Muscatine more pro-duction capacity. It also constructed 100,000 square feet of additional distribution space at the

As part of a management RCI (Rapid Continuous Improvement) exercise, Dave Burdakin, left, president of The HON Company, joined members on the production floor.

Cedartown, Georgia, plant to keep pace with shipping volume.[5]

Later that year, HON INDUSTRIES acquired Allsteel Inc., Bevis Custom Furniture Inc., and Panel Concepts Inc.—adding about $230 million in sales. The purchase of Allsteel was a stroke of marketing genius. Competitors at the high end of the office furniture market had always attempted to portray The HON Company as a supplier of "discount" merchandise for "low-end" consumers. This often made it difficult for The HON Company to penetrate the contract market, where furniture purchases are influenced by architects and designers is designed by contract. Allsteel was an established brand with strong engineering and marketing arms as well as an identity and presence in the design community.[6]

Bevis increased The HON Company's offerings in mid-priced folding tables, conference tables, panel systems, and computer furniture and provided some help in retail distribution channels,[7] and Panel Concepts manufactured panel systems at many price points.[8]

Early in 1998 Hearth Technologies acquired Aladdin Steel Products, a Colville, Washington, manufacturer of wood-, pellet-, and gas-burning steel stoves and inserts. It established the Aladdin Hearth Products division of Hearth Technologies to assemble Aladdin's Quadra-Fire brand with its existing Arrow and Dovre brands.[9]

In 1999 HON INDUSTRIES' Hearth Technologies embarked on a strategy to get closer to its customers, dealers, and builders. It acquired two lead-

Jack and the Frog

IF YOU ASKED DON MEAD WHY HE JOINED HON INDUSTRIES, he might answer, "It had a lot to do with the day Jack Michaels gave my son a frog."

It happened just after Mead, now president of The Gunlocke Company, and his family moved to Muscatine, Iowa. Their home sat across the street from two vacant lots that sloped down into a creek. Those lots were owned by HON INDUSTRIES Chairman, President, and CEO Jack Michaels.

"Like all 8-year-old boys, my son David hangs out at the creek all the time," Mead said. "Jack used to mow and maintain that lot himself. One day, I was out working in my yard, and David was at the creek trying to catch frogs."

When Mead looked up from his yard work, he saw a 6-foot-6-inch Michaels walking across the street with his son, about half Michaels' size. "Jack was listening patiently to my son, who was explaining things as an 8-year-old would explain something. I thought, 'Oh, Jack is probably going to tell me to keep my kid out of the creek.'"

But after Michaels introduced himself to Mead, he said, "Your son tells me he's hunting for frogs back there. Well, I've got a pond on my property [at home], and when I mow around it, there are frogs everywhere. So I just want to extend an invitation. Any time you want to take your son out there and catch frogs, you'll have a heyday."

About two weeks later, the Meads went out of town for the weekend. Upon their return, Mead's father-in-law reported that Michaels had contacted him. "Jack figured out that he was my father-in-law and contacted him to tell him that he'd been out mowing and caught a frog," Mead said. "He had put it in a bucket and saved it in his garage for David."

"Here's a guy with the responsibility of 10,000 members and a $2 billion organization. He has one interaction with my son, and two weeks later he's spending his time trying to figure this little boy's last name and how to get hold of him."

Mead continued, "The point is that when you work here, you're a HON member 24 hours a day. We are not only accountable to the shareholders and every HON member, but the community as a whole. We try to carry that perspective, that everyone is important. That's the way Jack operates, and it's a story I'll always remember."[1]

ing distributors—American Fireplace Company and the Allied Group—and formed Hearth Services Inc. to sell, install, and service gas- and wood-burning fireplaces, mantels, surrounds, and accessories. By adding sales, installation, and service, Hearth Technologies became the largest manufacturer *and* distributor of hearth products in the United States.

By 2000 Hearth Services had built relationships with home builders and 800 independent dealers in the Mid-Atlantic and Midwest. As a result, Hearth Technologies accounted for 25 percent of total HON INDUSTRIES sales. To keep pace, the 125,000-square-foot Aladdin plant at Colville, Washington, came on-line, expanding and streamlining production of the Quadra-Fire line and, by mid-2000, also producing Dovre stoves.[10]

In 2002 HON INDUSTRIES consolidated the BPI and Panel Concepts brands to form Maxon Furniture Inc., supplying office furniture systems to small and medium firms via commercial and contract markets. Maxon Furniture Group President Jean Reynolds called Maxon "the industry leader in fast response time, with mass customization in five days or less. Rapid turnaround is really our specialty. We're focused on being easy to specify and easy to install. So we're a good investment for our clients."[11]

James Knutson, Maxon's head of engineering, recalled the trials of the consolidation.

Above: The HON Company believes its people are its greatest asset. The company has assembled one of the best leadership teams in the industry, and its workforce is vested in the company's success.

Below: The HON Company takes demand from an end-user or channel partner, turns it around more efficiently, and delivers it faster and more dependably than any of its competitors.

Our biggest challenge was that we were two separate operating companies. BPI's old name, Budget Panels Incorporated, gave us a stigma to overcome. We did not want to be budget related. So we rebranded into Maxon, and we've been pretty successful.

From a manufacturing perspective, our biggest challenge is that we have a very broad product offering for a company our size. Within HON INDUSTRIES, Maxon is one of the smaller companies, and we're right on the cusp of having the ability to really leverage our size. So it's a challenge to know how to grow and gain more brand recognition within our industry.[12]

A Split and Focus

Realizing that it increasingly was serving two customer bases, in 1999 The HON Company was split into the HON group and the Allsteel group. The HON Company departments—from product engineering and industrial design to marketing, customer service, manufacturing, and distribution centers—were divided between the two. The two groups became independent operating units within HON INDUSTRIES early in 2000—The HON Company and Allsteel Inc.—and Allsteel logos appeared on their products.[13]

"Allsteel was a faded flower, but it still had the name and a little bit of cachet among architects and designers," said Thomas Miller, former president of HON International.[14]

Allsteel executives grappled with how best to serve different customers in fractured markets. "The challenge was to reestablish an old brand. The Allsteel brand had been dormant," said Don Mead, who joined Allsteel in 2000 as vice president of marketing.

We had a strong back wheel—strong engineering and manufacturing—and limited talent in the areas of marketing and branding. We all understood the power of the brand, the power of marketing the front wheel, and how key that was to our future. The challenge was to beef up our talent pool, and that was an ominous challenge.

We had formidable competition in Steelcase, Herman Miller, Knoll, and others, so it was important to find a segment of the market that wasn't being served well—those were the customers for whom we could differentiate ourselves. That is where the performance contract came up. We take the speed, the responsiveness, and the culture of HON INDUSTRIES and The HON Company and Allsteel, and combine it all with accelerating our product development and contracting quality products that customers would respect.[15]

The HON Company's Perpetual seating won "Best of Show NeoCon '02" for its comfort and user support.

The HON brand was broadly visible to wholesalers, national supply dealers, independent furniture dealers, state and local governments, and schools, added Dave Burdakin, president of The HON Company. "Allsteel, meanwhile, was a contracted line with limited distribution. It focused more on the architect and design [A&D] community and on corporate accounts. The A&D community looked at Allsteel as more of a design-oriented product line—more stylish than the HON brand. So the split helped both companies stop trying to be everything to everyone."[16]

Even as the office furniture industry's sales in 1999 declined for only the third year since the 1970s, The HON Company continued to grow, in substantial part because of restructuring. "Splitting The HON Company and Allsteel Inc. into separate companies with distinct markets was an uncommon idea and an unequivocal success in 2000," CEO Jack Michaels told investors. "The strategy made solid contributions to the top and bottom lines and improved inventory turns, even as retail and commercial sales slowed in the last quarter."[17]

International

Facing growing competition from lower-priced foreign products, increasingly from China, in 1998 The HON Company built its first plant outside the United States near Monterrey in northern Mexico. The 100,000-square-foot plant in the Monterrey Technology Park in suburban Ciénega de Flores opened in September with some 90 members manufacturing upholstered metal chairs.[18]

To position itself for global business development, rather than narrowly focusing only on export sales, HON International in 2002 sought alternative growth opportunities, including sourcing, alliances, and selective investments. With HON INDUSTRIES members already in Puerto Rico, Mexico, Venezuela, El Salvador, Singapore, and Japan, the company added managers responsible for each major foreign region to better support efforts to blend U.S. product with local content and design.[19]

"If a company wants to be a player in the world markets, it has to have the major pieces of furniture, the kinds of furniture that the world market wants," explained Thomas Miller. "We use the cubicles, the panels, in the United States. In other countries they use something called a desking system—it's basically a desk with European design. It's very sleek right now. It doesn't look like the old government-issue desks of the 1940s, and it's all loaded with wiring for computers and a lot of attachments."[20]

A Growing Force

By the new millennium HON INDUSTRIES had evolved into six companies serving three distinct markets, plus HON International, which marketed products outside the United States and Canada. Allsteel, The Gunlocke Company, and Holga served the contract furnishings market. Middle-market

In 2002 HON INDUSTRIES introduced the Heatilator I100—the industry's largest wood-burning fireplace at the time.

furnishings were manufactured and marketed by
The HON Company and Maxon. Hearth Technologies was comprised of Heatilator, Heat-N-Glo,
Aladdin Hearth Products (Quadra-Fire and Dovre),
and Hearth Services Inc.[21]

Seeing opportunity in the demand for office
furniture with quality wood finishes, in 2000 HON
INDUSTRIES formed the Wood Products Group.
The new division included the premium Gunlocke
brand plus the wood seating, veneer, and laminate
products marketed by The HON Company and
Allsteel. "In less than a year, it has improved profitability and the manufacturing process," Michaels
told investors in 2000.[22]

HON INDUSTRIES never stopped reinventing
itself. In 1997, HON INDUSTRIES brought out
nearly 300 new models, from innovative work surfaces to ceramic fiber fireplaces. That year, more
than 25 percent of revenues came from products

Allsteel's Terrace Workplace had a tile construction. Features
such as teaming tables helped companies create attractive,
functional environments.

that had been introduced in the preceding three
years. To maintain this product flow, in 1998 HON
INDUSTRIES began a more focused effort, according to its annual report, "to listen to—and hear—
our customers. . . . Our markets *are* changing. That
is why we have sharpened our focus and broadened
our vision."[23]

Addressing this goal in its 1999 annual report,
HON INDUSTRIES upgraded its dealer support
programs. "After proving its success in 1999, our
Express Solutions program, which offers high-speed
deliveries of . . . our most popular products, is now
being expanded." HON INDUSTRIES helped its

dealers create and fund new business development plans. Its field service engineers worked with dealers to ensure "flawless, on-time installations." To ensure "complete, on-time, undamaged" deliveries, HON teams managed each step from order to delivery and installation. They worked with carriers to improve planning, packaging, scheduling, and shipping. From 1992 to 1999 shipping lead times dwindled from four to five weeks to "as little as four days."[24]

A declining economy, however, took its toll on the office furnishings industry. HON INDUSTRIES closed four plants—including its operations in Williamsport, Pennsylvania; Tupelo, Mississippi; Santa Ana, California; and Jackson, Tennessee—between April 2001 and January 2002. This reduced overhead by some $12 million annually, with Tupelo's production load relocated to the Milan, Tennessee, and Muscatine plants.[25]

HON INDUSTRIES expanded the nomenclature for products in its market segments. In 1997 it was Mirati and Miles seating, Terrace Wave panel and teaming table, and improvements in CONCEN-SYS system furniture. In 1998 product introductions and redesigns included The HON Company's Tiempo and Talbot seating and Expectations commercial computer furniture; BPI's Cantilevered Systems, TL2 Floor to Ceiling systems, lateral files and conferences tables; Gunlocke's Prism systems, Harlow, and Credentials seating; and Holga's Opti-Stor rotating cabinet and FourFlex shelving.[26]

In 1999 The Gunlocke Company introduced ClearTech, which it dubbed the "finest wood furniture finish in the world." ClearTech was not only durable and low maintenance, it also enhanced the wood's beauty. Allsteel's Terrace systems of open-frame tile construction helped clients create attractive, functional environments.[27]

Meanwhile, Allsteel moved into its new headquarters in Muscatine in early 2001.[28] At Allsteel, 1999–2000 brought brand refinement, sharper marketing, and new showrooms. The HON Company also introduced a new dealer training program, as well as an e-commerce initiative, which helped the company communicate with both dealers and customers. Complete on-time deliveries improved by 50 percent in 1999–2000, and warranty costs dropped by 18 percent. HON International supported dealers in 53 countries in Latin America, Europe, Africa, the Middle East, and Asia-Pacific.[29]

At the same time, Hearth Technologies benefited from novel marketing initiatives. Its Customer Alliance Program identified high-potential U.S. markets, partnered with distributors in those markets, and aggressively pursued growth opportunities. The company also saw success from diversifying horizontally, creating and marketing hearth systems, not only fireplaces or stoves but facings, fans, remote controls, and more—"developing technology to enhance indoor quality" and outdoor lifestyle products.[30]

The HON Revolution 6200 series offered large proportioned seat and back cushions with integral lumbar support.

Hearth Technologies in1998 established an outdoor division to develop a new family of products, such as weatherproof fireplaces. Meanwhile, Heat-N-Glo introduced additional innovative direct-vent gas, top-vent gas, and electric fireplaces, and the Patio Campfire gas-log set. Heatilator premiered Accelerator Series wood fireplaces, Caliber Classic direct-vent gas fireplaces and Simplicity gas fireplaces. New Aladdin products included state-of-the-art gas inserts, gas stoves, and step-top gas stoves. Product introductions in 1999 included Heatilator's Maxus direct-vent gas series and portable campfire and grill; Heat-N-Glo offered HearthFire direct-vent insert series, Vantage multi-sided HV series, and Outdoor Hearth products.

Aladdin introduced a wood-burning stove and pellet fireplace insert. Heatilator broke new ground in 2000 with the Icon fireplace, which looked like real masonry. Heat-N-Glo introduced Crescent arched kitchen fireplaces, Intensity large-flame

fireplaces, and Everest vertical opening fireplaces. Aladdin's Quadra-Fire Columbia Bay gas stove featured a bay window, and the Dovre Sapphire gas stove could be top- or rear-vented.[31]

A number of products introduced in 2001 and 2002 won awards. Heat-N-Glo's Intensity was voted the industry's best gas fireplace and its Twilight indoor-outdoor see-through fireplace the most innovative product in 2001. An Aladdin Quadra-Fire won a 2001 Vesta Award, which honors innovation in design and technology, and the Castile pellet stove and Garnet gas stove were Vesta runners-up. Hearth Technologies products won four of 15

The 10700 series of contemporary laminate office furniture was accented with hardwood and rounded corners. The modular shelves and mobile pedestals were easy and quick to reconfigure.

HON INDUSTRIES' priority to get its product to end-users and channel partners where and when they want it ensures improved shipping performance and complete and on-time deliveries.

Gamut managerial seating. Allsteel inaugurated Pendulum seating, Persona storage products, Extension accessories, and Synchrony wood case goods. The Gunlocke Company brought out Volo and Cali executive seating. Holga introduced Apex integrated shelving and mobile aisle systems and SmartSpace carriages for lateral files.[33]

Allsteel's #19 Chair in 2002 impressed the design community. The Marcus Koepke design generated some 90 worldwide patents and patents pending from the #19 project to produce "a beautiful union of form and function." Koepke incorporated 18 custom-designed, integral parts, including a foam-gel-fabric cushion and height and reclining adjustments controlled with two easy-to-operate levers. Allsteel also introduced Landscape Surfaces for the Terrace panel system, which allowed designers to vary color, texture, and contrast. Meanwhile, The HON Company's Perpetual seating won "Best of Show NeoCon '02" for comfort and support. Its Park Avenue collection offered veneer desks, storage, and seating. The Gunlocke Seneca Chair was inspired by classic Adirondack chairs. Maxon's Whidbey Executive Chair combined top-grain leather and brushed aluminum with 21st-century ergonomics.[34]

awards at the 2001 Hearth, Patio and Barbeque Association show, including Best New Gas Fireplace and Product of the Year. Heatilator and Heat-N-Glo ranked first and second in a *Professional Builder* magazine brand awareness survey of its readers. A Heatilator fireplace, combining heat recovery with home ventilation, won a Vesta Award, as did a Quadra-Fire pellet insert.

Other hearth products included a Heatilator gas fireplace with "innovative flame technology," the Heat-N-Glo gas energy masters with an arched front and heat management system, Heat-N-Glo's direct-vent gas fireplace with a log set that filled its entire 49-inch firebox, and the company's largest cast-iron direct-vent gas stove, a 2002 Vesta finalist.[32]

In 2001 The HON Company introduced 25 new products, compared with ten in 2000 and 14 the year before. Its introductions included an Initiate panel system, Instinct task seating, Provisions mobile tables, Efficiencies filing systems, and

Allsteel Inc.

THE COMPANY THAT WOULD BECOME Allsteel Inc. started modestly in a small frame building in Aurora, Illinois, in 1912. It was named Allsteelequip Company. The original workforce of ten produced electrical cut-out boxes, shop tote boxes, and other made-to-order metal items.

For nearly two decades, drawing modest salaries and taking no dividends, John Knell, as president, and Charles H. Lembcke, as general manager, plowed all the profits back into the business.

Through 11 plant expansions from 1920 to 1959, Allsteelequip became a player in the electrical equipment supply industry. In 1929 the corporation revised its name to All-Steel-Equip Company. Gradually, the product line expanded to include water cooler cabinets, boiler jackets, kitchen cabinets, refrigerated food lockers, and custom-made sheet metal goods.

As customers buying All-Steel-Equip cabinets and lockers for their business offices began requesting filing cabinets, the company bought them from another Aurora supplier. As the volume of those purchases grew, All-Steel-Equip realized it should be making its own vertical files, so in 1936 it bought the Aurora Metal Cabinet Company. Not satisfied with the existing cabinets, the company shut down its new plant for three months, redesigned the products and the manufacturing process, and became a serious competitor in filing cabinets.

World War II delayed the move to desk manufacturing until 1947, but the company finally introduced its "knock-down" desk line with interchangeable components. Bookcases, telephone stands and credenzas followed. Meanwhile, the company's Los Angeles showroom served as a set for filming of the 1947 classic *Miracle on 34th Street.*

But All-Steel-Equip was just one product category shy of a full office furniture inventory—chairs. So in 1953 it bought the Shepherd Chair Co. of Melrose Park, Illinois. As it had with other acquisitions, All-Steel-Equip closed the plant and revamped the designs and the manufacturing process. Months later, its newest division reopened and introduced a line of new office chairs. That set the stage for nationwide sales and distribution for office furniture, and the decision to pursue the architectural-designer market.

In 1966 C.I.T. Financial Corp. bought the company, giving it a strong financial base for future growth. One of C.I.T.'s properties, B. K. Johl Inc. of Montreal, a major Canadian office furniture manufacturer, became a part of All-Steel-Equip.

In 1967, the company restructured into three divisions: office furniture, electrical products, and B. K. Johl. Six years later, the furniture divisions were renamed ALL-STEEL INC. and ALL-STEEL CANADA LTD., and simplified to Allsteel in 1986. Allsteel had several corporate parents, including RCA, before HON INDUSTRIES acquired it in 1997.

One of Allsteel's signature innovations, the lateral file, was developed in 1967 and rolled off the production line in 1969. Lateral files, modular desks, and panel systems—and myriad awards—are prime evidence of Allsteel's commitment to innovative design throughout the years, right down to the #19 chair.[1]

The #19 chair was "a sum expression of 18 integral parts, plus one equally integral human being."

Lean Manufacturing (RCI)

For all of The HON Company's marketing initiatives and dealer-support programs, it was the incredible array of products with which it flooded the downturned market that stimulated the company's rise to preeminence in the office furniture market-

Above: A production meeting at The HON Company's Geneva plant.

Below: Landscape Surfaces for the Terrace panel system were introduced in 2002. With this innovation, designers could vary colors and textures, such as Infinite Tech Fabric, Sand Hermosa Cherry, and Strata Espresso.

place.[35] Perhaps the chief driving force behind the innovative success, however, was the corporate mantra of Rapid Continuous Improvement (RCI).

HON INDUSTRIES' strong member-owner culture committed itself to applying the RCI process to eliminating waste and reducing costs, even at the administrative level. In 1997 HON INDUSTRIES' management reported that virtually all member-owners participated in RCI events. Results appeared everywhere in the organization, with sales-per-employee increasing by 50 percent from 1992 to 1998.

By 1998 the lead time from order to delivery of selected products had been trimmed to four days, and the delivery of mixed products to customer specifications approached two weeks. On the safety front, lost workday incidents fell 85 percent

from 1991 to 1997. The recordable accident rate dropped continually from 5.62 accidents per 100 workers in 1999 to 4.73 in 2000 and 3.59 in 2001. HON INDUSTRIES' success in 2000 in reaching $2 billion in net sales only four years after crossing the $1 billion threshold was a testament to the effectiveness of applying RCI to both marketing and manufacturing.[36]

Of course, these achievements did not go unnoticed. HON INDUSTRIES had weathered the economic storms of the early 2000s better than some of its competitors. HON INDUSTRIES Vice President and Chief Information Officer Malcolm Fields said, "When the company slows down, those compa-

Above: Member Olivia Marow.

Right: The exoskeletal aesthetics of the HON Mobius 4700 series bring the structural elements into plain view.

nies with lean principles are now making money." The HON Company President Dave Burdakin explained to the business press that the essence of RCI is "the attitude that we're never satisfied with where we are today. We are always looking for ways to improve. Lean management forces a company to eliminate all waste, whether it's non-value-added activity, extra handling, scrap, damage, or anything else that's not providing value or service for our customers." One reason RCI worked was because most HON INDUSTRIES plants had a system in which members could propose improvement ideas and were often given an opportunity to implement them personally.[37]

Advanced technology helped drive costs down as well. For example, using SynQuest supply chain planning software reduced HON INDUSTRIES' transportation costs by thousands of dollars as it improved on-time customer delivery. "With 18 production facilities and six distribution centers throughout North America, it was important for us to look at the most optimal way to supply each individual order," Jack Michaels said. The HON Company credited the manufacturing and transportation flexibility made possible by SynQuest for its ability to draw product from throughout the HON INDUSTRIES network to deliver a 20-truckload order to a New York City retailer shortly after the September 11, 2001, terrorist attack. HON INDUSTRIES cut delivery lead-times and operating costs even further by using managed wireless terminals in all its plants.[38]

A Profitable Performance

A side effect of HON INDUSTRIES' performance was an increasingly high national profile. Among other honors, in 1998 *Fortune* magazine placed HON INDUSTRIES on its list of "Most Admired" companies, and the company made *Forbes'* "Platinum List" for excellence in growth and profitability. The next year, *Industry Week* named HON INDUSTRIES one of the world's "100 Best Managed Companies"

based on such factors as financial performance, philanthropy, safety, research, and its relationship with employees and society. The company repeated that honor in 2000 when it made *Fortune's* "Most Admired" list again. The company also received recognition in 2000 from *Forbes* and *CFO* magazines. *Forbes* honored HON INDUSTRIES as one of its "400 Best Big Companies" in 2001.[39]

Among HON INDUSTRIES' subsidiaries, Heatilator and Allsteel were singled out for recognition. In 2000 Heatilator won the Governor's Iowa Industry Award for its use of technology, particularly applied

---

In 2003, The HON Company, Allsteel, and Gunlocke invested heavily to remodel their three Chicago showrooms. The brand-building exercise placed all three companies side-by-side on the 11th floor of the Merchandise Mart. Sister company, Maxon, kept its strategically placed showroom on the third floor.

When Allsteel members moved into the new Muscatine headquarters in 2000, they felt right at home. The new building, which won a *Business Week/Architectural Record* Award, was as sleek and stylish as the furniture it represented.

to production. The philosophy of Rapid Continuous Improvement, which permeated all of HON INDUS-TRIES, drew some of the credit for the award.[40]

Allsteel's new corporate headquarters in Muscatine received praise from the architecture profession. The company purchased the former Ring King Visibles plant in 1999 and recycled the 66,000-square-foot structure to contain executive offices, sales, marketing, engineering, industrial design, a showroom, and the training center. It was one of 11 recipients in 2000 of the *Business Week/Architectural Record* award for workplaces "designed to promote innovation and creativity." It was hailed for embracing "core midwestern values—honesty, fairness, and respect." In conjunction with the 2001 NeoCon furniture trade show, the Allsteel headquarters also received a Superlative Design Award from *Interior Design* magazine. *Architecture* magazine conferred an ACE Award on

Allsteel in 2002 as one of the best manufacturers in the building industry.[41]

A primary reason HON INDUSTRIES gained national attention was its financial performance. Through the 1990s, HON INDUSTRIES' net sales rose steadily toward $1 billion, finishing 1996—the end of its fifth decade of operation—just $2 million shy of that mark. The company more than doubled that performance in just four years, achieving $2.05 billion in net sales in 2000, only to be thwarted in the next two years by a weak economy that devastated the office furniture industry. Sales fell 12.4 percent in 2001 to $1.79 billion and slipped another 5.6 percent to $1.69 billion the next year. Through all those years, however, HON INDUSTRIES consistently outperformed the industries of which it was a part.

In 1997 the company's net sales skyrocketed 36.5%, but part of the increase was due to three recent acquisitions—Heat-N-Glo, Allsteel, Panel Concepts, and Bevis. The next year, HON INDUS-TRIES grew three times faster than the office furniture industry, but the Allsteel, Panel Concepts, and Bevis acquisitions were part of the reason.

Office furniture sales dropped 17.4 percent based on shipments in 2001–2002, and the economy continued to falter. Still, HON INDUSTRIES outperformed the industry. In the second year of double-digit decline in office furniture sales, the company emerged "with a solid balance sheet, strong margins, excellent cash flow and low debt." Further, its working capital was number one in the industry, and the stock price remained stable throughout the year, outperforming the S&P 500.[42]

When Iowa's largest newspaper asked the state's top companies how they continued to grow, Jack Michaels said the key to HON INDUSTRIES'

Member Alberta Axel.

success was its focus on value-priced furniture rather than top-dollar custom furniture contracts. "It's as important to know what a company won't do as it is to know what it will do," Michaels said. That focus led to steady growth. To be sure, a share of HON INDUSTRIES common stock purchased for $100 in 1947 had multiplied to 15,552 shares in 1997 and was worth $445,176. That value doubled again in March 1998 when the stock underwent a two-for-one split in the form of a 100 percent stock dividend. Stockholders received a quarterly dividend on February 28, 2003—the 192nd consecutive quarterly dividend paid since April 15, 1955.[43]

Each year, HON INDUSTRIES repurchased blocks of its common stock. Beginning in 1997 with the purchase of 483,154 shares at $4.1 million, the company spent more than $116 million to buy back a total of 5,346,131 shares over the next six years.[44]

Finally, in 1998 HON INDUSTRIES took steps to list its common stock on the New York Stock Exchange (NYSE). Feeling that Wall Street "underappreciated" HON INDUSTRIES, Michaels anticipated that the move to the NYSE from the Nasdaq Exchange would "increase awareness of the company... and prospects for profitable growth."[45] From then on, HON INDUSTRIES' unique corporate culture and tradition of innovation would no longer be a "member's only" proposition.

In addition to all their other benefits, HON INDUSTRIES members continued to participate in the Members' Stock Purchase Plan.[46]

Then in 1998 HON INDUSTRIES allocated the final shares in the HON Members Company Ownership Plan (ESOP), which had begun seven years earlier. That plan was merged into the company's defined contribution profit-sharing plan. Over the final three years of the ESOP, the company allo-

Member Bob Behrens.

HON INDUSTRIES is dedicated to improving the quality of life in communities where its members live, work, and raise their families. The company spearheads community improvement projects like this Weed Park playground in Muscatine, but projects are not limited to the town of its home base. Active participation of members in community affairs is a core value at HON INDUSTRIES.

cated 753,344 shares of common stock to participating members, contributing $7.74 million to the ESOP.[47]

"Our financial story speaks for itself," said Melinda Ellsworth, who joined HON INDUSTRIES in 2002 as vice president, treasurer, and head of investor relations.

The fact that we have been profitable is a testament to the strength of our management and flexibility of our company to streamline our cost structure, which we did at the front end before the industry really took a big dive. We benefited from that in addition to the fact that we're in a number of different channels that our competitors are not. We actually have a broader market penetration, and I think that with our HON INDUSTRIES companies focusing largely on small business, that has really helped to mitigate some of the significant hits that our competitors have taken because they really focus on the Fortune 100, *and while we are there, we also serve the small businesses, which have remained healthier in this downturn than the large corporations.*[48]

Giving Back

"HON INDUSTRIES is dedicated to improving the quality of life in the communities where our members live, work, and raise their families," the company annual report reiterated in 2000. As individuals, HON INDUSTRIES members volunteered to coach youth sports, lead scout troops, and read to elementary school pupils. The Boy Scouts of Muscatine in 2002 honored retired Chairman and CEO Stanley M. Howe for a lifetime of support. Until his retirement as head of HON International in December 2001, Tom Miller was chairman of Muscatine Appearance Projects, a city beautification effort. Junior Achievement honored The HON Company executive Roger Behrens in 2001 for his decades of leadership. Beyond these efforts to aid the local community, Chairman, President, and CEO Jack Michaels served as a director of the National Association of Manufacturers.[49]

"With Jack's encouragement, I am fortunate to serve on two boards," Ellsworth said. "They are a huge time commitment for me, and I come home with homework from every single board meeting. But it's important to the company that its executives are a part of the community—it's part of the culture here."[50]

As an organization, HON INDUSTRIES helped communities, educational causes, and needy families in many ways, commonly by matching members' contributions. Company-wide, HON INDUSTRIES donated $182,000—plus three truckloads of furniture—to help furnish offices for Federal Emergency Management Agency workers after the September 11 terrorist attacks in New York City.

Above and right: Artist Samuel Yates used 17 specially
treated four-drawer HON cabinets to create his *Minuet in
MG* sculpture.

Crossroads Hospice of Southeast Iowa received
$10,000 from the Heatilator Plant in Mount Pleas-
ant, Iowa. Jack Michaels put the weight of HON
INDUSTRIES behind efforts to build more housing
and improve education in Muscatine and Mount
Pleasant. In all its communities the HON INDUS-
TRIES Charitable Foundation supported schools
and gave scholarships to members' children. It also
helped support museums and other nonprofit organizations. For example, the Wayland, New York,
library received $50,000 in 1999 from HON INDUS-
TRIES on behalf of The Gunlocke Company.[51]
     In 1999 the HON INDUSTRIES Charitable
Foundation partnered with the Muscatine Community College Foundation to build a $600,000
new home for that city's Learning Tree Preschool,
which serves 150 children. In 2000 The Gunlocke
Company joined with the Veterans Administration

Medical Center in Bath, New York, to train veterans for careers in furniture upholstery.[52]

Sometimes HON INDUSTRIES received unexpected support from its sales force. In February 2001, an Owensboro, Kentucky, plant got a call from a Norfolk, Virginia, dealer who needed three executive high-back chairs in a hurry for the President of the United States, the Secretary of Defense, and the Chairman of the Joint Chiefs of Staff. They made the chairs in one day and delivered them to Norfolk with plenty of time to spare. Afterwards, a naval officer wrote to the dealer, New Day Office Products, to thank them for the chairs, which "proved to be a significant contribution to the success" of the meeting.

It took a bit more effort to fulfill the request of San Francisco artist Samuel Yates in 2002. To make his *Minuet in MG* sculpture, he needed 17 four-drawer HON cabinets able to withstand years of exposure to Northern California weather. The HON Company accepted the challenge. This required double-painting the cabinets with two layers of black powder coat and one of gloss clear coat. A crane was used to stack each cabinet to form a 65-foot-high steel column anchored in concrete. Yates filled each drawer with filings he made grinding up an MG Midget sports car. He then locked the drawers and sealed them shut to keep out rain. When finished, the slim column—possibly the world's tallest filing cabinet—was displayed at the DiRose Art and Nature Preserve in Napa, California.[53]

Whether rising to preeminence in the world's office furniture marketplace, making chairs for the president and his cabinet on a day's notice, or aiding in the vision of a California artist, HON INDUSTRIES has never backed down from a challenge—even the most difficult ones.

IN SUMMARY

IN 2000, UNDER JACK MICHAELS' leadership, HON INDUSTRIES solidified its niche atop the office furniture and hearth products industries.

In 1997 HON INDUSTRIES described itself as "the nation's largest manufacturer of value-priced office furniture, and fourth-largest office furniture manufacturer and marketer in North America." Later that year, HON INDUSTRIES acquired upscale Allsteel Inc., Bevis Custom Furniture Inc., and Panel Concepts Inc.—adding about $230 million in sales.

In 1999 HON INDUSTRIES' Hearth Technologies acquired two leading distributors—American Fireplace Company and the Allied Group—forming Hearth Services Inc. The new entity became the nation's largest manufacturer and distributor of hearth products.

By 2000 HON INDUSTRIES was comprised of six companies plus HON International, which marketed products outside North America. Allsteel, the Gunlocke Company, and Holga served the contract furnishings market. The HON Company and BPI Inc. made and sold middle-market furnishings. Hearth Technologies comprised Heatilator, Heat-N-Glo, Aladdin Hearth Products and Hearth Services Inc.

Facing growing competition, The HON Company in 1998 built a plant in Monterrey, Mexico. By 2002, HON INDUSTRIES members were in Puerto Rico, Mexico, Venezuela, El Salvador, Singapore, and Japan.

The Cadence desking line of furniture with Tolleson seating manufactured by Allsteel.

CHAPTER TEN

Vision and Values

1944–Present

*Values are where things begin and end, and if an enterprise isn't being
built on the basis of sound values, it's starting off in the wrong direction.*

—Dick Stanley, vice chairman of HON INDUSTRIES'
board of directors

BY 2003, HON INDUSTRIES was engaged in only the third leadership transition in its 60-year history. Stan Askren was elected president early that year, his eleventh year in management at HON INDUSTRIES, a career that included the presidency of two operating companies.

When he was first recruited by a headhunter looking for someone to join Michaels at HON INDUSTRIES, Askren had heard of the company but couldn't place the name. "So I hung up the phone, and as I'm walking to my office down the hallway I see HON, HON, HON," Askren recalled. "I walked along a row of file cabinets and saw that name and brand. That's when it moved from my subconscious to my conscious brain."[1]

In fact, Askren would find that HON INDUS-TRIES' vision and values had remained as steady as its leadership. Cofounder Max Stanley guided the company from its incorporation in 1944 until his death 40 years later. Stanley M. Howe, Max Stanley's protégé, applied his management talents for 50 years with the company. Jack Michaels, who came aboard in 1990 as president, succeeded Howe in 1996 as chairman.

Askren became HON INDUSTRIES' president, according to Michaels, "after a thorough review of several very capable internal candidates." These would not be easy shoes to fill. Michaels, a dynamic leader, had an imposing presence that filled a room and commanded attention. "Jack has become the embodiment of what HON stands for," Askren said of the man he would succeed.

The HON INDUSTRIES 2002 Annual Report pulled no punches, alluding to the scandals plaguing the leadership of other American corporations in a seemingly endless parade of headlines: "Setting the cultural climate is central to good governance. We sought to accomplish this years ago by adopting the HON INDUSTRIES Vision Statement, [which] represents much more than a traditional 'mission.' It represents the very foundation of our corporate culture."[2]

A close look at the Vision Statement and its underlying values showed how it guided the actions of HON INDUSTRIES' members. "HON was ahead

By 2003, Rapid Continuous Improvement events involving top HON INDUSTRIES officials had become a key element of management. Observing production in the Geneva plant were, from left, James Johnson, vice president, general counsel and secretrary; Malcom Fields, vice president and chief information officer; Eric Jungbluth, president, Allsteel Inc.; Stan Askren, president, HON INDUSTRIES; Jerald Dittmer, vice president and chief financial officer; and Brad Determan, president, Hearth & Home Technologies.

of the curve in its governance practices," said Richard Stanley, vice chairman of the HON INDUSTRIES board of directors and its longest serving member. "From the very early days, Max Stanley went out to find people to bring on the board who would bring points of view that were different from those of the managers of the company and people who were strong enough to challenge and test management recommendations."

Corporate Governance

Outside voices in corporate governance had been "a very good thing" for HON INDUSTRIES, Stanley said.

As these new regulations come out, such as Sarbanes-Oxley, HON INDUSTRIES is not in a position where it's having to change much. There are some legal niceties and paperwork that HON INDUSTRIES has to do now to be sure that we're complying with the letter of the law, but in the spirit of those, HON INDUSTRIES has been well ahead of the curve all along.[3]

The Olson Flex Stacker was named in honor of Ogden Olson, a furniture designer who had contributed designs to The HON Company's portfolio for 23 years.

Sarbanes-Oxley was landmark federal legislation mandating more fiscal accountability on the part of senior management of publicly held companies. The Sarbanes-Oxley Act of 2002 passed both houses of Congress—with overwhelming bipartisan support—in response to high-profile corporate scandals at Enron Corporation, Tyco International Ltd., WorldCom Inc., and other publicly held U.S. companies.

Articulating honest values in a short but far-reaching document was not easy, but the vision statement showed the way for members of the HON INDUSTRIES family. "It's ironic when we think about what we want the company to be in the next 100 years, but we felt it was important to capture that in the words that we did," Jack Michaels said.

Some ten years later, I know we've made three minor modifications to it. I wouldn't even call them

Olson Flex Stacker

NEW IN 2003, THE OLSON FLEX Stacker, a lightweight, versatile chair with applications for gatherings of 20 or 200, honored Ogden Olson, a 61-year-old designer who had been creating furniture for The HON Company for 23 years. Of the 30 to 40 new products The HON Company brought to market each year, "Ogden either drives or has his thumb print on at least half of them," said Jeff Jollay, The HON Company's vice president of marketing. As of early 2003, Olson had 46 patents to his name, many of them for chairs, workstations, or their components. Before becoming a member of The HON Company, Olson had designed ornamental salt and pepper shakers, a household brush, and a component of child-restraint systems.[1]

Allsteel's line of attractive and high-quality furniture is aimed at the architect and designer's market, including these Energy office chairs.

revisions. There are several key words, but two that stand out: fairness and respect, qualities that I felt were lacking in other organizations. A person is a member of our organization; he or she is not employed by the organization. Each is like part of our family.[4]

As a result, HON INDUSTRIES' members have a way of pulling together to make a project happen or meet a tight deadline. "I go back to some of the historical incidents that set the tone for how we think and act as a company," said Jeff Fick, vice president for member and community relations. "We've banded together through floods, tornadoes, and fires."

As a hands-on leader, Jack Michaels was always there in the thick of the action. "We had a torrential rain two years ago that subjected our machinery and production equipment to flooding," Fick recalled. "A number of people, our chairman and CEO, our current president, they were all work-ing to make sure there wasn't a problem. They saw that flooded area and worked together for probably six hours with pumps and other equipment to make sure it wasn't damaged. Jack ran out and got lunch for everybody."

"I think HON INDUSTRIES is very well prepared for the transition to new management," Jeff Fick said. "Jack Michaels insists that we be prepared for the transition and that we need to be positioned well to move forward. We have strong strategic planning. We have a very strong board of directors. Jack has assembled a management team that is pulling the organization forward. Our members throughout the organization understand what we need to do, where we're headed."[5]

No narrow specialists need apply here. In order to succeed, member-shareholders became immersed in all aspects of company management. The experience of chief financial officer Jerry Dittmer was typical. "I actually came in with a financial background," he recalled, "and I was told by Jack that if I ever wanted to be chief financial officer of the company, I had to know more than finance. He sent me out to Maxon [then BPI] as vice president and controller. I said, 'Well, I've already done that type of work,' to which he responded, 'You haven't done it for us!'"

The Allsteel GetSet nesting tables are easy to maneuver, easy to store, and attractive when combined with nesting chairs.

For the next several years, Dittmer learned from HON INDUSTRIES' master craftsmen and experienced managers about wood and systems furniture production then brought that knowledge to corporate headquarters, where he advanced from information technology to strategic planning, manufacturing, and finance. "It's easy to come to a corporate office and say, 'We're in corporate, we know everything,'" Dittmer said. "A person gets a much different perspective when he or she is out in the field, out in the business, out there day to day. They know what's going on. So we streamlined a lot of our operations even from an administrative standpoint. It also helped open up the lines of communication."[6]

Grounded in Solid Values

"In the building of successor leadership and bringing people into key positions," Dick Stanley said, "Stanley M. Howe and Jack Michaels and— I'm convinced now—Stan Askren, are three solid leaders who believe in and are solidly grounded in that value system and promote it and encourage

it and insist upon it among all of the people in the organization. If there's one message that ought to come out of this book, it's that values are where things begin and end, and if an enterprise isn't being built on the basis of sound values, it's starting off in the wrong direction."[7]

The HON INDUSTRIES Vision Statement, crafted in 1991 and updated in 2002, was articulate and simple.

We, the members of HON INDUSTRIES, are dedicated to creating long-term value for all of our stakeholders, to exceeding our customers' expectations and to making our company a great place to work. We will always treat each other, as well as customers, suppliers, shareholders, and our communities, with fairness and respect.

Our success depends upon business simplification, rapid continuous improvement, and innovation in everything we do, individual and collective integrity and the relentless pursuit of the long-standing beliefs.

The decision to stick to core values has not always been easy. After expanding during the 1990s, the North American office furniture industry shrank an estimated 40 percent by 2003, a chronic issue facing HON INDUSTRIES management in the new millennium. "A lot of it started post-9/11 when the economy trailed off," Eric Jungbluth, president of Allsteel, said in 2003. "People have been spending less on the infrastructure and the investment on the capital side. They're still projecting some declines this year yet in the industry, and we hope by the end of this year it starts to be a little more positive."[8]

Although net sales declined slightly in the first quarter of 2003, by the end of the third quarter HON INDUSTRIES had recorded a 4.3 percent increase over 2002 to $1.3 billion in sales for the first nine months of the year. Net income climbed $7.3 million over the previous year, to $70.5 million after three quarters, and the diluted share value rose from $1.07 in 2002 to $1.21 in 2003. Gross margins as of third quarter 2003 stood at 36.1 percent compared to 35.6 percent a year earlier. Making every effort to minimize the effect on HON INDUSTRIES members and their families, the company made the tough decision to implement cost reduction strategies, closing two Allsteel plants. The move was expected to save $13 million to $14 million per year, after one-time shut-down costs estimated at $11.5 million to $13 million. Consequently, in August 2003 HON INDUSTRIES was able to declare its 194th consecutive quarterly dividend on common stock, a dividend of 13 cents per share.[9]

People Make the Difference

CEO Jack Michaels analyzed what continually made HON INDUSTRIES profitable and a value-driven company in which to work.

In 1992, we began the Rapid Continuous Improvement aspect where that really means involving everybody. I've always contended that the person doing the job eight, ten, 12 hours a day knows more about it than anybody else, and if he or she wants to make improvements, management's role is to listen and then work to help implement the ideas. We're in an industry in which people are having successes, but a lot of them are not having successes. So what are the differences? I always contended, always, that it deals with the people. That's the difference.[10]

For Chief Financial Officer Jerry Dittmer, openness and accountability were always part of HON INDUSTRIES' corporate signature. "With Sarbanes-Oxley, a lot of new safeguards must be followed. The good news is, we don't feel we have anything to hide because of our controls. Part of the problems with the Tycos and the Enrons of the world is they didn't have an open environment. There were actually people who could manipulate things."

Dittmer recalled an incident in which "Jack Michaels said, 'Let's test our value system. Go down to payroll and tell them to pay you and me each a million dollars.' I explained to Jack that as the chief financial officer of this company, I couldn't get them to pay me $10, and it's a fact, because a person has to have the proper documentation. A person has to have the proper signatures. It's a very trusting environment, but we also have processes, policies, procedures, and we follow them no matter who a person is."[11]

The executive management team works with members to find new ways to run operations more efficiently while maintaining leadership in each of its core businesses.

Holga Inc. manufactures high-density storage, shelving, and mobile filing systems, as well as steel case goods. Pictured is the Holga Roll X.

Watch Out for Wall Street

Throughout the decades—and especially when the office furniture sector was hot—HON INDUSTRIES had earned the respect of the investment community. "We learned two and a half years ago that setting expectations to Wall Street can easily drive the management to run a company on a short-term basis. That's not what we're about," Michaels said.

In fact, in our vision statement, we talk about creating long-term shareholder value. We said, look, we're in a difficult period. We were, at that point, starting in the downturn of the industry. We're just going to do the best job that we can, but clearly we're going to create long-term shareholder value.

The analysts build their own models. We've been fortunate because we've been able to be within reason of their ranges. By doing that over an extended period of time and being very open and straightforward with them. I think they respect us because in this downturn we're gaining market share. We're still one of the most profitable, if not the most profitable.[12]

Because HON INDUSTRIES was scrupulously honest and maintained a conservative balance sheet, it enjoyed highly favorable relations with its banks. "We have a banker who came in here in the last year and was trying to help us with an acquisition," Dittmer said. "He was holding his briefcase, and he said, 'I have $2 billion in here. I want to loan this to you.' The point was, we were a very good credit risk. We work under very stringent financial goals and policies. Right now, we have a debt to [market] cap ratio of only 7 percent, which means it's very low. We are generating record amounts of cash in the corporation and feel that as long as we have a conservative balance sheet, honest and forthright, we'll have banks that will come trying to basically loan us money versus us going to ask for money."[13]

Run Like You're Scared

Despite its leadership position in the industry, the company refused to rest on its laurels. Institutional restlessness—of a positive variety—permeated HON INDUSTRIES. "The thing that we're always concerned about is, we've got to be sure we don't become arrogant, because it leads to complacency," Michaels said. "It leads to failure. Obviously, there's a fine line between being successful and being proud, but then the effects from being proud to being arrogant can be disastrous. It's kind of like a hidden asset. We're never satisfied."[14]

Through hard work, prudent risk-taking, and careful acquisitions, HON INDUSTRIES never held back, resulting in tremendous growth. It was a team effort. "We give members responsibility as well as authority," explained Dr. Malcom C. Fields, vice president and chief information officer of HON INDUSTRIES. "We share the rewards with them. Approximately a third of our profits have been given back to our members through profit sharing and another third through dividends to our shareholders."[15]

To ensure continued progress, HON INDUS-TRIES retained a brand consultancy, recalled Jim Kane, vice president of the wood seating and table business of The HON Company. "They've started with focus groups, basically with channel customers. Based on that, they continued with some

end users. Then, based on what they heard, to really confirm what they thought they were hearing, they did a quantitative survey with several hundred end users. We'll use those results then as we plan what comes next from a product point of view, a service point of view, and so forth."[16]

The HON INDUSTRIES network can be compared to a microcosm of the Internet, Malcolm Fields said. "We have, I expect, more than 50 sites that are connected via networks, dedicated network connections, throughout the corporation. Then that network, if one thinks of that as a small pile of spaghetti, is all connected."

HON INDUSTRIES in the early part of the millennium turned its management attention to the company's relationship with its marketplaces. The move toward more people-oriented marketing and

---

This HON Park Avenue desk is finished with natural maple, a new option for the collection. It is designed to offer maximum working space, filing and storage space, and computer compatibility.

customer relations was true to HON INDUSTRIES' original vision and values, recalled HON INDUSTRIES President Stan Askren.

> We have such a tremendous operational model, such a strong, powerful 'back wheel.' We bolt that on to a very strong 'front wheel.' We talk about it on a daily basis: What do we need to do to be building stronger brands? What do we need to do to understand the people who use our products? What needs are we meeting? What needs are we not meeting? What do we need to do to respond or talk, communicate better, with the decision makers? What are they buying? What are they not buying? Why are they buying? Where are they buying? What are the products they'd like to have? What are the services they'd like to have with that?[17]

At the market's upper tier—where custom furniture is ordered by contract—this meant staying abreast of the needs of clients such as American Express, the state of California, Deloite and Touche, Gucci, and Coca-Cola.

Askren was confident that HON INDUSTRIES could acclimate itself to its markets' changing economic landscapes.

> If a person looks at the history of this company, and I've had the opportunity to do that, it's all

The Allsteel Team Space concept offers a flexible and attractive working environment for multiple group members. The furniture is designed to be attractive yet totally ergonomic and functional.

> about continuous reinvention. I can even look at my tenure here, what Jack has done to reinvent this company. He basically has put in place a new, very strong management team. Look at the hearth business. When he came in here, we had a little operation down in Mount Pleasant, Iowa, that really wasn't realizing its potential, and now we have a hearth business that's the world leader. You have the reinvention of office furniture with the advent of 'split and focus' and with the creation of Allsteel and The HON Company. You have the introduction, full implementation, full enculturation of Rapid Continuous Improvement—a very sophisticated set of tools that has allowed us to reduce our cost, improve our quality, improve our speed to market— and then to just continuously regenerate.[18]

Company Culture Fosters Success

Through that history of continual reinvention and growth—whether rocketing from $1 billion to $2 billion in sales in just four years in the '90s or adjusting during a shrinking economy in the next decade—

HON INDUSTRIES maintained the vibrant company culture that fostered success. "I think it has to do with following our vision statement," Dave Burdakin said. "It gives us a core set of principles that guide our behavior. You know, whether the company is one billion, two billion, or three billion, the same core principles apply. I think all the top executives in HON INDUSTRIES believe that the HON culture is a competitive advantage—and something that makes us special and something we want to continue."[19]

HON INDUSTRIES grew in large part through acquisitions, but the company's culture and values drove critical decision-making on which firms to acquire. "We only buy profitable companies," Jerry Dittmer said. "It's important that they have a culture that can relate to ours. The culture in Muscatine, Iowa, is different than the culture in Van Nuys, California, different than the culture in Cedartown, Georgia. But at the end of the day, we have this

membership culture. So when we go in to look at an acquisition, we'll go through our vision statement and say, 'Do they have this, do they have this?' They'd better have most of those items, or we don't even need to bother going to the next step."[20]

Expanding on that theme, Dick Stanley said, "A few years ago, HON INDUSTRIES was considering the acquisition of another company, and it was at the point where four of us directors went out to meet the president and CEO. He had a value statement that was framed and on his wall there. Good sounding PR. I asked him, 'What process did you use to develop that?' He said, 'Oh, I went home and wrote it.' To me, that was a big 'no' in terms of going forward, because a value system isn't something in which you can write the beautiful flowery words and say, 'Here's what we're going to do.' The value system has to be grass roots up, understood, and really internalized by all the people involved."[21]

HON INDUSTRIES' vision of ever more people-oriented products appeared to be working. On the product development front, HON INDUSTRIES revitalized its offerings by introducing or updating a number of products in 2003. The company unveiled Nuance and Unanimous seating lines

Allsteel's Personal Space concept offers a one-person office suite, complete with a work station, waiting area, desk, and working table.

and an ergonomic go-everywhere chair. A natural maple finish and additional pieces rounded out the Park Avenue Collection. The Perpetual Line offered many contemporary, mobile office solutions. To help market its products, The HON Company opened a Washington, D.C., showroom and revamped its showrooms in New York and Chicago.

HON Products Win Designer Applause

Closely listening to its customers' needs—an important focus of HON INDUSTRIES' culture—undoubtedly helped to make the company's case. The Gunlocke Company's Amalfi chairs won a Silver Award at the 2003 NeoCon. Its Mantra line of case goods gracefully blended ash wood with aluminum legs and bases. Maxon produced desks and work tables, panel systems, and task or managerial seating for myriad office settings. From the Roll-X mobile aisle system to simple open wire shelving, vertical to lateral to pedestal files, Holga solved document storage problems. Heatilator, Heat-N-Glo, and Quadra-Fire led the markets for fireplaces, stoves, inserts, and related products. That year, the division changed its name from Hearth Technologies to Hearth & Home Technologies to reflect its broader focus on products for the home.[22]

Maxon Furniture specialized in panel systems and workstation products. "We're the industry leader in fast response time. So we offer mass customization in five days or less, a very lean enterprise, and rapid turnaround," said Maxon President Jean Reynolds. "That really helps your end user. It also helps our distributors because they're able to market and sell the product quickly," added Josh Slowick, vice president, sales and marketing.

"We've all got to look at growth in different ways," Reynolds continued. "I think we'll be doing that by getting closer to our customers, understanding their needs, and designing product more specifically to fit the needs of the client rather than more of a push through distribution channels."[23]

Meanwhile, further branding efforts, perhaps overdue, were underway at The HON Company. "Going forward, I think you'll see we're going to invest more in building the HON brand name," Burdakin said. "You'll see more improved styling in HON products. We've started to introduce products like Perpetual, which we introduced at NeoCon, that have more contemporary styling. We won a design

The Gunlocke Company's Amalfi chairs won a Silver Award at the 2003 NeoCon.

Above: Gunlocke Company's Mantra line of case goods gracefully blends ash wood with aluminum legs and bases.

Right: Unveiled by The HON Company in 2003, the Nuance line of chairs features ergonomic, go-everywhere chairs. The chair features a hard back and lumbar region support.

award for innovation with it." The HON Company also received the Manufacturer of the Year Award from the Office Furniture Dealer Alliance based on the vote of all the furniture dealers in America, Burdakin said. Allsteel won that award in 2002.[24]

For Allsteel, focused on the architects and designers' market, the HON INDUSTRIES culture was a competitive advantage. Jungbluth said, "I've heard it repeatedly from customers and people with whom I've met. We have an approach with our customers externally. We're willing to listen. We're willing to try to do things differently to meet their needs. I think that's powerful; a lack of arrogance where some of our competitors, as they've gotten bigger, have begun to take on more of an arrogant approach. And I hear that day in, day out with our customers, whether it's dealers or end users—that it's kind of refreshing to deal with us."[25]

At Holga, according to Tom Head, vice president and general manager, "We're focused on what we call high-density filing and storage, which right now makes up about 40 percent of our business—and we're trying to get it to be more than that. That's kind of a specialty niche type product. We really want to be the performance leader in that segment: 'You will have the best total experience if you buy a Holga system.' "[26]

The Gunlocke Company faced a different challenge, according to President Don Mead. "It has a strong brand in the marketplace, good reputation, but it has not achieved and maintained the financial performance that other companies within HON INDUSTRIES would expect to see. The big challenge is to continue with the product performance, but to focus very heavily on making sure that the shareholders get out of it what they expect, which is a well-managed, well-led company that delivers good financial performance."[27]

Hearth & Home Technologies was a HON INDUSTRIES company that implemented a number of strategies to encourage growth. The company introduced two new products under the brand name Heat-N-Glo Lifestyle Products. "It's targeted at living spaces outside of the home, outdoor kitchens, patios," said President Brad Determan. "We've launched a variety of hearth products that are tailored at that. Outdoor livable square footage can be built for 25 percent of what indoor footage costs."

Additionally, Heatilator Home Products were bannered and targeted at maintaining the quality of air inside the home. Determan explained, "It involves devices like air exchangers that are inte-

grated to recover the waste heat off gas fireplaces, central vacuum cleaners that are very efficient in terms of removing particles from a home."[28]

Through HON International, HON INDUSTRIES achieved sales in about 53 countries, primarily in the Caribbean and in South America, Central America, and Mexico. "We do some business in the Middle East, a little bit in Ireland and a little bit in Asia-Pacific," Tom Miller, president, HON International, said. "If one wants to be a player in the world markets, your company has to have the kinds of furniture that the world market wants."

The European Continent has many older buildings with odd corners, making them harder to reconfigure than North American buildings with predominantly square corners, Miller said. To be truly competitive in Europe, which Miller sees as the next big development market, "A company has to start from scratch. It can't bring its products over. It can't bring its tooling. Moreover, Europe is not a single market. It's still a lot of little individual markets."

Vision: New Technologies Sought

"One idea we're working on now is a more advanced data management system so that engineers can collaborate better on designs and get prod-

The first fireplace designed specifically for the kitchen, Heat-N-Glo's arched-front Crescent offered a masonry style bi-fold door attachment with a flip-down warming shelf.

Members Stephanie Lossi, Linda Franklin, Rodney Kleindolph, and Sylvia Snyder.

ucts to market more effectively," Pete Atherton, chief technology officer, said. HON's technology team looked at cutting-edge technology and projected its possible impact on working environments. "Take an example of voice input," Atherton said. "If in the future people communicate with their computers by voice, we've got to be able to provide an environment where the devices can pick up the voice very well." For that and other reasons, the team investigated acoustics. "We're always looking for better materials to absorb sound," Atherton said. "As computing devices get faster—they're not fast enough yet—we'll be able to actually measure sound as it hits and generates another sound, which cancels it."[29]

Atherton lauded HON INDUSTRIES' ethic of Rapid Continuous Improvement, which "allows for people to generate new ideas to go to products." He founded a group of technical and marketing leaders at HON INDUSTRIES, the Future Technology Leadership Team, to evaluate ideas submitted to a Web site from members throughout HON INDUS-TRIES. Among ideas submitted, said Atherton, was one from the company's patent attorney, who came up with the question, "How do I easily pick up my files from where I'm working and carry them somewhere else?" "It actually was really clever the way he did the presentation," Atherton said. "He had photographs of himself and all the pieces he'd have to carry, and how this device would make his life so much easier."[30]

An Enlightened Workplace

With a 60-year tradition of respect and fairness for all of its members, HON INDUSTRIES has always been, by design, a good place to work. Fick gave this assessment:

I think we have healthy discontent with the status quo. We're always looking for a better way. It's part of our culture. It's accepted. There aren't barriers to people challenging how we do something. In fact, there is encouragement. There are rewards. There is recognition for people who can figure out a better way to do something, who can save money, who can improve service, who can improve a product. That's a big part of our culture.[31]

Julie Zielinski, vice president of marketing for Allsteel, recalled her first meeting with Michaels.

I was a product manager for systems, and I had a meeting to review our product plans with Jack

Michaels, the CEO. Each of the product managers had to take him through this room, and I'd show him our current product development projects. After the meeting, I went back to my desk, and the phone rings, and it's Jack Michaels calling me to say, "Well, Julie, I just wanted to let you know I'm really glad you're here. I enjoyed getting to know you. So, welcome." The chairman is calling, and I'm sitting there, and I almost didn't know how to respond. Wow! That was so incredibly powerful to me, having come from a different environment.

"The other part that struck me," Zielinski recalled, "was, here are all these Iowans, unpretentious, hanging out. They don't look like they're anything special. They don't talk like they're any-

The HON Company's Tercero conference room suite of products is a comprehensive solution for boardrooms. In addition to a conference table and executive chairs, it offers side tables, a lectern, a coffee cart, and a large multimedia armoire.

thing special, and I got to know them and they're incredibly special. They're incredibly talented. Their skills are absolutely up to date, and I realized here is this guy who's leading this manufacturing team. He grew up on a farm, and he is leading this manufacturing team that is clearly the cream of the crop of all lean manufacturing in all the United States. It's the sweet surprise of HON INDUSTRIES."[32]

Of course, the cornerstone of HON INDUSTRIES' corporate citizenship was the company members and the communities in which they lived. "The members come from the communities, and we want to be sure we are a good corporate citizen in these communities," Michaels said. "So the first real effort was organized internally. It focused on members and communities. Secondly, we really promote volunteerism. We have volunteers—I'm just astounded—in all the communities, from scouting to Little League baseball to peewee this and peewee that, to church groups, to every facet of the community. Then we have been able, through our charitable foundation, to give funding to charitable organizations within those communities. We must ensure

Member Barb Nielsen.

that we have good communities for our people to live in and to operate in and to work in. We actually give up to 2 percent of each year's profits to our charitable foundation."[33]

Values: Giving Begins at Home

Fick elaborated. "We focus our charitable giving on communities where our members live and work, on children, on families, on education. We're much more apt as a foundation to contribute money if a member is involved in a significant way. We want to leverage both the dollars and the volunteerism. Muscatine is a key community because our headquarters group is here, and about a third of our workforce is here."

Among other philanthropic efforts, HON INDUSTRIES helped support the building of playgrounds in Muscatine city parks, along with a $10 million improvement project on Muscatine's scenic Mississippi riverfront that included recreational facilities and a river environmental learning center.

On a smaller scale, the company and individual members worked on Habitat for Humanity houses and helped to fund a domestic abuse shelter. In 2003 HON INDUSTRIES donated funds to buy school supplies for children and gave monies toward development of a disk golf course.[34]

Reflecting back, Fick said, "We were founded not with a concept for a product, but with a concept of how to treat people. It was an idea to provide employment for people returning from World War II who needed employment, and with the concept that there was a better way to work with your workforce—make them part of the team. Communicate with them often. Share your profits with your workforce. That's how we started, and that's how we've grown over time."[35]

Vision: "The North Star"

Looking to HON INDUSTRIES' future, Askren said, "First we need to make sure that we preserve—not only preserve, but enhance—our member culture, our vision statement. Our vision statement is analogous to Polaris. It's the North Star."[36]

"I think we are the predominant player in office furniture and in the hearth business," Askren said.

Jack Michaels discusses safety issues with members as part of "Project Hat," a company-wide initiative in the workplace. Under Michaels' leadership, work-related injuries to members were reduced significantly.

"I think we will continue to generate strong, consistent growth and returns for all of our stakeholders. I think we want to be a place where people look at us and say, 'That's a great place to work.' As long as we have this sort of solid core foundation of the right people, focused on the right elements, with the right values, I think it would be very, very difficult to feel anything other than optimism and positive feelings for the future of our organization."[37]

"The publication of this book coincides with shareholder approval to change the name of HON INDUSTRIES to HNI Corporation," Askren continued. "The new name will serve to better align the corporate identity with the direction of the company as a strategic manager of multiple, distinct, and independent brands. We feel the HNI Corporation name will accomplish this, yet keep us connected to our past and true to our culture, our values, and our vision."[38]

Our Vision

WE, THE MEMBERS, ARE DEDICATED to creating long-term value for all of our stakeholders, to exceeding our customers' expectations, and to making our company a great place to work. We will always treat each other, as well as customers, suppliers, shareholders, and our communities, with fairness and respect.

Our success depends upon business simplification, rapid continuous improvement, and innovation in everything we do, individual and collective integrity, and the relentless pursuit of the following long-standing beliefs:

WE WILL BE PROFITABLE.

We pursue mutually profitable relationships with customers and suppliers. Only when our company achieves an adequate profit can the other elements of this Vision be realized.

WE WILL CREATE LONG-TERM VALUE FOR SHAREHOLDERS.

We create long-term value for shareholders by earning financial returns significantly greater than our cost of capital and pursuing profitable growth opportunities. We will safeguard our shareholders' equity by maintaining a strong balance sheet to allow flexibility in responding to a continuously changing market and business environment.

WE WILL PURSUE PROFITABLE GROWTH.

We pursue profitable growth on a global basis in order to provide continued job opportunities for members and financial success for all stakeholders.

WE WILL BE A SUPPLIER OF QUALITY PRODUCTS AND SERVICES.

We provide reliable products and services of high quality and brand value to our end-users. Our products and services exceed our customers' expectations and enable our distributors and our company to make a fair profit.

WE WILL BE A GREAT PLACE TO WORK.

We pursue a participative environment and support a culture that encourages and recognizes excellence, active involvement, ongoing learning, and contributions of each member; that seeks out and values diversity; and that attracts and retains the most capable people who work safely, are motivated, and are devoted to making our company and our members successful.

WE WILL BE A RESPONSIBLE CORPORATE CITIZEN.

We conduct our business in a way that sustains the well-being of society, our environment, and the economy in which we live and work. We follow ethical and legal business practices. Our company supports our volunteer efforts and provides charitable contributions so that we can actively participate in the civic, cultural, educational, environmental, and governmental affairs of our society.

TO OUR STAKEHOLDERS:

When our company is appreciated by its members, favored by its customers, supported by its suppliers, respected by the public, and admired by its shareholders, this Vision is fulfilled.

Notes to Sources

Chapter One

1. "Millennium: The Innovators," *Muscatine Journal*, 20 November 1999, 6D; C. Maxwell Stanley, James H. Soltow, *The HON Story* (Ames, IA: Iowa State University Press, 1991), 3–4; Richard Stanley, interview by Fred Anderson, recording, 1 July 2003, Write Stuff Enterprises.
2. Stanley and Soltow, *The HON Story*, 3–4; Richard Stanley, interview.
3. "Datelines... January–June 1943," www.pw1.netcom.com; "Atlantic—June 1943," "Mediterranean—June 1943," "Indian & Pacific Oceans—June 1943," www.naval-history.net; "American Coal Miners Strike," www.onwar.com.
4. Stanley and Soltow, *The HON Story*, 4.
5. Ibid.
6. Richard Stanley, interview.
7. Stanley and Soltow, *The HON Story*, 4–5.
8. James Hanson, interview by Fred Anderson, recording, 11 July 2003, Write Stuff Enterprises.
9. Stanley and Soltow, *The HON Story*, 5.
10. Richard Stanley, interview.
11. Stanley and Soltow, *The HON Story*, 6.
12. Ibid., 59.
13. Harvey Allbee Jr., interview by Fred Anderson, recording, 30 June 2003, Write Stuff Enterprises.
14. Stanley and Soltow, *The HON Story*, 7; "Iowa Charter Asked by Home Appliance Concern," *Rock Island Argus*, 14 January 1944; "Law Firm Celebrates Century in Muscatine," *Quad-City Times*, 19 June 2003, A13.
15. Stanley and Soltow, *The HON Story*, 7.
16. Ros Jensen, *Max: A Biography of C. Maxwell Stanley* (Ames, IA: Iowa State University Press, 1990), 60.
17. Stanley and Soltow, *The HON Story*, 5; Richard Stanley, interview.
18. Stanley and Soltow, *The HON Story*, 7–8.
19. Ibid.; "Cabinets for Modern Kitchens," sales brochure of the Home-O-Nize Company, 1944.
20. Stanley and Soltow, *The HON Story*, 9
21. Ibid., 10.
22. Jensen, *Max: A Biography of C. Maxwell Stanley*, 11.
23. Stanley and Soltow, *The HON Story*, 11.
24. Lyle McCullough, interview by Fred Anderson, recording, 26 June 2003, Write Stuff Enterprises.
25. Stanley and Soltow, *The HON Story*, 11.
26. Ibid., 12.
27. Ibid., 15.
28. McCullough, interview.
29. Ibid.
30. Ibid.
31. Ibid.
32. Stanley and Soltow, *The HON Story*, 15; Ros Jensen, *Max: A Biography of C. Maxwell Stanley*, 68.
33. Stanley and Soltow, *The HON Story*, 15.
34. "Four Building Permits Totaling $15,000 Issued," *Muscatine Journal*, November 1946.
35. Stanley and Soltow, *The HON Story*, 14–15.
36. Ibid., 14.
37. Ibid., 15; "Machinery Arriving for New Home-O-Nize Firm," *Muscatine Journal*, 19 November 1946.
38. Richard Stanley, interview.
39. Stanley and Soltow, *The HON Story*, 12–13.
40. Ibid.
41. McCullough, interview.
42. Stanley and Soltow, *The HON Story*, 16–17.
43. Ibid., 17.
44. McCullough, interview.
45. Stanley and Soltow, *The HON Story*, 17–18.
46. Hanson, interview, 11 July 2003.
47. Stanley and Soltow, *The HON Story*, 18–19; "Metal and Press Time Available," display advertisement in *Des Moines Register*, 9 February 1947.
48. Stanley and Soltow, *The HON Story*, 19.
49. Ibid.; Annual Report 1959, The Home-O-Nize Co., 6–7 (margin notes).

Chapter One Sidebar

1. Helen Weiershauser, "Muscatine's Stubborn Hero," *Muscatine Journal* 7 August 1997; "Button Capital of the World," American Museum of Natural History, www.amnh.org; "Mussels, Clams Produce River Pearls," www.greatriver.com; "The Old Pioneer," www.pearlbuttoncapital.com.

Chapter Two

1. Stanley and Soltow, *The HON Story*, 20; "The D-1," Stampings Inc. product sheet, 1947; Jensen, *Max: A Biography of C. Maxwell Stanley*, 60.
2. Richard Stanley, interview.
3. Stanley and Soltow, *The HON Story*, 20.
4. Ibid., 20–21.
5. Ibid., 15, 19, 20, 22; Photo, 1947, boxes of Home-O-Nize coasters.
6. Richard Stanley, interview; Robert Carl, interview by Fred Anderson, recording, 26 June 2003, Write Stuff Enterprises; Stanley and Soltow, *The HON Story*, 22.
7. Stanley and Soltow, *The HON Story*, 22–23.
8. Ibid.; Richard Stanley, interview; Carl, interview; Home-O-Nize advertising flier for "Three by Fiver," the card index file, 1947; "Home-O-Nize

Company Is Releasing First Item," *Muscatine Journal*, September 1947.

9. Hanson, interview, 11 July 2003.

10. Jensen, *Max: A Biography of C. Maxwell Stanley*, 67; "Facts About The Home-O-Nize Co., Makers of Home Conveniences," 1947, 2.

11. "Facts About The Home-O-Nize Co.," 3, 5, 6.

12. Ibid.; Jensen, *Max: A Biography of C. Maxwell Stanley*, 67.

13. "Facts About The Home-O-Nize Co.," 7–8.

14. Jensen, *Max: A Biography of C. Maxwell Stanley*, 67; Richard Stanley, interview.

15. Carl, interview.

16. Stanley and Soltow, *The HON Story*, 23, 26.

17. Ibid., 23, 25.

18. Ibid., 26.

19. Ibid., 24, 25; Annual Report 1959, The Home-O-Nize Co., 6–7 (margin notes).

20. Stanley and Soltow, *The HON Story*, 24, 25.

21. Ibid., 27; Annual Report 1959, The Home-O-Nize Co., 6–7 (margin notes).

22. Richard Stanley, interview.

23. Stanley and Soltow, *The HON Story*, 25.

24. Ibid., 26.

25. Richard Stanley, interview.

26. Carl, interview; Jensen, *Max: A Biography of C. Maxwell Stanley*, 69.

27. Richard Stanley, interview.

28. Stanley and Soltow, *The HON Story*, 25.

29. Stan Howe, interview by Jeffrey L. Rodengen and Fred Anderson, recording, 10 June 2003, Write Stuff Enterprises.

30. McCullough, interview.

31. Stanley and Soltow, *The HON Story*, 28.

32. Ibid.

33. McCullough, interview.

34. Ibid.

35. Stanley and Soltow, *The HON Story*, 28.

36. Ibid., 29.

37. Ibid.

38. Ibid., McCullough, interview; Annual Report 1950, The Home-O-Nize Co., 3; Annual Report 1951, The Home-O-Nize Co., 2.

39. Annual Report 1959, The Home-O-Nize Co., 6–7 (margin notes).

40. Ibid.

41. Stanley and Soltow, *The HON Story*, 30–31.

42. Hanson, interview, 11 July 2003.

43. Stanley and Soltow, *The HON Story*, 31; Jensen, *Max: A Biography of C. Maxwell Stanley*, 65, 142.

44. Stanley and Soltow, *The HON Story*, 30; Carl, interview.

45. Stanley and Soltow, *The HON Story*, 30.

46. Howe, interview.

47. Richard Stanley, interview.

48. Stanley and Soltow, *The HON Story*, 31; Jensen, *Max: A Biography of C. Maxwell Stanley*, 65.

49. Stanley and Soltow, *The HON Story*, 31; Jensen, *Max: A Biography of C. Maxwell Stanley*, 71.

50. Stanley and Soltow, *The HON Story*, 31–32; Annual Report 1950, The Home-O-Nize Co., 2–3.

51. Stanley and Soltow, *The HON Story*, 32.

52. Annual Report 1950, The Home-O-Nize Co., 2–3; Stanley and Soltow, *The HON Story*, 33.

53. Carl, interview.

54. Richard Stanley, interview.

55. Stanley and Soltow, *The HON Story*, 32–33.

56. Ibid., 33; Jensen, *Max: A Biography of C. Maxwell Stanley*, 60; Annual Report 1950, The Home-O-Nize Co., 2–3.

57. Stanley and Soltow, *The HON Story*, 31, 34; Jensen, *Max: A Biography of C. Maxwell Stanley*, 65–66; Annual Report 1950, The Home-O-Nize Co., 2–3.

58. Annual Report 1950, The Home-O-Nize Co., 3.

59. Information supplied by HNI Corporation.

60. Howe, interview.

Chapter Two Sidebar

1. Jensen, *Max: A Biography of C. Maxwell Stanley*, 71–75.

Chapter Three

1. Stanley and Soltow, *The HON Story*, 35.

2. Jensen, *Max: A Biography of C. Maxwell Stanley*, 69.

3. Richard Stanley, interview.

4. Stanley and Soltow, *The HON Story*, 54; Richard Stanley, interview.

5. Stanley and Soltow, *The HON Story*, 55, 160, 170; Jensen, *Max: A Biography of C. Maxwell Stanley*, 70.

6. Administrative Memo No. 8, 1 December 1954, "Personnel Assignments and Designations" (including Stanley Howe); Administrative Memo No. 10, 1 September 1955, "Plant Engineering Dept.; Prime-Mover Engineering Dept." (including Rex Bennett).

7. Stanley and Soltow, *The HON Story*, 43–44. Annual Report 1952, The Home-O-Nize Co., 3.

8. Stanley and Soltow, *The HON Story*, 45; Annual Report 1953, The Home-O-Nize Co., 2.

9. Stanley and Soltow, *The HON Story*, 46.

10. Annual Report 1954, The Home-O-Nize Co., 2.

11. Stanley and Soltow, *The HON Story*, 45.

12. Ibid., 45–46.

13. Annual Report 1951, The Home-O-Nize Co., 1; Annual Report 1955.

14. Stanley and Soltow, *The HON Story*, 43.

15. Ibid.

16. Ibid., 47.

17. Annual Report 1952, The Home-O-Nize Co., 3; Annual Report 1955, The Home-O-Nize Co., 3; Stanley and Soltow, *The HON Story*, 47–48.

18. Howe, interview; Stanley and Soltow, *The HON Story*, 48.

19. Stanley and Soltow, *The HON Story*, 52.

20. Ibid., 51-52; Annual Report 1953, The Home-O-Nize Co., 3; Annual Report 1954, The Home-O-Nize Co., 3.

21. Annual Report 1951, The Home-O-Nize Co., 4.

22. Stanley and Soltow, *The HON Story*, 38–42, 51.

23. Ibid., 37–38; Annual Report 1951, The Home-O-Nize Co., 2; Annual Report 1955, The Home-O-Nize Co., 3; Annual Report 1956, The Home-O-Nize Co., 2.

24. Stanley and Soltow, *The HON Story*, 37–38, 49; Annual Report 1951, The Home-O-Nize Co., 4; Annual Report 1952, The Home-O-Nize Co., 3; Annual Report 1953, The Home-O-Nize Co., 2.

25. Stanley and Soltow, *The HON Story*, 56–57, 59; Annual Report 1951, The Home-O-Nize Co., 2.

26. Stanley and Soltow, *The HON Story*, 58–59; Annual Report 1955, The Home-O-Nize Co., 4; Annual Report 1953, The Home-O-Nize Co., 2.

27. Annual Report 1955, The Home-O-Nize Co., 4; Stanley and Soltow, *The HON Story*, 52–53.

28. Stanley and Soltow, *The HON Story*, 35–36; Annual Report 1951, The Home-O-Nize Co., 1; Annual Report 1956, The Home-O-Nize Co., 1–2.

Chapter Three Sidebar

1. Stanley and Soltow, *The HON Story*, 53; Annual Report 1951, The Home-O-Nize Co.

2. Transcription of recording by Clem Hanson, 1975, 8.

3. Howe, interview.

Chapter Four

1. Stanley and Soltow, *The HON Story*, 63, 73.

2. Hanson, interview, 11 July 2003.

3. Stanley and Soltow, *The HON Story*, 65–66; *HON–PM Management News*, 17 March 1961; 1962 Annual Report, The Home-O-Nize Co., 3; 1965 Annual Report, The Home-O-Nize Co., 3.

4. Hanson, interview, 11 July 2003.

5. Stanley and Soltow, *The HON Story*, 67.

6. Annual Report 1956, The Home-O-Nize Co., 3; Stanley and Soltow, *The HON Story*, 76; Annual Report 1960, The Home-O-Nize Co., 4.

7. Annual Report 1955, The Home-O-Nize Co., 4.

8. Jensen, *Max: A Biography of C. Maxwell Stanley*, 1990.

9. Howe, interview.

10. Ibid.; Hanson, interview, 11 July 2003; Jensen, *Max: A Biography of C. Maxwell Stanley*, 66; Annual Report 1959, The Home-O-Nize Co., 4; Stanley and Soltow, *The HON Story*, 67–70.
11. Stanley and Soltow, *The HON Story*, 68–69.
12. Ibid., 70–71; 1964 Annual Report, The Home-O-Nize Co., 3; Jensen, *Max: A Biography of C. Maxwell Stanley*, 66.
13. Howe, interview.
14. Stanley and Soltow, *The HON Story*, 80–84; Annual Report 1958, The Home-O-Nize Co., 11; *HON–PM Management News*, 7 December 1959; Annual Report 1959, The Home-O-Nize Co., 3; Annual Report 1960, The Home-O-Nize Co., 2; 1963 Annual Report, The Home-O-Nize Co., 3; *HON–PM Management News*, 2 August 1965.
15. Stanley and Soltow, *The HON Story*, 84–85.
16. Ibid., 86–89.
17. Howe, interview
18. Stanley and Soltow, *The HON Story*, 86–87.
19. Ibid., 98–99.
20. Ibid., 96–98.
21. Richard Stanley, interview.
22. Stanley and Soltow, *The HON Story*, 99.
23. Ibid., 99–100; *HON–PM Management News*, 25 May 1965.
24. *HON–PM Management News*, 27 October 1965; *HON–PM Management News*, 3 December 1965; "A Journey to the Future," HON Industries 50th Anniversary Timeline, 6; Stanley and Soltow, *The HON Story*, 101; *HON–PM Management News*, 4 October 1961; *HON–PM–Luxco Management News*, 2 November 1962.
25. *HON–PM–Luxco Management News*, 18 December 1963; *HON–PM Management News*, 25 May 1965; *HON–PM Management News*, 9 December 1960; *HON–PM–Luxco Management News*, 4 December 1963.
26. Howe, interview.
27. Ken Meyerholz, interview by Jeffrey L. Rodengen, recording, 9 June 2003, Write Stuff Enterprises.
28. Stanley and Soltow, *The HON Story*, 101–103.
29. Ibid., 105; Susan Cradick, interview by Richard F. Hubbard, recording, 21 July 2003, Write Stuff Enterprises; "Vision & Mission," The Stanley Foundation, www.stanleyfoundation.org.
30. Stanley and Soltow, *The HON Story*, 90–91; 1965 Annual Report, The Home-O-Nize Co., 6–7.
31. Stanley and Soltow, *The HON Story*, 93; 1965 Annual Report, The Home-O-Nize Co., 6–7; 1963 Annual Report, The Home-O-Nize Co., 3.
32. HON Industries 1986 Annual Report, 5; Stanley and Soltow, *The HON Story*, 94–95.
33. Howe, interview.

Chapter Four Sidebar: The Stanley Foundation

1. Jensen, *Max: A Biography of C. Maxwell Stanley*, 75.
2. Ibid., 80–81.
3. Richard Stanley, interview.
4. "Reaching Far Beyond Muscatine," *Muscatine Journal*, 24 October 2000; "Patient but Persistent," *Muscatine Journal*, 25 October 2000.

Chapter Four Sidebar: Wood Miller's Legacy

1. Obituary, "H. Wood Miller, 93," *Quad-City Times*, 3 May 1994, 2M.
2. "Meet One of Those Fellows Called—'A Designer,' " *The Home-O-Nizer*, No. 2.
3. Stanley and Soltow, *The HON Story*, 1991, 96–97.

Chapter Five

1. 1972 HON INDUSTRIES Annual Report, 8–9.
2. Stanley and Soltow, *The HON Story*, 115.
3. Ibid.
4. Annual Report 1967, The Home-O-Nize Co., 5.
5. Annual Report 1968, The Home-O-Nize Co., 3, 5.
6. Stanley and Soltow, *The HON Story*, 120; 1971 HON INDUSTRIES Annual Report, 4.
7. Stanley and Soltow, *The HON Story*, 121–122; 1968 HON INDUSTRIES Annual Report, 4.
8. *HON INDUSTRIES Management News*, 19 May 1969.
9. 1969 HON INDUSTRIES Annual Report, 4.
10. 1972 HON INDUSTRIES Annual Report, 4–5, 7.
11. Annual Report 1966, The Home-O-Nize Co., 3; *HON–PM Management News*, 25 February 1966. *HON–PM Management News*, 31 October 1966; Stanley and Soltow, *The HON Story*, 122–123.
12. Stanley and Soltow, *The HON Story*, 124–125; Annual Report 1967, The Home-O-Nize Co., 3; *HON INDUSTRIES Management News*, 24 June 1968.
13. Stanley and Soltow, *The HON Story*, 123–125; 1968 HON INDUSTRIES Annual Report, 1; 1969 HON INDUSTRIES Annual Report, 1; *HON INDUSTRIES Management News*, 15 September 1969; *HON INDUSTRIES Management News*, 8 November 1969.
14. Stanley and Soltow, *The HON Story*, 123; 1972 HON INDUSTRIES Annual Report, 4; *HON INDUSTRIES Management News*, 4 January 1972.
15. 1969 HON INDUSTRIES Annual Report, 5.
16. Stanley and Soltow, *The HON Story*, 131.
17. Ibid., 135.
18. Ibid., 132–134; 1971 HON INDUSTRIES Annual Report, 2–3; *HON INDUSTRIES Management News*, 27 May 1971.
19. Stanley and Soltow, *The HON Story*, 134–135; *HON INDUSTRIES Management News*, 27 May 1971; *HON INDUSTRIES Management News*, 14 July 1971.
20. Stanley and Soltow, *The HON Story*, 121; 1972 HON INDUSTRIES Annual Report, 5.
21. Stanley and Soltow, *The HON Story*, 135–137.
22. Ibid., 125–126; 1970 HON INDUSTRIES Annual Report, 1.
23. 1968 HON INDUSTRIES Annual Report, 3.
24. *HON–PM Management News*, 26 July 1967; Stanley and Soltow, *The HON Story*, 113–114.
25. *HON INDUSTRIES Management News*, 16 May 1972; Stanley and Soltow, *The HON Story*, 115–116; 1972 HON INDUSTRIES Annual Report, 3.
26. Annual Report 1966, The Home-O-Nize Co. 2; 1968 HON INDUSTRIES Annual Report, 12; 1969 HON INDUSTRIES Annual Report, 12.
27. *HON–PM Management News*, 2 June 1966; *HON–PM Management News*, 14 June 1968; Annual Report 1966, The Home-O-Nize Co., 3; Annual Report 1967, The Home-O-Nize Co., 3; 1968 HON INDUSTRIES Annual Report, 1; 1969 HON INDUSTRIES Annual Report, 1; 1970 HON INDUSTRIES Annual Report, 11; 1971 HON INDUSTRIES Annual Report, 13; 1972 HON INDUSTRIES Annual Report, 15; Stanley and Soltow, *The HON Story*, 110–111; *HON–PM Management News*, 31 March 1966.

Chapter Five Sidebar: Fun Facts About Holga

1. Thomas D. Head, interview by Fred Anderson, recording, 19 August 2003, Write Stuff Enterprises.

Chapter Six

1. George B. Tindall and David E. Shi, *America*, 2nd ed. (New York: W. W. Norton & Company, 1989), 911–912.
2. Ibid.
3. Ibid.
4. "Inflation and Deflation." Microsoft Encarta 97 Encyclopedia.
5. Stanley and Soltow, *The HON Story*, 145.

6. 1973 HON INDUSTRIES Annual Report, 5; 1980 HON INDUSTRIES Annual Report, 5, 18–19.
7. Stanley and Soltow, *The HON Story*, 142.
8. Ibid., 141.
9. 1975 HON INDUSTRIES Annual Report, 3.
10. Meyerholz, interview.
11. "Geneva Plant Extension," *HON INDUSTRIES Management News*, 26 March 1973; "Geneva Plant Property," *HON INDUSTRIES Management News*, 10 November 1978; "People of HON Are Visible in Muscatine," *Muscatine Journal*, 27 January 1979.
12. Stanley and Soltow, *The HON Story*, 164–165.
13. Ibid., 145–146; 1974 HON INDUSTRIES Annual Report, 2.
14. 1974 HON INDUSTRIES Annual Report, 2; 1977 HON INDUSTRIES Annual Report, 9; "Norman Bates Inc.," *HON INDUSTRIES Management News*, 11 November 1974.
15. 1977 HON INDUSTRIES Annual Report, 2; *Wall Street Journal*, 27 April 1977, 5, col. 4; "Murphy-Miller," *HON INDUSTRIES Management News* (undated); "Murphy-Miller Co., *HON INDUSTRIES Management News*, 25 April 1977.
16. Howe, interview.
17. 1976 HON INDUSTRIES Annual Report, 5; 1978 HON INDUSTRIES Annual Report, inside cover.
18. *Wall Street Journal*, 10 November 1980, 39, col. 4; Stanley and Soltow, *The HON Story*, 146; 1980 HON INDUSTRIES Annual Report, 2–3, 12; "Acquisition of Hiebert Inc.," *HON INDUSTRIES Management News*, 14 October 1980.
19. 1973 HON INDUSTRIES Annual Report, 6; 1975 HON INDUSTRIES Annual Report, 5–6; 1975 HON INDUSTRIES Annual Report, 3, 6–7.
20. 1976 HON INDUSTRIES Annual Report, 3, 6–7; 1977 HON INDUSTRIES Annual Report, 10; 1978 HON INDUSTRIES Annual Report, 3, 10; 1979 HON INDUSTRIES Annual Report, 10.
21. 1980 HON INDUSTRIES Annual Report, 14; Stanley and Soltow, *The HON Story*, 180.
22. Stanley and Soltow, *The HON Story*, 148, 187; Jensen, *Max: A Biography of C. Maxwell Stanley*, 52, 58, 80.
23. Cradick, interview.
24. Ibid.
25. 1976 HON INDUSTRIES Annual Report, 5; 1973 HON INDUSTRIES Annual Report, 5.
26. Stanley and Soltow, *The HON Story*, 154–156; "Wage and Salary Increases," *HON INDUSTRIES Management News*, 11 November 1974.
27. Stanley and Soltow, *The HON Story*, 154, 171; Jensen, *Max: A Biography of C. Maxwell Stanley*, 67; "Corry Jamestown's Strike Ends," *HON INDUSTRIES Management News*, 18 September 1978.
28. Stanley and Soltow, *The HON Story*, 155, 157; "Scholarship Program," *HON INDUSTRIES Management News*, 19 January 1976.
29. *HON INDUSTRIES Management News*, 20 November 1974.
30. 1977 HON INDUSTRIES Annual Report, 3.
31. Ibid., 4.

Chapter Seven

1. 1981 HON INDUSTRIES Annual Report, 2, 6.
2. Howe, interview.
3. Phillip E. Hecht, interview by Jeffrey L. Rodengen and Fred Anderson, recording, 10 June 2003, Write Stuff Enterprises.
4. Stanley and Soltow, *The HON Story*, 181–182; 1981 HON INDUSTRIES Annual Report, 2; 1982 HON INDUSTRIES Annual Report, 2, 7.
5. Stanley and Soltow, *The HON Story*, 181–182.
6. Hecht, interview.
7. Ibid.
8. Ibid.
9. Howe, interview.
10. 1985 HON INDUSTRIES Annual Report, 2, 11; "Arrow Tualatin, Inc.," *HON INDUSTRIES Management News*, 15 November 1985.
11. 1981 HON INDUSTRIES Annual Report, 3; *HON INDUSTRIES Management News*, 11 December 1981.
12. Stanley and Soltow, *The HON Story*, 176; 1981 HON INDUSTRIES Annual Report, 2; 1982 HON INDUSTRIES Annual Report, 9; 1983 HON INDUSTRIES Annual Report, 3; 1984 HON INDUSTRIES Annual Report, 3, 6; 1985 HON INDUSTRIES Annual Report, 2, 6; "Board of Directors Meeting," *HON INDUSTRIES Management News*, 9 February 1982.
13. *HON INDUSTRIES Management News*, 23 February 1972; *Wall Street Journal*, 24 February 1982, 24, col. 3; "Rishel Acquisition," *HON INDUSTRIES Management News*, 30 August 1982; 1982 HON INDUSTRIES Annual Report, 3; Stanley and Soltow, *The HON Story*, 177; 1984 HON INDUSTRIES Annual Report, 3, 6; 1985 HON INDUSTRIES Annual Report, 2.
14. 1986 HON INDUSTRIES Annual Report, 3, 8; 1988 HON INDUSTRIES Annual Report, 2.
15. "Purchase of Ring King Visibles Common Stock," *HON INDUSTRIES Management News*, 10 May 1983; Stanley and Soltow, *The HON Story*, 184–185.
16. 1984 HON INDUSTRIES Annual Report, 3; 1986 HON INDUSTRIES Annual Report, 3.
17. 1986 HON INDUSTRIES Annual Report, 3–4; "XLM Company," *HON INDUSTRIES Management News*, 17 November 1986; 1988 HON INDUSTRIES Annual Report, 11.
18. Thomas Miller, interview by Jeffrey L. Rodengen, recording, 23 May 2003, Write Stuff Enterprises.
19. "HON Buys Budget Panels," *Des Moines Register*, 8 October 1986, 5S; HON INDUSTRIES 1986 Annual Report, 3.
20. Jean Reynolds, interview by Richard F. Hubbard, recording, 17 July 2003, Write Stuff Enterprises.
21. Miller, interview.
22. "Oak Street Warehouse Addition," *HON INDUSTRIES Management News*, 25 February 1981; 1981 HON INDUSTRIES Annual Report, 3; Stanley and Soltow, *The HON Story*, 164.
23. "Property Acquisition," *HON INDUSTRIES Management News*, 10 April 1981; "South Gate Property Purchased from Firestone," *HON INDUSTRIES Management News*, 14 April 1981; Stanley and Soltow, *The HON Story*, 165–166, 172; 1981 HON INDUSTRIES Annual Report, 3; 1982 HON INDUSTRIES Annual Report, 3; *Washington Post*, 2 April 1981, D2.
24. "Board of Directors Meeting," *HON INDUSTRIES Management News*, 9 February 1982. Stanley and Soltow, *The HON Story*, 164.
25. "Texas Plant Site Acquisition," *HON INDUSTRIES Management News*, 11 June 1985; 1986 HON INDUSTRIES Annual Report, 3.
26. Jack Michaels, interview by Jeffrey L. Rodengen and Fred Anderson, recording, 10 June 2003, Write Stuff Enterprises.
27. 1988 HON INDUSTRIES Annual Report, 3.
28. "Sale of The Prime-Mover Co.," *HON INDUSTRIES Management News*, 7 December 1988; 1988 HON INDUSTRIES Annual Report, 3; 1987 HON INDUSTRIES Annual Report, 13.
29. Jensen, *Max: A Biography of C. Maxwell Stanley*, 180.
30. Ibid., 180–183.
31. Dispatch from The Associated Press, 21 September 1984, p.m. cycle; Dispatch from United Press International, 25 September 1984, p.m. cycle; "C. Maxwell Stanley," *HON INDUSTRIES Management News*, 20 September 1984.
32. Hanson, interview, 11 July 2003.
33. Stanley and Soltow, *The HON Story*, 155.
34. Hanson, interview, 11 July 2003.
35. 1984 HON INDUSTRIES Annual Report, 28; Jim Hanson, interview by

Fred Anderson, telephone conversation, 8 September 2003, Write Stuff Enterprises.

36. 1981 HON INDUSTRIES Annual Report, 3.

37. "Work Sharing/Cost Reduction Program," *HON INDUSTRIES Management News*, 23 March 1982.

38. "Work Sharing Plan," 1982 HON INDUSTRIES Annual Report, 14; *HON INDUSTRIES Management News*, 2 September 1982.

39. 1983 HON INDUSTRIES Annual Report, 21; 1984 HON INDUSTRIES Annual Report, 17; "Efficiency Key to Success of HON Firms," *Business Record*, 13 October 1986, Sec. 1, 22.

Chapter Seven Sidebar: Philanthropy Abounds

1. "Facts About The Home-O-Nize Co.," 7–8.

2. Cradick, interview; "HON INDUSTRIES Charitable Foundation," *HON INDUSTRY Management News*, 20 March 1986.

3. Jeff Fick, interview by Jeffrey L. Rodengen, recording, 10 June 2003, Write Stuff Enterprises.

4. Ibid.

5. Ibid.

Chapter Seven Sidebar: Heatilator's History

1. "Since 1928, Heatilator Has Been a Fireplace Fixture," *The Hawk-Eye*, Burlington, Iowa, 24 February 2002; Fred Wohlleber, "The Origin of Vega Industries," 11 May 1981; "Who We Are," Hearth Technologies Inc., April 2000.

Chapter Seven Sidebar: Rishel's Rich History

1. Lou Hunsinger Jr., "The HON Plant Closing: The End of an Era," *Sun-Gazette*, Williamsport, Pa., 3 May 2001; Dr. Michael Clark, and Jill Thomas-Clark, "The J.K. Rishel Furniture Company," *Style 1900: The Quarterly Journal of the Arts & Crafts Movement*, Summer/Fall 1998, 18–20.

Chapter Eight

1. Michaels, interview.

2. Fick, interview.

3. 1991 HON INDUSTRIES Annual Report, 2, 8; "Wage & Salary Freeze," *HON INDUSTRIES Management News*, 19 February 1991; "Wage and Salary Freeze," *HON INDUSTRIES Management News*, 29 May 1991; "Suspension of Wage and Salary Freeze," *HON INDUSTRIES Management News*, 20 August 1991.

4. 1995 HON INDUSTRIES Annual Report, 2, 12, 13; "HON Workers Lose Jobs,"

Muscatine Journal, 8 December 1995, 1.

5. 1992 HON INDUSTRIES Annual Report, 7.

6. Ibid., 9–15.

7. Thomas Hammer, interview by Richard F. Hubbard, recording, 9 June 2003, Write Stuff Enterprises.

8. Ibid.

9. Ibid.

10. Dave Burdakin, interview by Jeffrey L. Rodengen, recording, 16 July 2003, Write Stuff Enterprises.

11. Stan Askren, interview by Jeffrey L. Rodengen, recording, 10 June 2003, Write Stuff Enterprises.

12. Michaels, interview.

13. Tony Hayden, interview by Jeffrey L. Rodengen, recording, 9 June 2003, Write Stuff Enterprises.

14. 1992 HON INDUSTRIES Annual Report, 9–11; 1993 HON INDUSTRIES Annual Report, 2–3.

15. 1995 HON INDUSTRIES Annual Report.

16. Ibid., 3; 1996 HON INDUSTRIES Annual Report, 7–8. Stewart B. Leavitt, "HON Industries: Capturing an Expanding Middle Market," *Office Products International*, June 1995, 42.

17. Michaels, interview.

18. "The Gunlocke Company," *HON INDUSTRIES Management News*, 16 October 1989; 1989 HON INDUSTRIES Annual Report, 2, 8, 20.

19. Don Mead, interview by Jeffrey L. Rodengen, recording, 10 June 2003, Write Stuff Enterprises.

20. "Corry Hiebert Situation," *HON INDUSTRIES Management News*, 10 March 1989; "Holga Inc.," *HON INDUSTRIES Management News*, 20 June 1989; "CorryHiebert Sales and Marketing Functions Assumed by Gunlocke," *HON INDUSTRIES Management News*, 19 May 1993; "CorryHiebert to Close," *HON INDUSTRIES Management News*, 13 October 1993; "CorryHiebert Corporation," *HON INDUSTRIES Management News*, 20 December 1993; 1989 HON INDUSTRIES Annual Report, 2–3; 1993 HON INDUSTRIES Annual Report, 3.

21. Robert Hayes, interview by Jeffrey L. Rodengen, recording, 23 May 2003, Write Stuff Enterprises.

22. 1989 HON INDUSTRIES Annual Report, 3; "Development Center," *HON INDUSTRIES Management News*, 26 April 1991; "HON INDUSTRIES Technical Center," *HON INDUSTRIES Management News*, 28 June 1991; "HON INDUSTRIES Board of Directors Meeting," *HON INDUSTRIES Management News*, 15 May 1996.

23. Pete Atherton, interview by Jeffrey L. Rodengen, recording, 10 June 2003, Write Stuff Enterprises.

24. Atherton, interview.

25. Hayden, interview.

26. "Rishel," *HON INDUSTRIES Management News*, 20 June 1989; "Board of Directors' Actions," *HON INDUSTRIES Management News*, 7 May 1990; 1989 HON INDUSTRIES Annual Report, 3; 1990 HON INDUSTRIES Annual Report, 3.

27. 1990 HON INDUSTRIES Annual Report, 3, 21; "Board of Directors' Actions," *HON INDUSTRIES Management News*, 7 May 1990; "XLM Company Headquarters Move to Avon," *HON INDUSTRIES Management News*, 17 January 1991; "XLM Company Relocates Headquarters to Mt. Pleasant," *HON INDUSTRIES Management News*, 10 June 1991; "XLM Company to Operate as Part of The HON Company," *HON INDUSTRIES Management News*, 18 April 1994; 1994 HON INDUSTRIES Annual Report, 22.

28. 1990 HON INDUSTRIES Annual Report, 3, 12, 21; 1991 HON INDUSTRIES Annual Report, 3, 9.

29. "Chandler Attwood Ltd.," *HON INDUSTRIES Management News*, 27 December 1991; 1992 HON INDUSTRIES Annual Report, 3; 1993 HON INDUSTRIES Annual Report, 3; "Archer Bond," *HON INDUSTRIES Management News*, 15 June 1994; 1994 HON INDUSTRIES Annual Report, 22; "Chandler Attwood Limited," *HON INDUSTRIES Management News*, 27 January 1995; "Chandler Attwood Limited," *HON INDUSTRIES Management News*, 18 August 1995; "Chandler Attwood Limited Ceased Operations at Dallas, Texas," *The HON Company Management News*, 1 May 1996.

30. Jerry Dittmer, interview by Jeffrey L. Rodengen, recording, 9 June 2003, Write Stuff Enterprises.

31. "Plymouth Office Products," *HON INDUSTRIES Management News*, 17 January 1992; 1991 HON INDUSTRIES Annual Report, 8; "Ring King Visibles Inc.," *HON INDUSTRIES Management News*, 3 January 1996; "HON Sells Ring King," *Muscatine Journal*, 4 January 1996, 1A; "HON Quits Computer Line To Focus On Office Furniture," *Investors' Business Daily*, 12 July 1996.

32. Fick, interview.

33. "Heatilator/Dovre," *HON INDUSTRIES Management News*, 23 November 1993; "Acquisition of Hearth Products Business," *HON INDUSTRIES Management News*, 30 July 1996; "Who We Are (internal information flier)," Hearth Technologies Inc., April

2000; "HON INDUSTRIES Merges Heat-N-Glo Fireplace Products, Inc., with Heatilator Inc.," *HON INDUSTRIES Management News*, 4 October 1996; "HON Quits Computer Line."

34. Askren, interview.

35. "HON INDUSTRIES Learning Center," *HON INDUSTRIES Management News*, 29 December 1994.

36. Askren, interview.

37. "HON INDUSTRIES Learning Center"; "Learning Center Relocation," *HON INDUSTRIES Management News*, 30 October 1995; *HON INDUSTRIES Management News*, 5 August 1996.

38. "HON INDUSTRIES Board of Directors Meeting," *HON INDUSTRIES Management News*, 13 February 1995.

39. 1989 HON INDUSTRIES Annual Report, 4–5; 1992 HON INDUSTRIES Annual Report, insert, "Our Vision"; 1996 HON INDUSTRIES Annual Report, 7.

40. 1994 HON INDUSTRIES Annual Report, 6.

41. Mike DeRosier, interview by Jeffrey L. Rodengen, recording, 15 July 2003, Write Stuff Enterprises.

42. "HON Studying Export Market," *Cedar Rapids Gazette*, Cedar Rapids, Iowa, 15 March 1990, 1D; "HON Export Limited," *HON INDUSTRIES Management News*; 18 March 1991; 1992 HON INDUSTRIES Annual Report, 3; 1993 HON INDUSTRIES Annual Report, 3; 1994 HON INDUSTRIES Annual Report, 3; 1996 Annual Report, HON INDUSTRIES, 29; Leavitt, "HON Industries: Capturing an Expanding Middle Market," 43; "HON Export Limited," *HON INDUSTRIES Management News*, 30 December 1996.

43. 1992 HON INDUSTRIES Annual Report, 15.

44. 1996 HON INDUSTRIES Annual Report, 2.

45. 1989 HON INDUSTRIES Annual Report, 2–3; 1990 HON INDUSTRIES Annual Report, 2, 4; 1991 HON INDUSTRIES Annual Report, 3; 1992 HON INDUSTRIES Annual Report, 2, 16; 1993 HON INDUSTRIES Annual Report, 2; 1994 HON INDUSTRIES Annual Report, 2; 1995 HON INDUSTRIES Annual Report, 2; 1996 HON INDUSTRIES Annual Report, 2, 7.

46. 1993 HON INDUSTRIES Annual Report, 6; 1996 HON INDUSTRIES Annual Report, 4.

47. 1994 HON INDUSTRIES Annual Report, 22.

48. 1990 HON INDUSTRIES Annual Report, 3; "Governor's Award for Pellet Mill," *HON INDUSTRIES Management News*, 18 September 1992; 1991 HON INDUSTRIES Annual Report, 3; 1992 HON INDUSTRIES Annual Report, 15; 1993 HON INDUSTRIES Annual Report, 14; "HON INDUSTRIES Joins EPA Energy Conservation Program," *HON INDUSTRIES Management News*, 28 October 1993; 1994 HON INDUSTRIES Annual Report, 5.

49. 1993 HON INDUSTRIES Annual Report, 5.

50. "HON INDUSTRIES Members Company Ownership Plan (ESOP)," *HON INDUSTRIES Management News*, 3 January 1992; 1991 HON INDUSTRIES Annual Report, 4, 9; 1992 HON INDUSTRIES Annual Report, 3; 1992 HON INDUSTRIES Annual Report, 20; 1996 HON INDUSTRIES Annual Report, 24.

51. 1991 HON INDUSTRIES ANNUAL REPORT, 3–4; 1992 HON INDUSTRIES Annual Report, 3.

52. 1992 HON INDUSTRIES Annual Report, 3.

53. "Fortune Magazine," *HON INDUSTRIES Management News*, 20 February 1996.

Chapter Eight Sidebar: The Gunlocke Chair Company

1. "Gunlocke; Capturing the Spirit of Every Age," company promotional brochure; "100 Years of Gunlocke, 1902–2002" (insert), *Evening Tribune*, Hornell, N.Y., 2002; PR Newswire, "LADD Announces Agreement to Sell McGuire Furniture," 8 November 1989; Robert J. Roberts, "Furniture Manufacturer Gunlocke Turns 95 With Giant Bash," *Evening Tribune*, Hornell, N.Y., 21 September 1997; Janice Bullard, "Going With the Grain," *Democrat & Chronicle*, Rochester, N.Y., 14 March 1999, 1E; "Style Comes to the Office (The Gunlocke Company profile)," *US Industry Today*, June 2000, 99; "Oval Office Chair Highlights Gunlocke's Anniversary," *The Evening Tribune*, Hornell, N.Y., reprinted in *Genesee County Express*, 2 May 2002, 7.

Chapter Eight Sidebar: Stanley M. Howe

1. "Chairman of the Board," *HON INDUSTRIES Management News*, 13 February 1996; Howe, interview; "2002 Distinguished Citizen: Stanley M. Howe," Boy Scouts of America program, Muscatine, Iowa; "Stan Howe Gives Major Gift to MHS Construction Project," *Muscatine Journal*, 31 December 2002; "Stan Howe Honored by University of Iowa," *HON INDUSTRIES Management News*, 13 June 1995; "Millennium: The Innovators"; "Stanley M. Howe Named BIFMA President," *HON INDUSTRIES Management News*, 24 June 1988;

"HON's Howe Moves Aside," *Muscatine Journal*, 14 February 1996, 1.

Chapter Eight Sidebar: Allsteel Inc.

1. "A Legacy of Leadership," Allsteel Company Background, www.allsteeloffice.com/background.html; "Allsteel, 1912–1987," (company-published history).

Chapter Nine

1. 1997 HON INDUSTRIES Annual Report, 1, 6–7.

2. Ibid., 7; 1998 HON INDUSTRIES Annual Report, 1–7; 2000 HON INDUSTRIES Annual Report, 2.

3. 1997 HON INDUSTRIES Annual Report, 3–4.

4. Ibid., 7; 1998 HON INDUSTRIES Annual Report; 1–7; 2000 HON INDUSTRIES Annual Report, 2.

5. 2000 HON INDUSTRIES Annual Report, 10; 2001 HON INDUSTRIES Annual Report, 1, 5.

6. 1998 HON INDUSTRIES Annual Report, 12; 1999 HON INDUSTRIES Annual Report, 4; "HON INDUSTRIES Selected by *Industry Week* Magazine as One of the World's 100 Best-managed Companies," *HON INDUSTRIES Management News*, 16 August 1999; "HON INDUSTRIES Was Selected One of the World's 100 Best-Managed Companies by *INDUSTRY WEEK*," HON INDUSTRIES News Release, 17 August 2000; 2000 HON INDUSTRIES Annual Report, 11; "HON INDUSTRIES Makes Forbes List," *Muscatine Journal*, 4 January 2001.

7. "Heatilator Wins Industry Award," *Mt. Pleasant News*, Mt. Pleasant, Iowa, 19 October 2000.

8. "Winning Workplaces," reprint from *BusinessWeek*, 4 November 2002; "Allsteel Headquarters Honored for Its Design," *Muscatine Journal*, 4 August 2001; "Allsteel Recognized as Best Manufacturer," *Muscatine Journal*, 5 October 2002.

9. 1997 HON INDUSTRIES Annual Report, 2, 3; 1998 HON INDUSTRIES Annual Report, 13, 16; 1999 HON INDUSTRIES Annual Report, 2, 16; 2000 HON INDUSTRIES Annual Report, 8, 9; 2001 HON INDUSTRIES Annual Report, 2–4; 2002 HON INDUSTRIES Annual Report, 2–4.

10. "HON Expands Production," *Muscatine Journal*, 3 April 1997; "The HON Company Systems Plant Expansion," *HON INDUSTRIES Management News*, 13 May 1997; "The HON Company

Cedartown, Georgia, Plant Warehouse Expansion," *HON INDUSTRIES Management News*, 12 August 1997.

11. "Consolidation of Heat-N-Glo Plants," *HON INDUSTRIES Management News*, 24 February 1997; 1997 HON INDUSTRIES Annual Report, 5, 11, 17.

12. "HON Buys Bevis Furniture," *World Herald*, Omaha, Neb., 7 October 1997, Business Sec., 14; "HON INDUSTRIES to Acquire Bevis Custom Furniture, Inc.," *HON INDUSTRIES Management News*, 7 October 1997; 1997 HON INDUSTRIES Annual Report, 11; 1998 HON INDUSTRIES Annual Report, 30; "HON INDUSTRIES Acquired Bevis Custom Furniture, Inc.," *HON INDUSTRIES Management News*, 13 November 1997.

13. "HON INDUSTRIES to Acquire Panel Concepts, Inc.," *HON INDUSTRIES Management News*, 10 November 1997; 1997 HON INDUSTRIES Annual Report, 11; 1998 HON INDUSTRIES Annual Report, 30; "Iowa's HON INDUSTRIES Buying California Office Furniture Panel Maker," *The Gazette*, Cedar Rapids, Iowa.

14. Reynolds, interview.

15. James Knutson, interview by Jeffrey L. Rodengen, tape recording, 15 July 2003, Write Stuff Enterprises.

16. "HON INDUSTRIES Announced Plans to Acquire Aladdin Steel Products," *HON INDUSTRIES Management News*, 9 February 1998; "HON INDUSTRIES Acquires Aladdin Steel Products Inc.," PR Newswire, 20 February 1998; 1997 HON INDUSTRIES Annual Report, 12.

17. "Plans to Expand in Retail Market," *HON INDUSTRIES Management News*, 28 May 1998; "HON Starts up New Plant in Mexico," *Muscatine Journal*, 23 September 1999; "Arranca Operaciones en Nuevo León," *El Norte*, Monterrey, Nuevo León, Mexico, Sec. G. 1.

18. "The HON Company Creates Allsteel Group and HON Group to Support Continued Growth," *HON INDUSTRIES Management News*, 23 August 1999; 1999 HON INDUSTRIES Annual Report, 2, 3; "The HON Company/Allsteel Inc.," *HON INDUSTRIES Management News*, 22 February 2000; "Allsteel of a Deal," *Muscatine Journal*, 25 March 2000.

19. Miller, interview.

20. Mead, interview.

21. Burdakin, interview.

22. 1999 HON INDUSTRIES Annual Report, 3–4, 13; 2000 HON INDUSTRIES Annual Report, 22; "Aladdin Hearth Gets Okay for New Colville Plant," *Statesman Examiner*, Colville, Wash., 4 August 1999; "Aladdin Hearth Settles Into New Multi-million Dollar Plant," *Statesman Examiner*, Colville, Wash., 13 July 2000.

23. 1999 HON INDUSTRIES Annual Report, 15.

24. 2000 HON INDUSTRIES Annual Report, 10.

25. "We Are Very Excited..." *Muscatine Journal*, 13 January 2001.

26. 2001 HON INDUSTRIES Annual Report, 3, 25, 31; "HON Will Close Pennsylvania Plant," *Muscatine Journal*, 30 April 2001. "HON to Close a Third Plant," *Muscatine Journal*, 25 July 2001; "Closing of Tupelo Plant: Means 100 New Jobs at Milan Allsteel," *Mirror Exchange*, Milan, Tenn., 7 August 2001; "Allsteel Plant to Shut Down in Jackson," *Jackson Sun*, 5 January 2002.

27. "HON International Structure," *HON INDUSTRIES Management News*, 20 November 2002.

28. Miller, interview.

29. 1997 HON INDUSTRIES Annual Report, 4; 1999 HON INDUSTRIES Annual Report, 4.

30. 1999 HON INDUSTRIES Annual Report, 9, 11.

31. 2000 HON INDUSTRIES Annual Report, 13–16.

32. 2001 HON INDUSTRIES Annual Report, 18–19.

33. 1997 HON INDUSTRIES Annual Report, 8; 1998 HON INDUSTRIES Annual Report, 13, 41.

34. 1999 HON INDUSTRIES Annual Report, 7, 15.

35. 2000 HON INDUSTRIES Annual Report, 19.

36. 2001 HON INDUSTRIES Annual Report, 10, 21; "Who Has the Best Filing Cabinets?" *Office Solutions and Environments*, July 2001, 22.

37. "Readjusting the Office Chair," *Chicago Tribune*, 11 June 2002; "#19 Chair from Allsteel Redefining Seating for the 21st Century," *Forma Interiors*, Vol. 2, No. 1, 009; David Elbert, "Iowa Firm Allsteel Hopes Many Will Take a Seat," *Des Moines Register*, 15 April 2002, 1D; 2002 HON INDUSTRIES Annual Report, 7, 23.

38. 1998 HON INDUSTRIES Annual Report, 13, 41; 1999 HON INDUSTRIES Annual Report, 15; 2000 HON INDUSTRIES Annual Report, 19.

39. 2001 HON INDUSTRIES Annual Report, 10, 18–19, 21; 2002 HON INDUSTRIES Annual Report, 23; "Hearth Technologies Heats up Its Industry," *Manufacturing Today*, November–December 2002, 114.

40. 1997 HON INDUSTRIES Annual Report, 8; 2002 HON INDUSTRIES Annual Report, 1.

41. 1997 HON INDUSTRIES Annual Report, 4, 8–9; 1998 HON

INDUSTRIES Annual Report, 14; 2001 HON INDUSTRIES Annual Report, 11; 2002 HON INDUSTRIES Annual Report, 11.

42. "The War on Waste: Is It Sustainable?" *Start*, March 2002, 36; "Interview: Dave Burdakin, President, The HON Company," *ConCurrents*, 21 November 2001.

43. "HON INDUSTRIES Reduces Transportation & Distribution Costs with SynQuest Supply Chain Planning Software," *Business Wire*, 13 August 2001; "HON Reduces Costs With Transportation Software," *Muscatine Journal*, 18 August 2001; "Road to Recovery," *Supply Chain Systems*, January 2002; "HON INDUSTRIES Reduces Costs and Increases Customer Satisfaction Through Wireless Technology," *Business Wire*, 11 December 2001.

44. 1997 HON INDUSTRIES Annual Report, 5; "Investors: Maytag Leads the Way," *Des Moines Register*, 25 July 1999, G-1; 1998 HON INDUSTRIES Annual Report, 23; "HON INDUSTRIES Declares 12.5 Cents Per Share," *Muscatine Journal*, 6 August 2002., 3A; 2002 HON INDUSTRIES Annual Report, 27.

45. 1997 HON INDUSTRIES Annual Report, 17; 1998 HON INDUSTRIES Annual Report, 23, 32; 1999 HON INDUSTRIES Annual Report, 23; 2000 HON INDUSTRIES Annual Report, 23; 2001 HON INDUSTRIES Annual Report, 25; 2002 HON INDUSTRIES Annual Report, 27.

46. "New York Stock Exchange," *HON INDUSTRIES Management News*, 12 May 1998; 1998 HON INDUSTRIES Annual Report, 12.

47. 1998 HON INDUSTRIES Annual Report, 33; 1999 HON INDUSTRIES Annual Report, 33; 2000 HON INDUSTRIES Annual Report, 31–32; 2001; 2001 HON INDUSTRIES Annual Report, 34.

48. 1998 HON INDUSTRIES Annual Report, 34–35.

49. 2000 HON INDUSTRIES Annual Report, 41; "Boy Scouts Honor Stan Howe," *Muscatine Journal*, 4 October 2002. "MAPS' Miller Moves On, But His Legacy Remains," *Muscatine Journal*, 10 December 2001. "Local Man Honored by Junior Achievement," *Muscatine Journal*, 13 October 2001; "Michaels Elected to National Board," *Muscatine Journal*, 1 December 2001.

50. Melinda Ellsworth, interview by Richard F. Hubbard, tape recording 10 June 2003, Write Stuff Enterprises.

51. "Despite Economic Downturn, Gunlocke Vows to Be Around for Its Centennial," *Evening Tribune*, Hornell,

N.Y., 8 November 2001; "Gunlocke Gives $20,000 to St. James Mercy Foundation Founders Club," *The Evening Tribune*, Hornell, N.Y., 5 January 2000; "Allsteel Employees Raised $25,000 for UW," *Mirror-Exchange*, Milan, Tenn., 15 February 2000; "HON Donates Money and Product for East Coast Recovery Efforts," *Muscatine Journal*, 4 October 2001; "Heat-N-Glo, HON Contribute $182,000 to East Coast Fund," *Lake City Graphic*, Lake City, Minn., 18 October 2001, 20; "HON Company Makes Donation to Club Efforts," *Cedartown Standard*, Cedartown, Ga., 6 January 2000; "Heatilator Donates $10,000 to Crossroads Hospice," *Mt. Pleasant News*, Mt. Pleasant, Iowa, 19 May 2000; "Housing Shortage Must Be Addressed," *Mt. Pleasant News*, Mt. Pleasant, Iowa, 6 October 1999; 2000 HON INDUSTRIES Annual Report, 41; "Gunlocke: Tomorrow's Industry Leader Today," *Genesee Country Express*, Dansville, N.Y., 11 November 1999.

52. "Learning Tree Preschool," *HON INDUSTRIES Management News*, 2 August 1999; "One to Grow On; MCC, HON Team up to Put Down New Roots for Learning Tree Preschool," *Muscatine Journal*, 29 July 1999; "Company Leadership," *The Hawk Eye*, Burlington, Iowa, 27 November 1999; "Bath VA, Gunlocke Join Forces," *Leader*, Corning, N.Y., 26 January 2000.

53. "HON Rescues the Seats of Power," *Messenger-Inquirer*, Owensboro, Ky., 28 February 2001; "File High; Artist, HON INDUSTRIES Make Art," *Muscatine Journal*, 24 August 2002.

Chapter Nine Sidebar: Jack and the Frog

1. Mead, interview.

Chapter Ten

1. 2002 HON INDUSTRIES Annual Report, 51; "HON Directors Select New President," *Quad-City Times*, 13 February 2003.
2. HON INDUSTRIES Company Directory, 2003.
3. Richard Stanley, interview.
4. Michaels, interview.
5. Fick, interview.
6. Dittmer, interview.
7. Richard Stanley, interview.
8. Eric K. Jungbluth, interview by Jeffrey L. Rodengen and Fred Anderson, recording, 9 June 2003, Write Stuff Enterprises.
9. "HON INDUSTRIES Announces Results for Third Quarter—Fiscal 2001," *Business Wire*, 22 October 2003; "HON INDUSTRIES Announces 184th Consecutive Quarterly Dividend," *Business Wire*, 4 August 2003; "HON plans two closings," *Quad-City Times*, 30 July 2003.
10. Michaels, interview.
11. Dittmer, interview.
12. Michaels, interview.
13. Dittmer, interview.
14. Michaels, interview.
15. Malcolm Fields, interview by Richard F. Hubbard, recording, 9 June 2003, Write Stuff Enterprises.
16. Jim Kane, interview by Richard F. Hubbard, recording, 10 June 2003, Write Stuff Enterprises.
17. Askren, interview.
18. Ibid.
19. Burdakin, interview.
20. Dittmer, interview.
21. Richard Stanley, interview.
22. "Manufacturer Has Showroom in D.C.," *Quad-City Times*, 30 July 2003; Earth Technologies Changes Name, Prepares to Add Jobs," *Mt. Pleasant News*, 3 January 2003;

www.hon.com/newproducts; www.allsteeloffice.com/products; www.gunlocke.com/seating; www.gunlocke.com/casegoods; www.maxonfurniture.com/products; www.holga.com/products; www.heatilator.com/products; www.heatnglo.com/products; www.aladdinhearth.com.
23. Reynolds, interview; Josh Slowik, interview by Richard F. Hubbard, recording, 21 July 2003, Write Stuff Enterprises.
24. Burdakin, interview.
25. Jungbluth, interview.
26. Tom Head, interview by Jeffrey L. Rodengen, recording, 16 July 2003, Write Stuff Enterprises.
27. Mead, interview.
28. Brad Determan, interview.
29. Atherton, interview.
30. Ibid.
31. Fick, interview.
32. Julie Zielinski, interview by Richard F. Hubbard, recording, 6 June 2003, Write Stuff Enterprises.
33. Michaels, interview.
34. Fick, interview; "Program Helps Parents Buy School Supplies," *Muscatine Journal*, 21 August, 2003; "Weed Park Has a Course of a Different Color," *Muscatine Journal*, 10 June 2003; "University of Iowa Renames Lab for C. Maxwell Stanley," Stanley Consultants news release, 24 July 2003.
35. Fick, interview.
36. Askren, interview.
37. Ibid.
38. Ibid.

Chapter Ten Sidebar: Olson Flex Stacker

1. Craig Cooper, "Olson's Creations Stack Up," *Quad-City Business Journal*, 3 February 2003; www.hon.com/product.

Index

Page numbers in italics indicate photographs.